Credit Markets for the Poor

Credit Markets for the Poor

Patrick Bolton and Howard Rosenthal
Editors

Russell Sage Foundation
New York

The Russell Sage Foundation

The Russell Sage Foundation, one of the oldest of America's general purpose foundations, was established in 1907 by Mrs. Margaret Olivia Sage for "the improvement of
social and living conditions in the United States." The Foundation seeks to fulfill this
mandate by fostering the development and dissemination of knowledge about the
country's political, social, and economic problems. While the Foundation endeavors
to assure the accuracy and objectivity of each book it publishes, the conclusions and
interpretations in Russell Sage Foundation publications are those of the authors and
not of the Foundation, its Trustees, or its staff. Publication by Russell Sage, therefore,
does not imply Foundation endorsement.

Library of Congress Cataloging-in-Publication Data

Credit markets for the poor / Patrick Bolton and Howard Rosenthal, editors.
    p. cm.
    Includes bibliographical references and index.
    ISBN 0-87154-132-7
    1. Credit. 2. Poor. 3. Commercial loans. 4. Credit control. I. Bolton,
Patrick, 1957– II. Rosenthal, Howard, 1939–
HG3751.C7293 2005
332.7'086'942—dc22   2004061486

The paper used in this publication meets the minimum requirements of American
National Standard for Information Sciences—Permanence of Paper for Printed Library Materials. ANSI Z39.48-1992.

Text design by Suzanne Nichols.

RUSSELL SAGE FOUNDATION
112 East 64th Street, New York, New York 10021
10 9 8 7 6 5 4 3 2 1

CONTENTS

CONTRIBUTORS

Patrick Bolton is John H. Scully '66 Professor of Finance and professor of economics in the Bendheim Center for Finance at Princeton University.

Howard Rosenthal is Roger Williams Straus Professor of Social Sciences and professor of politics at Princeton University and distinguished visiting professor of economics and political science at Brown University.

Raisa Bahchieva is research director at the New York City Department of Housing Preservation and Development.

Timothy Bates is Distinguished Professor of Urban and Labor Studies at Wayne State University.

John P. Caskey is professor of economics at Swarthmore College.

Daniela Fabbri is assistant professor of finance at HEC-University of Lausanne and research fellow at International Center for Financial Asset Management and Engineering (FAME).

Robert Kaestner is professor in the Department of Economics and member of the Institute of Government and Public Affairs at the University of Illinois, Chicago, and research associate for the National Bureau of Economic Research.

Malgosia Madajewicz is assistant professor of economics and international affairs in the Department of Economics and School of International and Public Affairs and fellow at the Institute for Social and Economic Research and Policy at Columbia University.

Mario Padula is associate professor of econometrics at the University of Salerno.

Loïc Sadoulet is professor of economics at INSEAD.

Lisa J. Servon is associate professor and associate director of the Community Development Research Center at New School University.

Robert M. Townsend is Charles E. Merriam Distinguished Service Professor in Economics at the University of Chicago.

Susan M. Wachter is professor of real estate and finance at the Wharton School at the University of Pennsylvania.

Antwuan Wallace is a doctoral candidate in policy analysis at New School University.

Elizabeth Warren is Leo Gottlieb Professor of Law at Harvard Law School.

ACKNOWLEDGMENTS

This book reflects the efforts of many more than the editors and contributors. The entire project should be credited to Eric Wanner, president of the Russell Sage Foundation, who urged us to hold a conference on "Credit Markets for the Poor" at a time when our own objectives were far more limited. This volume represents that conference, which took place on May 2–3, 2003, at Princeton University. Gracefully and flawlessly organized by Nancy Danch of the Mahmadoua Bobst Center for Peace and Justice, the conference was held at the Bobst Center. We thank Nancy and the center's director, Jameson Doig, for two days that ran without a hitch in a splendid venue. We thank the discussants, Erik Berglöf, Ngina Cheteji, Paul DiMaggio, Erica Field, Eric Maskin, Ailsa Röell, Gérard Roland, Julia Rubin, Jose Scheinkman, David Skeel, and Peter Tufano. Their comments greatly improved the final versions of the chapters of this book. Very useful comments were also provided by the external reviewer for the Russell Sage Foundation. Finally, Suzanne Nichols, director of publications at Russell Sage, has been a pesky but very welcome thorn in our sides throughout the entire publication process.

Chapter 1

Introduction

Patrick Bolton and Howard Rosenthal

Even when they are just as creditworthy as others, poor and minority borrowers are sometimes excluded from formal credit markets. As Oded Galor and Joseph Zeira (1993), Abhijit Banerjee and Andrew Newman (1993), and Philippe Aghion and Patrick Bolton (1997)—among others—have argued, excluding such individuals is all the more troubling if it permanently impedes their rise from poverty.

The exclusion of poor borrowers can indicate inefficiency in credit markets and the existence of credit rationing. Economists and policy makers have long worried about problems related to credit rationing. A large literature in economics and finance establishes a fundamental link between it and imperfect information (Stiglitz and Weiss 1981; Jaffee and Stiglitz 1990). The key assumption underlying early ideas of credit rationing is that lenders are imperfectly informed about borrowers' creditworthiness. Coupled with that assumption is the observation that, with rising interest rates, the risk pool of credit applicants worsens, because only riskier and more desperate borrowers are willing to borrow at the more onerous terms. A fairly intuitive conclusion is that under such circumstances lenders may prefer to ration credit at lower interest rates than to extend loans to the highest bidders. The main concern with this form of credit rationing, then, is that it might exclude the poor and minorities from formal credit markets even when many of them are just as creditworthy as other borrowers. A related concern is that credit rationing may also arise from discrimination and out of lenders' exaggerated concerns about minority borrowers' creditworthiness. Although it is difficult to substantiate these claims conclusively, there is some recent evidence supporting this view (see Blanchflower, Levine, and Zimmerman 2003).

The recent literature in development economics has put the spotlight on this potential inefficiency and identifies credit rationing as a key cause of underdevelopment (see Banerjee 2003 for a recent survey). On the policy front, many also see the emergence of Grameen Banks—which specialize in small, short-term loans to relatively poor individuals or groups—as the main innovation in development policy in the last two decades and the new hope for the poor in developing countries (see Armendariz and Morduch 2004).

Another cause of credit rationing is imperfect enforcement of loan repayments and strategic defaults (see, for example, Hart 1995). According to this view, the poor are more likely to be excluded from formal credit markets because they are less able to provide collateral to alleviate the risk of default. This perspective also emphasizes that the poor may often be the main victims of excessively lenient loan enforcement policies, weak courts, and weak debt-collection rights. While these policies obviously help a poor borrower in dire straits, they can also raise the cost of borrowing and lead to poor borrowers' being excluded altogether from credit markets. The contrast between the thriving market for automobile loans and the anemic mortgage market in Brazil provides a telling illustration of this problem. While under Brazilian law it is relatively easy to repossess a car ` following default on an automobile loan, it is very difficult to evict occupants of a dwelling who have defaulted on their mortgage. This latter source of credit rationing calls for different policy responses, such as improving debt collection or enforcing debt contracts. Another proposed response, emphasized especially by Hernando de Soto (2003), is to give legal ownership claims to poor squatters that could be used as collateral in a loan agreement. In chapter 5, Daniela Fabbri and Mario Padula present evidence of the effects of inadequate procedures for debt collection in Italy, a developed economy.

More generally, despite the wide acceptance of the notion that credit rationing is an important problem in economic development, little is known on how the poor are dealing with barriers to borrowing in developed economies. The same is true on how policy intervention should be designed to best address inefficiencies in credit markets. The contributions in this book are an attempt to fill this gap.

As the chapters by John P. Caskey (chapter 2), Lisa J. Servon,

Robert Kaestner, and Antwuan Wallace (chapter 3), Timothy Bates (chapter 6), and Robert M. Townsend (chapter 7) vividly illustrate, there is an extensive set of credit markets for the poor in the United States that is almost entirely separated from the mainstream. They operate below the radar screen of most researchers, who study the larger, more formal, financial markets. But, as this volume highlights, these markets are very important for the poor, who rely on them. Improvements in these markets could bring substantial benefits. It is also apparent from the studies in this volume that credit rationing in practice does not simply manifest itself as a sharp dividing line between those who have access to credit and those who have not. In reality, there is a range of alternative credit options open to poor borrowers, some involving fairly sophisticated institutional arrangements.

These markets are especially important in nations with weak social safety nets. The United States, in particular, is widely acknowledged as providing only minimal redistributive transfers to the poor. Credit markets, albeit imperfectly, can substitute for the lack of direct redistribution. They have the potential to provide both for short-term consumption smoothing in the face of job loss, unexpected health care expenses, and other personal reverses. Credit is also thought of as a motor for entrepreneurship, providing the funds to allow the poor to escape poverty.

The poor who borrow to smooth consumption have limited access to formal credit markets. They are likely to have bad credit histories or to have reached the limit of their borrowing capacity. They therefore might face rates as high or higher than 350 percent if they engage in payday loans, a popular form of short-term "bridge" lending (see chapter 2 for a detailed description). If they are members of a marginal racial, ethnic, or immigrant group, they may depend more on informal credit channels. They may also lack the wherewithal to benefit from low-cost transactions available via the Internet. If they borrow to finance a subprime residence, such as a mobile home, they will borrow at higher rates than their more affluent peers. These poor, it should be stressed, are nonetheless not the very bottom of the economic ladder. A checking account, for example, is required to obtain a payday loan or subsidized use of the Internet. The homeless, by definition, do not have mortgages on dwellings, whether mobile or fixed.

A basic shortcoming of credit markets as a vehicle for redistribution is that they require the participation of lenders. As capitalists, lenders lend only if the loan is expected to be profitable. To start a small business the poor often need government subsidies or loan guarantees. But to ensure that a business looking for a subsidy is at least minimally viable, government programs may demand minimum training and skills in the borrowers. Inevitably, these requirements often mean that the loans wind up going to only a subset of the targeted population.

Nonetheless, even if credit markets for the poor are only an imperfect substitute for redistribution, they can have an important impact on poverty levels and social inequality. It is therefore important to consider how these markets operate, how they affect poverty and inequality, and how they might be made more efficient.

This book reports on research in the operation of these markets along several dimensions. The writers have backgrounds in economics, political science, business, law, urban planning, and government. Their work here addresses three broad issues.

First is the exclusion of poor households from the banking sector and more generally the mainstream formal credit markets. This volume asks what types of credit arrangements are available to the poor who do not borrow through bank loans or credit card debt. How do these alternative lending arrangements compare to more mainstream credit? How easy is it to obtain such loans? How large is the spread over typical bank loans or credit card debt? What is the risk of default?

The second major theme relates to how debt repayment is enforced. Here the main economic question is whether legal or nonlegal obstacles to debt collection lead to inefficiency in credit markets. Is the unavailability of credit for the poor driven by the lack of effective enforcement of debt collection? If so, should enforcement be strengthened, as the personal bankruptcy "reform" bill debated by the last five Congresses proposes? Or are existing limitations on debt collection justified as basic protections for those driven into debt by desperation?

The third issue deals with credit for investment and entrepreneurship. Here the central economic question is whether, as is often assumed, low levels of business creation and self-employment among poor households are explained by the inability to produce collateral for the first bank loan to launch a business. Part III of the book makes it clear that the determinants of entrepreneurship among the poor are complex and that the dearth of business creation in that segment of society cannot be attributed solely to credit rationing. For example, social networks among the poor play an important role in the supply of financing. Also, when the poor borrow with collective responsibility, as in the Grameen Bank and its multiple offshoots, they may be able to self-enforce repayments via group monitoring and thus make lending more viable. Interestingly, as successful as these group-lending schemes have proved in some developing countries, their performance in more developed countries is at best mixed and raises the question whether the poor in developed countries are better off borrowing alone. Other questions are taken up in part III of this volume. One is how one can provide financing that allows the poor to default in exceptional circumstances, as a safety valve, without hurting their reputations for credit worthiness. Another is how important human capital is as a complement to financial capital.

Credit and Banking Services at the Fringe

The chapters by John Caskey and by Lisa Servon, Robert Kaestner, and Antwuan Wallace both focus on households at the fringe of the formal banking sector. In chapter 2, Caskey builds on his earlier Russell Sage volume, *Fringe Banking: Check-Cashing Outlets, Pawnshops, and the Poor* (1994), and documents important changes that have occurred in the last decade in small-scale lending to poor households. He highlights a major shift away from lending by pawnshops to so-called "payday lending." The phrase refers to very short-term loans taken out by workers who run out of cash before payday. In a typical arrangement, the lender advances cash in exchange for a personal check made out by the borrower to the lender. The lender then holds on to the check for a limited time before depositing it. As Caskey documents, this form of short-term lending has now outgrown lending by pawnbrokers. Caskey's study raises a number of interesting positive and normative economic questions. An immediate first question is why has this form of lending gradually supplanted lending by pawnbrokers? Another question is why banks appear to be unwilling to cover this segment. Bank behavior is all the more puzzling given that payday lending requires that the borrower open a checking account at a bank. Caskey suggests that the rise in direct pay deposits by employers to employee checking accounts is the main reason for the relative growth in payday lending, and regulatory restrictions may explain why banks have not entered this lucrative market.

His study also reveals that many poor are repeat, even habitual, borrowers even though the costs are prohibitive. This raises the question of whether payday lenders are taking advantage of the lack of self-control or other behavioral biases of some poor borrowers. A related question is why the costs of borrowing for repeat borrowers are not brought down by competition.

In chapter 3, Servon, Kaestner, and Wallace are concerned with the general question of how poor households' exclusion from formal mainstream credit markets, whether as borrowers or savers, can be alleviated through policy. They point to the digital divide as an increasingly important factor in that bank policies of encouraging depositors to switch to online banking may have the unintended effect of excluding the poor, who do not have easy online access. They study an attempt of a major bank to tackle this issue by facilitating Internet access for poor depositors through grants of computers, Internet access, and training. As their study reveals and as one might have expected, the results of this laudable initiative are unfortunately somewhat disappointing. Although participants were conscious of the benefits of online access, insufficient resources toward training and toward subsidized online access were devoted by the bank to make this experiment work. It is hardly surprising that a profit-motivated bank would not set up an effective but loss-inducing program. Nonetheless, this study reveals that poor households would be responsive to such a program if it were adequately funded. It also points to an increasingly important divide, which is yet another factor excluding the poor from formal credit markets.

Legal Institutions and Household Borrowing

How do legal institutions affect the borrowing of households? How does the impact of the institution vary as a function of the borrower's income and wealth? These questions are addressed in part II in chapters by Raisa Bahchieva, Susan M. Wachter, and Elizabeth Warren, and Daniela Fabbri and Marco Padula. In chapter 4, Bahchieva, Wachter, and Warren study another potential form of exclusion—from home ownership via mortgage markets. They examine recent trends in home ownership and in mortgage debt for homeowners, painting a mixed picture of the spread of homeownership in the last decade or so. While undoubtedly homeownership has grown among poorer households and has facilitated the integration of those households into credit markets, it has also been accompanied by a rise in mortgage debt and greater financial fragility. The authors demonstrate that, among low-income households, the rising indebtedness was not so much a consequence of the changing tax status of low-income debt as it was of government policy that facilitated borrowing by low-income households. The chapter suggests that these policies may have led to too much indebtedness among lower income households.

Overindebtedness is reflected in the relatively higher growth in the number of personal bankruptcy filings in recent years versus the growth in home ownership. Thus, although poor households have benefited ex ante from a greater access to mortgage debt, the authors hint that ex post a large fraction of these households might have ended up worse off. They may be highly vulnerable to even small negative income shocks that would push them into bankruptcy and result in the loss of their homes. Furthermore, as the authors suggest, they might have ended up in this exposed financial state for lack of foresight and for imprudent borrowing encouraged by aggressive loan-marketing policies of lenders. About half of all bankruptcies are now homeowners or were homeowners shortly before bankruptcy. In their sample of households, average debt has risen faster than average assets. This finding, however, should be balanced against other evidence showing that median net worth has increased significantly over the past decade.

The authors find that loan-to-value ratios are lower in states where a large amount of home equity is protected in bankruptcy. Homeowners in those states are less likely to lose their homes. The authors therefore propose that higher homestead exemptions in bankruptcy may be called for as a way of protecting poor households against themselves, by discouraging them from borrowing too irresponsibly against their homes.

In chapter 5, and in contrast to Bahchieva, Wachter, and Warren's argument, Fabbri and Padula point to the benefits of better enforcement of debt contracts in Italy. Indeed, their analysis reveals how Italian jurisdictions with stricter legal enforcement of creditor rights also have more developed credit markets and, in particular, more lending to poor households. Most of the loans in their sample are secured loans, but creditor costs in seizing the collateral against which they have lent vary across provinces.

That is, Fabbri and Padula argue that the variation in the backlog of pending cases in district courts across provinces is a proxy for the variation in debt collection costs across these same provinces. The higher the backlog, the longer the time to get court approval to seize collateral following default and therefore the higher the debt collection costs. Their study finds a positive statistical relation between this backlog variable and a variable indicating the fraction of poor households that have been denied a loan application. They also suggest that the variation in court backlogs is itself driven by variations in regional economic development, with poorer regions having more backlogs.

Small Business Loans

Part III of this volume deals with the other major function of credit markets for the poor: allowing poor households to take advantage of investment opportunities and thus exit poverty. A common concern among social scientists is that poor households may be disadvantaged in accessing investment opportunities that may be open to them and that they may be "trapped in poverty" because they are not able to borrow to fund their initial investment outlays. In response to these concerns several policy initiatives have been set up to provide subsidies towards business creation by "disadvantaged" households. The chapter by Timothy Bates (chapter 6) studies government subsidized loans. Robert Townsend (chapter 7) explores how community networks affect credit markets. Loïc Sadoulet (chapter 8) explores how borrowers can be insured against short-term reverses. Malgosia Madajewicz (chapter 9) asks when group loans can succeed.

In chapter 6, Bates provides an illuminating assessment of some of these initiatives and a healthy warning, pointing to major flaws and deficiencies of existing subsidized business creation programs. He argues that there is little evidence to date that the facilitation of small-business creation is an effective strategy towards poverty reduction. A basic problem with these programs, he observes, is that it is far from obvious that the typical disadvantaged household has the expertise to run a small business. In addition, these households might not have profitable investment opportunities available that would dominate other job opportunities. As a result, programs that subsidize small business creation often end up targeting the wrong households, those that might well have successfully set up a business even in the absence of a subsidy. Worse still, these programs may lure inexperienced households into entrepreneurship, thus setting them up for failure, and ultimately making them worse off. His chapter discusses the Economic Opportunity Lending (EOL) programs set up under the Johnson administration as a part of the War on Poverty and points out that the businesses created under these programs have been beset by high failure and default rates, so much so that the programs were eventually phased out in 1984.

If lack of financial resources is only part of the explanation for the low rates of small-business creation among the poor, it is important to identify the other factors that are relevant for entrepreneurship. Are the high failure rates in the EOL programs due to a lack of training, or to low levels of education? Or are there other critical factors?

These questions are taken up in Townsend's study (chapter 7), which compares patterns of formal and informal lending to poor households in three ethnically diverse neighborhoods in Chicago and Minneapolis. Interestingly, his study points to extensive use of informal credit. Family and nonfamily connections are called on both to help face adverse income shocks due to illness or layoffs and to help start new business ventures. His study shows, however, that these informal lending relations cannot be a perfect substitute for more formal lending arrangements and cannot perfectly overcome credit rationing in the formal credit markets. Perhaps the most striking finding is that the extent to which households do rely on informal networks to smooth consumption or raise funds for investment varies considerably with the ethnic composition of the neighborhood. His study compares lending and small-business creation in three neighborhoods. The first is a predominantly Hispanic district in Chicago, with also some Korean businesses. The second is another Chicago neighborhood dominated by lower middle-class African American households. The third is a neighborhood in Minneapolis–St. Paul dominated by Hmong, an ethnic community from Laos. Townsend describes how in Hispanic communities informal lending networks are highly developed but involve relatively small transactions. Consistent with Bahchieva, Wachter, and Warren's findings, he reports that the homeowners (or the households with higher incomes) tend to substitute away from these informal networks and rely more on formal credit markets. In the Hmong community these informal networks are, if anything, stronger and more persistent. Among Koreans, financial transactions rely less on family ties, are more formal, and involve larger amounts. In contrast, the African American communities appear more fragmented and seem to rely much less on lending through informal ethnic-based networks.

The importance of informal lending and ethnic- or community-based networks underlined in Townsend's study has also been stressed in recent years in developing countries. Indeed, the most striking recent innovations in development finance are related to the microcredit movement around the Grameen Banks, which tries to exploit these community ties to initiate less default-prone credit to poor households. Some of these microcredit experiments have been so successful in raising very poor communities' living standards that they have encouraged similar experiments in poor neighborhoods in developed countries.

In chapter 8, Sadoulet begins by pointing out the limited success of existing microcredit programs in developed countries. More often than not financial institutions specializing in this form of group lending to the poor have found that they could not generate a sufficiently high rate of return and have closed down. Sadoulet singles out several reasons—ranging from the higher costs of setting up a sufficiently dense branching network, poor contract design, inadequate processing of claims and lack of institutional credibility—why these programs could not be as successful as their counterparts in some developing countries. He argues that these programs would be more effective if they were run by regular banks rather than specialized institutions.

For banks to run successful group lending programs, however, Sadoulet argues that they need to set up a complementary repayment insurance program. He observes that group lending programs, while taking advantage of existing informal community networks and getting the network involved in monitoring the start-up business by imposing joint liability on the group, also impose unwanted default risk on the credit group. He argues that this risk is more efficiently shared with the lending institution. He proposes that, to share this risk, the bank issue an experience-rated insurance policy along with the loan, giving the group borrower some protection against the joint liability risk. Should the individual borrower be unable to repay then he would be able to draw on his insurance policy. However, each draw on the policy would result in higher insurance premiums and/or lower future protection to preserve incentives.

As appealing as this proposal sounds, Sadoulet is aware of at least two potential obstacles to its implementation. First, he points out that the first bank who offers such an insurance policy may be seen as a "weak" debt enforcer and may thus encourage hit-and-run borrowing. Second, repayment insurance may be discouraged by bank regulators if it raises complex accounting and prudential regulation issues.

In chapter 9, Madajewicz points to another potential drawback of group lending, negative incentive effects of joint liability. She argues that group borrowers have reduced incentives to limit the risk of the individual projects they undertake to the extent that this risk is shared with other group members. Furthermore, she contends that this negative incentive effect is likely to be larger for relatively wealthier borrowers. She suggests that this incentive effect may be one reason for the observed better growth record of small businesses funded through individual loan than through group loan contracts. The reason is that the incentive problem under group lending induces lenders to lend smaller per-capita amounts as a way of mitigating risk-taking incentives. Thus, in her analysis, joint liability under group lending has both a positive and a negative effect. Madajewicz provides some supporting evidence for her analysis from Bangladesh and argues that the negative incentive effect she identifies may be one reason why microcredit has not been as successful in developed countries. Indeed, she points out that microcredit schemes in the United States have always taken the form of group lending. She suggests that perhaps individual loans might have been better in the more developed economies, where the poor have relatively more assets.

Taken together, the four studies in part III identify a number of important conditions for small-business lending to be successful.

Borrowing needs to be complemented by human capital. As Bates documents in chapter 6, subsidized loans to small businesses are much less likely to succeed if the borrower has no training and a low level of education. Borrowing needs to be complemented by social capital. At the same time, group effects cannot be artificially imposed from the outside. The experience of the Grameen Bank has led to many programs where a group of poor have joint liability for all the loans issued to the group. Townsend documents in chapter 7 the striking variety of informal lending across ethnically diverse neighborhoods, with family or community-based credit much more widely available to the Hmong living in Minneapolis, who have a tight interpersonal network, and to first-generation Mexicans in Chicago than to the more fragmented African American communities in Chicago. As Sadoulet and Madajewicz discuss in chapters 8 and 9, these programs are notoriously unsuccessful in the United States. Defaults, in particular, are rife. The low success rate of these programs in more developed countries may be due to higher administrative costs, as both Sadoulet and Madajewicz stress, but also to the fact that the constituency of poor group-borrowers is those households who have been denied other sources of credit, which in developed countries are relatively easier to get. Therefore, group borrowers in developed countries are likely to be on average less well suited to small-business creation through these programs.

Political Economy of Credit Markets

Part IV completes the volume with chapter 10 by Howard Rosenthal, who explores how political forces shape policy intervention in credit markets. His chapter provides an overview of political economy analyses of credit markets. A valuable backdrop for the previous, mostly empirical, studies of credit markets for the poor, it lays out the policy questions related to the exclusion of the poor from credit markets and the protection of debtors in financial distress. Rosenthal focuses mainly on positive analyses of the link between inequalities in wealth, the operation of credit markets, and political intervention. He highlights how the interaction of credit markets and politics with inequality can be quite subtle. He points out, for example, that a high degree of initial inequality might prevent credit markets from operating altogether if the political process offers opportunities for the subsequent abrogation of debt obligations. At the other extreme, if the debtor constituency is not strong enough the political process will not deliver adequate relief to debtors in a financial crisis.

In several of the theoretical studies that Rosenthal summarizes, the model economies have the property that, when budding entrepreneurs borrow, the credit market will reduce poverty but lead to an increase in inequality. A few borrowers get lucky and reap huge returns. The models suggest that while the supply of credit to the poor may substitute for redistribution in terms of poverty reduction, the very success of a credit market may increase pressures to redistribute.

Other theoretical work discussed examines the effect of government regulation and political intervention. Usury laws, which limit the ability of the poor to borrow, can be seen as improving welfare. Lax enforcement, in the form of "fresh start" personal bankruptcy protections or of limitations on ability to collect debts and attach collateral, can be seen as largely beneficial to borrowers with high ability or endowments. The worst off, in terms of initial ability or endowments, will be unaffected, because they are always credit rationed. Intermediate types, however, may become credit rationed as laxity is increased. In many cases, the relevant political coalitions could thus involve the "rich" and "poor" intervening in debt markets against the interests of the middle.

Summary

Credit markets for the poor operate largely apart from the mainstream credit markets. They are mostly invisible to the wealthier borrowers and lenders as well as to most financial researchers, who study the larger and more formal financial markets. Small improvements in these markets, however, can be of great importance for the poor, who are constrained to rely on them. As this volume highlights, these are not simple markets with simple financial transactions. Their efficiency and competitiveness could conceivably be improved along many different dimensions. However, to determine appropriate political interventions in these markets with greater confidence more research into these understudied markets is called for.

Credit markets transfer resources from the haves to have-nots.

Unlike transfers, however, they may not reduce inequality. Some funded projects succeed and others fail. The successes escape poverty. The failures, at best, default and are no better off than they were before borrowing. Even worse, as with repeated payday borrowers, the poor may get into a vicious cycle of borrowing that drains their resources.

This book provides many new insights into how borrowing by the poor might be made more productive. Promising steps include fostering investment in both human and social capital that complements financial capital, and carefully designing laws and institutions that structure incentives and protect the poor from the temptation to borrow more than they can repay.

References

Aghion, Philippe, and Patrick Bolton. 1997. "A Theory of Trickle-Down Growth and Development." *Review of Economic Studies* 64(2): 151–72.

Armendariz, Beatriz, and Jonathan Morduch. 2004. *The Economics of Microfinance*. Cambridge, Mass.: MIT Press.

Banerjee, Abhijit. 2003. "Contracting Constraints, Credit Markets, and Economic Development." In *Advances in Economics and Econometrics: Theory and Applications, Eighth World Congress of the Econometric Society,* Vol. III, edited by Mathias Dewatripont, Lars Peter Hansen, and Stephen J. Turnovsky. New York: Cambridge University Press.

Banerjee, Abhijit, and Andrew Newman. 1993. "Occupational Choice and the Process of Development." *Journal of Political Economy* 101(2): 274–98.

Blanchflower, David, Phillip Levine, and David Zimmerman. 2003. "Discrimination in the Small Business Credit Market." *Review of Economics and Statistics* 85(4): 930–43.

Caskey, John P. 1994. *Fringe Banking: Check-Cashing Outlets, Pawnshops, and the Poor.* New York: Russell Sage Foundation.

de Soto, Hernando. 2003. *The Mystery of Capital: Why Capitalism Triumphs in the West and Fails Everywhere Else.* New York: Basic Books.

Galor, Oded, and Joseph Zeira. 1993. "Income Distribution and Macroeconomics." *Review of Economic Studies* 60(1): 35–52

Hart, Oliver. 1995. *Firms, Contracts, and Financial Structure.* Clarendon Lectures in Economics. New York: Oxford University Press.

Jaffee, Dwight, and Joseph E. Stiglitz. 1990. "Credit Rationing." In *Handbook of Monetary Economics,* edited by Benjamin M. Friedman and Frank H. Hahn. Amsterdam: North-Holland.

Stiglitz, Joseph E., and Andrew Weiss. 1981. "Credit Rationing in Markets with Imperfect Information." *American Economic Review* 71(3): 393–410.

Part I

Credit and Banking Services
at the Fringe

Chapter 2

Fringe Banking and the Rise of Payday Lending

John P. Caskey

Ten years ago I wrote a book entitled, *Fringe Banking: Check-Cashing Outlets, Pawnshops, and the Poor* (Caskey 1994). It focused on the operations of check-cashing outlets and pawnshops, explained who used these "fringe banks" for financial services and why, and documented the rapid growth in fringe banks in the 1980s and early 1990s.

Here I review major changes in fringe banking that have occurred in the decade since then. My focus now, however, is not just on pawnshops and check-cashing outlets (CCOs) but also on payday lending. I made this change for two reasons. First, payday lending has been the most rapidly growing segment of fringe banking for the past ten years and now is probably as large as, or larger than, pawnbroking. Second, one cannot discuss changes in pawnbroking and check cashing without discussing the influence that the explosive growth in payday lending has had on these industries.

Rise of Payday Lending

In a traditional payday loan, a customer writes a personal check made out to the lender, which the lender agrees to hold for about two weeks before depositing. In exchange, the payday lender advances to the customer a cash payment that is somewhat less than the amount of the check. The difference, which is the "finance charge," combined with the maturity of the loan determines the annualized interest rate. In the states where payday lending thrives, lenders typically charge $15 to $25 for each $100 they advance. That is, in a typical transaction, a borrower might write a check for $235 that the lender agrees to hold for two weeks and the lender then provides the borrower with a $200 cash advance on that check. In most cases, the loan process is very quick. A first-time borrower who arrives with the necessary information (a check, recent pay stub, copies of recent bank statements, identification, and a series of utility bills or other evidence of a stable place of residence) can walk out with his cash in less than thirty minutes.

Before the loan matures, the borrower can pay the lender the face value of the check in cash, extinguishing the debt, and concluding the transaction. If the borrower does not repay the loan by its maturity, the lender may deposit the check. Assuming that the check clears, the loan is fully repaid and the transaction complete.

If a borrower does not want to or cannot repay a loan at maturity, a lender will frequently allow him or her to renew the loan by "rolling it over." In a rollover, the borrower pays the lender the finance charge due at maturity and the lender agrees to hold the check for another specified period. Another way to extend the maturity of a loan is a "same-day" advance. That is, the borrower repays an existing loan with its finance charge and, on the same day, takes out a new cash advance equivalent to the previous one.

Under either method, the interest on the loan is paid with each renewal. There is no compounding of interest. This makes the calculation of the annual percentage rate quite simple. For example, the annual percentage interest rate on a two-week $200 loan for which the lender charges $30 is 390 percent (15 percent for 2 weeks multiplied by 26). Given the short maturity of the loans and the size of the finance charge relative to the size of the loan, the annual percentage rate on payday loans commonly falls between 350 and 1,000 percent.

Researchers have conducted several surveys of the characteristics of payday loan customers and their findings are broadly consistent.[1] All payday loan customers have bank accounts, for this is what makes them eligible for the service. The vast majority is employed and has a household income between $15,000 and $60,000. The customers tend to be young adults; most are under forty years old. Most have children in the household. A strong majority has a high school education; about half have some higher education. Somewhat more than half are women. About half carry major credit cards.

Information on why people seek payday loans is more limited. Payday lenders say that their clients have almost no money in their bank accounts and face pressing expenditure needs. Such a situation may arise because of an unexpected expense, an unexpected income shortfall, or poor budgeting habits. The vast majority of their customers do not have access to convenient lower-cost credit from mainstream lenders because they either have severely impaired credit histories or have reached the limit of the credit lines these lenders are willing to extend. Payday lenders emphasize that their customers, rather than taking out a payday loan, could pay bills with checks they know will bounce or pay some bills late. These measures, however, can be more costly than a payday loan. Banks commonly charge $20 to $30 for each bounced check and the firms to which the checks were written also typically impose "returned check" charges, often around $20.[2] In addition, utility companies, landlords, and other firms commonly impose stiff financial penalties for late payments.

Not surprisingly, given that payday lenders make unsecured loans to high-risk borrowers, the lenders incur substantial loan losses, but not as high as one might expect. Most lenders report that loan losses are about 10 to 20 percent of their annual payday loan revenues. Such losses reflect a number of steps the lenders use to limit their risk. Most, for example, will lend only to applicants with steady employment records who have maintained checking accounts in good standing for at least six months. Many lenders limit first-time customers to loans of $200 or less but gradually increase the size of cash advances to customers who develop a history of repaying or renewing loans on time. Lenders commonly limit the size of loans, even to well-established customers, to under $500. With first-time applicants, many lenders will pay a fee to obtain a report from TeleTrack, a credit bureau that focuses on the fringe banking market. The report will tell a lender whether the applicant has failed to repay other payday lenders and whether the applicant has other outstanding payday loans. Lenders further reduce their risk by responding quickly when there are indications that a borrower might default. In discussions with such customers, lenders will encourage them to repay or renew their loans by emphasizing possible penalties tied to a failure to do so. A lender will, for example, point out that if he deposits a customer's check and it bounces, the resulting fall of dominoes will include a "non-sufficient funds" (NSF) fee from the borrower's bank, a returned check charge from the lender, and—possibly—legal expenses. In addition, the bank may force a borrower to close her account if she has a history of writing NSF checks.[3]

In surveys of payday loan customers and in focus groups, the customers commonly report that they find a number of features of the loans attractive (Elliehausen and Lawrence 2001; Wilson 2002). They like the fact that there is no traditional credit check. They like the fast loan decision and disbursal. They like the closed-end, short-term structure of the loan because they think that this meets their needs and reduces the chances that they will incur a long-term debt-service burden. They view the loan as much more convenient and respectable than a pawnshop loan since they do not have to leave collateral in the possession of the lender. Customers consistently report that they do not like the high cost of the loans.

People strongly disagree over whether payday lending provides a useful service for most customers. Defenders of the industry argue that payday lenders provide a form of short-term emergency liquidity insurance to people who have no better alternatives. Acknowledging that the loans appear to be outrageously expensive when stated in terms of the annual percentage rate, they argue that this is misleading. Payday advances, they explain, are intended to be very short-term loans. They also emphasize that there is a fixed cost to processing a closed-end unsecured loan of any size and, because payday loans are small, this cost is bound to be high relative to the size of the loan. Further contributing to the high cost of the loans are the loss rates on them and the extensive portfolio monitoring that the lenders do to minimize the losses.

Critics of payday lending argue that most customers do not use payday loans solely as an occasional short-term emergency source of credit. They say that instead, whatever their initial intent, many take out such loans frequently. They may borrow once to meet an unexpected emergency or a cash shortfall caused by careless budgeting. In many cases, however, when the next pay period comes they face a difficult choice. They can use their available cash to repay the loan. If they do, given their limited income available for discretionary expenditures, they are likely to run short again before the next pay period and need to take out another advance. Alternatively, they can simply pay the finance charge and extend the loan another pay period, that is, "roll over" the loan. Either approach leads them, very likely, to the next pay period facing the same set of choices. This way, a short-term emergency loan becomes either a medium-term loan through a series of rollovers or a series of briefly interrupted short-term loans.

The data clearly indicate that, unless external limits prevent it, most payday loan customers take out such loans frequently. State regulators from Indiana, Illinois, North Carolina, and Wisconsin collected time series data from individual payday loan outlets to document how frequently customers use the loans.[4] They find that most payday loan customers entered into seven or more loan transactions over the course of a year and that about a quarter entered into fourteen or more. The Wisconsin Department of Financial Institutions provided me with its raw data after eliminating all information that could possibly identify a particular lender or borrower. The data were collected in the fall of 2000 from seventeen payday loan offices across the state. At each of the offices, examiners from the department attempted to gather information from twenty randomly selected active loan files and five closed ones. The examiners asked the lenders to provide a history of all transactions for the selected borrowers for the previous year. The active files were outstanding loans that were not in arrears at the time of the examination. The closed files were loans that had already matured; whether they were paid off in full was not specified. In some cases, the closed files included loans that fell due only within the month before the examination. In cleaning the data, the department eliminated the data from three lenders because these lenders were too young to have data going back a full year.

After eliminating a small number of observations with extensive missing or obviously erroneous data entries, I retained the records for 322 loan clients, 283 with active accounts and 39 with closed accounts. There were a total of 3,832 reported loan transactions (originations or renewals), about 11.9 per customer. The average term for the loan originations and renewals was 14 days; nearly 90 percent were for between 12 and 16 days. The average cash advance was $245.03 and the average finance charge $49.37, implying an

Table 2.1   Distribution of Wisconsin Payday Loan Customers by Number
of Transactions

Number of Loans per Borrower Within Previous Year	Number Borrowers in Category	Percentage Borrowers in Category
1 to 5	84	26.1%
6 to 10	79	24.5
11 to 20	101	31.4
More than 20	58	18.0

Source: Author's estimates using data from Wisconsin Department of Financial Institutions (2001).

average APR of 528 percent. Table 2.1 shows the distribution of the customers by number of loan transactions. About 26 percent of the clients had fewer than six transactions over the previous year and 18 percent had more than twenty.[5]

The data in table 2.1, which as noted are similar to the data from other state agencies, can be somewhat misleading. Recall that 283 (88 percent) of the borrowers in the data set had active accounts at the time of the data collection. What is not shown in the table is that 16 percent of the active borrowers had taken out their first loan from the payday lender within only two months. Another 61 percent initiated their first loan between two and six months prior to the examination date. These relatively new customers are bound to take out fewer loans over the previous year. Thus, the borrowers in the first category of table 2.1, those taking out five or fewer loans over the previous year are primarily short-term customers, not long-term customers who borrowed infrequently. In fact, of the 127 customers in the data set who were customers at least once ten months or more before their most recent loan, only four took out five or fewer loans over the course of the year. But 56 (44 percent) of these long-term customers had more than twenty loan transactions. The median long-term customer had nineteen loan originations or renewals over the course of the year.[6]

The department's data also permit an examination of patterns with respect to loan renewals, defined to be a rollover or same-day advance. Of the 322 customers, 20.2 percent never renewed a loan in the relevant period, 38.5 percent had four or more sequential renewals, and 15.5 percent had seven or more. If we limit the analysis to customers who took out at least one loan ten or more months before their most recent loan, 11.8 percent never renewed a loan, 54.3 percent had four or more sequential renewals, and 23.6 percent had seven or more. Moreover, as noted earlier, some customers consistently repay their loans on the due dates but take out new loans before their next payday, remaining out of debt only a few days between paydays. Of the 3,832 transactions, 53 percent were rollovers or same-day advances. But an additional 26 percent were loan originations made within one to thirteen days of the termination of the previous loan.

A few states set limits on the number of times a payday lender can renew a loan (Fox and Mierswinski 2001). In those that do, typically the cap is three or four times. Even in states that do not, some lenders set their own limits.[7] But most payday loan customers probably find the limits only a mild inconvenience. If state law, or lender policy, restricts only rollovers, a lender can renew the loan with a same-day advance. If same-day advances are not permitted, a borrower can create one by repaying one lender and, on the same day, going to another to take out a new loan. Finally, a borrower can repay one lender, wait a few days, and borrow again from the same lender or a different one.

Although payday lending in its modern incarnation began to emerge and grow explosively only in the mid-1990s, variants of it have been around a long time. In the early 1900s some lenders would "buy" a worker's next salary at a discount a few days before it was paid out. These early payday loans were structured as salary-purchases in an effort to avoid state usury laws (Neifeld 1939). In a 1975 master's thesis on the check-cashing industry in New York City, Irving Wolf (1975, 21) reported that in the 1930s some check cashers "cashed postdated checks and charged a 'fee' for each day the check was not negotiated."

It appears that in the early 1990s only a small share of check cashers engaged in payday lending in states where check-cashing fees were unregulated or loosely regulated (Caskey 1994). There are, however, no firm data to document its evolution from 1990 to 1995. Before 1995, almost no state regulatory authorities collected data on payday lenders. One cannot use yellow-page listings to document the rise of the industry because most list themselves under "check cashing" or under "loans," categories that include other businesses as well. Payday lenders have told me that between 1993 and

1995, an increasing number of check cashers began to enter the business. At the same time, in a small number of states without restrictive usury laws, some entrepreneurs opened "monoline" stores that specialized in payday lending, rather than combining this service with commercial check cashing. The evidence indicates that, by 1995, the industry was growing very rapidly in many states, and it sustained this growth through 2001.

Wisconsin's Department of Financial Institutions (2001), for example, reports that in 1995 there were seventeen payday loan offices in the state. In early 2003, the licensee list on the department's website listed 278. The North Carolina Office of the Commissioner of Banks (2001b) reported that there were 307 payday loan offices in that state in 1997. By year-end 2001, there were 1,204. The rapid spread of payday loan offices caught the attention of journalists. My own search for news articles, under the "business and finance" category of Lexis-Nexis, using the term "payday loan" in the article title or first paragraph found that before 1996 there were no such articles and in 1996 there were two. In 1999, there were 111.

By 2002, payday loan offices were found in all but a few states. The exact number nationally is not known because many states do not require the lenders to hold licenses or do not report the number of licensees. In 2001, an investment banker who helps finance the industry estimated that there were 10,000 payday loan offices nationwide, about half of which also function as CCOs (Robinson 2001). About 4,400 of these belonged to firms that operate 200 or more offices across multiple states.

In states where usury laws are not restrictive, many payday lenders operate as state-licensed lenders.[8] But some, including nearly all in states with restrictive laws, function as agents for banks that are in states with permissive usury rules. Under such arrangements, a customer completes a loan application in the payday lender's office, but the out-of-state bank approves and books the loan. The bank may subsequently sell a substantial share of the loan back to the lender or kick back a substantial share of the interest payments on the loans. In exchange, the lender agrees to reimburse the bank for most of its associated loan losses. Payday lenders argue that, under such arrangements, the relevant usury ceiling is that of the state where the bank is because, like banks that offer credit cards across state lines, the bank can "export" its interest rates to customers in other states.[9]

These bank–payday lender partnerships, often referred to by critics as "rent-a-charter" deals, have been challenged on a number of fronts. A few states have restricted the ability of local businesses to operate as agents of out-of-state banks. In addition, the chartering authorities for national banks and thrifts—Office of the Comptroller of the Currency (OCC) and the Office of Thrift Supervision (OTS)—have indicated that they think such arrangements almost inevitably bring excessive risk to the banks. By early 2003 they had forced all banks and thrifts with national charters to exit the business (Ben Jackson, "OCC Payday Purge Done; Lenders Eye State Banks," *American Banker*, February 3, 2003, p. 2). Many payday lenders continue to have partnerships with state-chartered banks. These arrangements will be threatened, however, if the Federal Deposit Insurance Corporation decides to apply as much pressure to the banks as the OCC and the OTS did to deposit institutions with federal charters. If bank–payday lender partnerships are terminated by bank regulators, the industry will have to withdraw to the approximately thirty states where payday lenders can operate profitably under state laws. Given its large size, the industry would undoubtedly launch a major lobbying campaign to change the laws in states where the industry cannot operate profitably and to pressure the federal bank regulatory agencies to take a more benign view of bank–payday lender partnerships.

Another threat to payday lending comes from the development of payday-loan-like overdraft programs that large numbers of community banks and credit unions have begun to offer in recent years (Alex Berenson, "Banks Encourage Overdrafts, Reaping Profit," *The New York Times*, January 22, 2003, pp. A1, C7). These programs carry such trademark names as "Bounce Protection," "Overdraft Privilege," or "Courtesy Pay," and are marketed to banks by firms that help the banks implement and manage the programs. A bank that offers an overdraft privilege informs selected customers that it will honor NSF checks as long as customers do not overdraw their accounts by more than a specified amount, such as $300. Each time the bank honors one of these checks, it charges its standard "overdraft fee," typically $20 to $25. The bank requires that the customer return the account to a positive balance within a relatively short time, commonly thirty days.[10] Some banks impose a fee of usually between $2 and $5 for each day that an account carries a negative balance. Because the fee income can be significant, banks encourage their eligible customers to make use of the service whenever they need it. As far as I am aware, banks and bank regulators have provided no data to date indicating the extent to which customers who use the overdraft privilege do so frequently.

Effectively, the overdraft privilege is a short-term loan. The banks offering the service claim that it is not a credit product and that there is no finance charge, simply an overdraft fee. The overdraft fee is much higher than what the banks would earn in finance charges on a line of credit, enabling the banks to offer the product to customers with higher risk profiles. A customer might, for example, write an NSF check for $100 that the bank honors while charging a $20 overdraft fee. If the customer returns the account to a positive balance within two weeks, the fee equates to charging a 520 percent annualized interest rate.[11]

Some payday lenders say they do not see the entry of banks into this market as particularly threatening. In the case of the overdraft privilege, they argue that their finance charges are often lower than the banks' overdraft fees. In theory, someone with a $300 limit on an overdraft privilege could write one overdraft check for $280 and incur only a $20 fee. Most payday lenders would charge somewhat more than $45 for a $280 cash advance. In practice, however, many customers may overdraw their accounts by writing several smaller checks, such as three checks for $65 each. In this case, the fee for the overdraft privilege would aggregate to $60 for a $195 advance, well over what payday lenders would charge. Other payday lenders do worry about the spread of payday-loan-like overdraft policies. They point out that even if the bank overdrafts carry higher finance charges than their own loans, they are more convenient because the customer simply writes an NSF check and does not need to visit a payday loan office. These lenders worry that they could lose some of their most creditworthy customers to the banks and credit unions offering payday-loan-like overdraft programs.

Changes in Pawnbroking

When *Fringe Banking* (Caskey 1994) was published, the pawnbroking industry was growing rapidly. Recent data indicate that this growth continued until about 1997. In many states, the number of pawnshops actually declined between 2000 and 2002.

Table 2.2 Listings of Pawnshops Across the Country

Year	Number of Listed Pawnshops	Growth Rate
1986	4,849	
1987	5,189	7.0%
1988	5,550	7.0
1989	6,171	11.2
1990	6,863	11.2
1991	7,354	7.2
1992	7,760	5.5
1993	8,787	13.2
1994	9,616	9.4
1995	10,425	8.4
1996	11,075	6.2
1997	11,537	4.2
1998	11,529	−0.1
1999	Missing	
2000	12,092	
2001	12,356	2.2
2002	Missing	
2003	11,683	

Source: American Business Information (1986–2002); InfoUSA (2003).

Almost all states require pawnshops to be licensed, but only a few issue public documents reporting the number of active pawnshops in the state. Even fewer provide a time series of pawnshop licenses in the state. One can, however, track rather closely the number of pawnshops nationally by using the services of businesses that sell business mailing lists. American Business Information (ABI), for example, uses local yellow page listings and other sources to produce a mailing list of businesses in thousands of different business categories, broken down by geographic area. Table 2.2 provides ABI's data on the number of pawnshops in its lists for each year between early 1986 and early 2003.[12] As indicated in the table, the number of pawnshops nationally grew at about 6 percent or more per year through 1996. After that, it either grew much more slowly or declined. By 2003, the number of pawnshops nationally barely exceeded the number in 1997.

One journalist attributed the marked slowing in the growth of pawnbroking to strong economic growth from 1992 through 1999 (John Pletz, "Strong Economy Makes Business Difficult for Pawnshops," *Austin American-Statesman*, August 24, 1999, p. D1). The argument is that this raised the incomes of many pawn customers so that they no longer needed to borrow. But this claim overlooks a number of offsetting effects. Partly due to strong economic growth, there were high levels of immigration during the 1990s, and many working-class immigrants are natural customers for pawnshops. In addition, strong economic growth can benefit pawnshops. More optimistic individuals are more likely to borrow for discretionary reasons, confident that they will be able to redeem their pledged property within a short time. A strong economy also tends to increase pawnshop sales. This, in turn, permits pawnshops to make larger loans relative to the value of the collateral. Finally, the data indicate that, among families earning less than $25,000 in 1998 prices, the percentage with debt service payments that were 40 percent or more of household income showed a steady increase between 1989 and 1998 (Kennickell, Starr-McCluer, and Surett 2000). And the percentage of these families who reported being overdue on a debt service payment by 60 days or more increased between 1992 and 1998. Because the natural customer base of pawnshops consists of individuals whose debt burdens or payment histories restrict their access to mainstream credit, these trends suggest that the strong economy did not diminish that population.

In my view, the major reason pawnbroking lost its momentum was the rise of payday lending. As noted, most pawnshop customers have credit profiles that prevent them from obtaining lower-cost credit from mainstream lenders. But survey data indicate that a majority of pawnshop customers have bank accounts, and many might be eligible for payday loans.[13] Those eligible to borrow from a payday lender would likely prefer to do so. Payday lenders are generally willing to make larger loans—their loans average about $250 versus about $75 for pawnshops. Their loans carry interest rates similar to most pawn loans, but are more convenient because the customer leaves a check rather than a personal possession. They may also be considered more respectable than pawnshops. In a nutshell, when payday lenders became common, pawnshops lost a significant share of their customer base, slowing the growth of pawnbroking and even reversing it in some states.[14]

Two close observers of the pawnbroking industry agree with my analysis of the major factor behind the recent stagnation of the industry. A recent newspaper article (Debbie Blossom, "Pawnshops

Fill a Niche," *The Tulsa World*, January 20, 2002, p. E1), for example, quotes the executive secretary of the Oklahoma Pawnbrokers Association as saying, "What has hurt the industry . . . is competition from a burgeoning crop of small check cashing and loan companies that offer quick money." The article notes that there were 451 pawnshops in Oklahoma in 1997. By year-end 2001, there were 387. Similarly, Joseph Rotunday, the CEO of EZCorp, a publicly traded corporation that operated 280 pawnshop outlets as of June 2002, explained his company's performance. "The company had been progressing very nicely until the late 1990s . . . the cash and credit constrained consumer found that they had more choices by which to satisfy their need for cash . . . in the late 1990s a rapidly emerging new product called payroll advance/payday loans came along and provided our customer base an alternative choice. Many of them elected the payday loan over the traditional pawn loan" (Interview by Lynn Fosse, *Wall Street Corporate Reporter*, Vol. 7, Issue 16, July 15, 2002, p. 1).

Even more telling is the behavior of the pawnbrokers themselves. By the late 1990s, many began to offer payday loans. Cash America, for example, is a publicly traded corporation with the largest number of pawnshops in the United States. At year-end 1987, it had 82 shops. By 1998, it had 414. Reflecting the general trends in the industry, it then stopped growing. By year-end 2002, the number of its pawnshops had declined to 396. Obviously concerned with the flagging demand for its pawn loans, Cash America began to offer payday loans in ten of its pawnshops in 1999, advancing $3.2 million in such loans over the course of the year. As it gained experience, it brought the product to more shops; in 2002 it advanced $124 million from 391 of its locations (10-K filing of Cash America International, Inc. for fiscal year ended December 31, 2002, pp. 4–5). The CFO explained his company's decision to offer the product by saying, "The payday loan is a product . . . [our customers] want, a product they need. It's not appropriate for us not to offer it to them" (Hang Nguyen, "Dallas Area Pawnshops Offer Payday Advances as Good Economy Cuts Business," *Dallas Morning News*, August 23, 2000, p. 1A).

Similarly, EZCorp, the second largest pawnshop company, grew from 57 shops in 1991 to 331 by 1999. After that, it began to close more than it opened and by June 2002 it operated 283. The CEO attributed much of this retrenchment to the rise of the payday loan alternative. EZCorp responded by beginning to offer payday loans in 2000. The third largest publicly traded pawnshop corporation, First Cash Financial, grew from 23 pawnshops in 1992 to 114 in 1999. After that, its business stagnated; at the end of 2001 it still operated 114 pawnshops. According to a *Dallas Morning News* account, "First Cash reports that its pawn business is not growing at all . . . 'We're hustling to keep it steady,' said Scott Williamson, executive vice president" (Hang Nguyen, "Dallas Area Pawnshops Offer Payday Advances as Good Economy Cuts Business," *Dallas Morning News,* August 23, 2000, p. 1A). First Cash entered the payday loan business in 1998 when it purchased eleven check-cashing and payday loan stores in California and Washington. By year-end 2001, it owned forty-four CCOs and payday advance stores. In 1999, pawn service charges accounted for 60 percent of the company's total loan service charge revenues and payday loans for the other 40 percent. By 2001, the numbers had essentially reversed, to 37 percent and 63 percent. In its 2001 10-K filing, the company explained that its "primary business plan is to significantly expand its short-term advance operations" (10-K filing of First Cash Financial Services, Inc. for fiscal year ended December 31, 2001, p. 1).

Beyond the new competition from payday lenders and the growing tendency for pawnbrokers to offer payday loans themselves in states where the business is feasible, pawnbroking has changed in another way over the past decade. In addition to selling items from their inventories to people shopping in their pawnshops, many pawnbrokers regularly sell their goods through the Internet, especially the eBay auction site. One journalist (Mike Tierney, "Pawn Shops in Atlanta Provide Quick Cash When Going Gets Rough," *Atlanta Journal and Constitution*, November 1, 2001, p. F1) interviewed Jerry Adelman, the owner of two pawnshops in Atlanta, about his business: "'My third store' is how Adelman describes eBay, on which he peddles tools and such, largely to small-town Americans outside the reach of Home Depot or Lowe's. Adelman's crowded back room . . . contains a machine for wrapping items purchased via the web." Similarly, *The Tulsa World* quoted a local pawnbroker as saying, "Today, half of store sales are through eBay" (Debbie Blossom, "Pawnshops Fill a Niche," *The Tulsa World*, January 20, 2002, p. E1).

Changes in the Check-Cashing Industry

As I explained in *Fringe Banking* (Caskey 1994), CCOs cash checks, mainly paychecks and government-issued checks, for a fee. Most charge a check-cashing fee that is a percentage of the face value of the check. Outside of a few states with more restrictive fee ceilings, it is common for CCOs to charge between 1.5 and 3.5 percent of the face value of the check for cashing payroll or government checks.[15] CCOs also commonly sell a variety of related payment services and convenience items. At almost all CCOs, for example, customers can pay utility bills, wire money, purchase money orders, make photocopies, and buy prepaid telephone calling cards. And, as noted earlier, CCOs in many states have in recent years begun to offer payday loans.

Over the past decade, research has provided substantially more information on the characteristics of people who use CCOs, and the findings largely confirm the picture common in the early 1990s. In 1998, for example, the Office of the Comptroller of the Currency (OCC) conducted a high quality survey on the use of financial services by residents in low- and moderate-income census tracts in New York City and Los Angeles. The survey sampled 2,006 adults asking, among other things, numerous questions about how they receive and make payments. The one drawback to the survey is that it covered only two large cities that are not representative of the country. Both, for example, have much larger than normal Hispanic and immigrant populations. New York also has a markedly lower than normal percentage of homeowners. Nevertheless, the results are similar to those from surveys covering other areas of the country (Caskey 2002a).

Table 2.3 provides an overview of the ways in which people in the OCC survey receive their incomes and where people cash checks.[16] It presents the data for all survey respondents and for two subgroups—those with deposit accounts of any type, labeled "banked," and those without, labeled "unbanked." As the table shows, about half of the adults in the survey population receive most of their income in the form of checks. Among those who sometimes cash checks, 39 percent report that they usually do so at a check-cashing outlet. Not surprisingly, among those who do not

Table 2.3 Forms of Income and Locations for Cashing Checks Among Residents of Lower-Income Census Tracts in New York City and Los Angeles

	Percentage Among the Survey Population	Percentage Among Banked Individuals	Percentage Among Unbanked Individuals
Way in which most income was received			
Direct deposit	23.8%	37.7%	0.0%
Check	49.4	48.7	50.5
Cash	10.9	6.2	18.8
Electronic transfer to nonbank	6.4	0.4	16.6
None of these ways or no income	8.6	5.9	13.1
Total number surveyed	2,006	1,369	637
Most common location for cashing checks (among those who cash checks)			
Bank	53.1%	79.1%	21.2%
Workplace	2.0	1.9	2.1
Check-cashing outlet	39.3	15.6	68.4
Friend or family	0.8	0.0	1.9
Supermarket	3.3	1.8	5.1
Total number surveyed	832	513	319

Source: Author's estimates using data from OCC.
Note: Percentages may not sum to 100 due to rounding, nonresponses, or other factors.

have accounts, significantly more usually cash their checks at CCOs than those who do. Almost 80 percent of those with accounts usually cash checks at banks.

Data from the OCC survey and other surveys conducted in the 1990s are consistent in indicating the socioeconomic characteristics of individuals who cash checks at CCOs (Caskey 2002a). They tend to be younger and less well educated than those who use banks. They are also more likely to rent their homes. They tend to have lower household incomes. In the OCC survey, for example, most had household incomes below $30,000. They are substantially more likely to be African American or Hispanic. Most do not have bank accounts. In the OCC survey, only about 22 percent of the regular users of CCOs had deposit accounts; about half of these had savings accounts but not checking accounts. Among the regular CCO customers, 74 percent reported that they did not have any financial savings. The corresponding percentage among regular bank customers was 24 percent.

There are no satisfactory formal surveys asking people why they go to a CCO to cash their checks rather than to a bank, but available information points to a common-sense explanation. In the case of those without bank accounts, many urban banks refuse to cash checks for nondepositors unless the check is drawn on the bank to which it is presented. In addition, banks commonly charge $1 to $3 for money orders; CCOs usually charge $1 or less.[17] Unlike CCOs, banks do not sell stamped envelopes in which to mail the money orders and they do not serve as payment agents for utility companies. That is, those without bank accounts who go to CCOs to cash their paychecks can conveniently address all of their payment needs at the same time. They cannot do so at most banks.

Why, then, would the 20 percent of the people who regularly cash checks at CCOs yet have deposit accounts go to a CCO? There are two explanations. First, as indicated in the surveys, many have only savings accounts. They may cash their checks at a CCO because they also need to purchase and mail money orders or want to pay utility bills in person. CCOs are one-stop centers for such services; banks are not. Second, even someone with a checking account may want to cash a paycheck at a CCO if the balance in the account is less than the check. In this case, many banks would refuse to cash the check insisting, instead, that the customer deposit it and wait a few days for it to clear before gaining access to the cash.

Over the past decade, the major change in the commercial check-cashing industry has been the entry of many check-cashing outlets into payday lending. For many, revenues from payday lending now represent a third or more of store revenues. This development, along with strong economic growth between 1992 and 2000, permitted the check-cashing industry to sustain the growth of the 1980s, though at a slower pace than the 1990s.

As with pawnshops, most states do not provide official counts of the number of check-cashing outlets operating within their borders. Until about 1998, however, data from business-listing services provided a good indication of national CCO growth trends. Most dedicated CCOs are listed in their local yellow pages, listing under "check cashing" or, as the business is known in Illinois, "currency ex-change." Business-listing services also typically use the yellow pages as their major source of information. Grocery stores and other firms that cash checks as a sideline to their main business generally do not list under the "check cashing" category in the yellow pages. After 1998, however, in many states the yellow page listings under "check cashing" began to include many monoline payday loan stores that do not cash paychecks. Undoubtedly, much of the growth in yellow page–listed CCOs that occurred within the last five years represents listings of monoline payday loan stores, but it is difficult to say ex-actly how much.

Nevertheless, it is interesting to review trends in the listings pro-vided by business listing services. Table 2.4 provides a time series of data from ABI. As shown in the table, CCOs grew strongly between 1986 and 1998. The 1992 growth slowdown may reflect the 1991 recession. In recessions, CCOs are typically hurt because they cash fewer and smaller paychecks. The somewhat slower growth rates between 1994 and 1998 compared to the earlier period may reflect contrasting forces. For one, CCOs may have saturated many major markets by the early 1990s. In addition, the trend toward direct de-posit over the 1990s may have also undercut the check-cashing busi-ness. Offsetting these factors were the strong growth in the econ-omy between 1992 and 2000 and the rise of payday lending as an additional source of revenue for many CCOs.

As noted, much of the explosive growth in CCOs that appears to have occurred between 1998 and 2003 undoubtedly reflects in-creasing numbers of payday lenders listed as check-cashing busi-nesses. A number of observations support this hypothesis. First, a small number of states require payday lenders to hold check-cashing licenses but distinguish between the licenses held by pure CCOs, CCOs that engage in payday lending, and payday lenders that do not cash paychecks. The North Carolina Office of the Commissioner of Banks (2001a), for example, reported that 233 firms, with 1,131 lo-cations, held check-cashing licenses in that state as of year-end 2000. Of these 233 license holders, 114 were CCO–payday lender hybrids, 68 were check cashers that did not make payday loans, and 51 were monoline payday lenders. Similarly, the Tennessee Depart-ment of Financial Institutions (2001) reported that there were 309 active check cashing outlets in the state as of year-end 2001 and

Table 2.4   Listings of CCOs Across the Country

Year	National Count of CCO Listings	Growth Rate in CCO Listings in Percentage	National Count of "Currency Exchange" Listings[a]
1986	1,202		Missing
1987	1,538	28.0%	Missing
1988	1,958	27.3	Missing
1989	2,487	27.0	643
1990	2,991	20.3	679
1991	3,425	14.5	691
1992	3,593	4.9	696
1993	4,125	14.8	718
1994	4,361	5.7	726
1995	4,786	9.7	771
1996	5,127	7.1	785
1997	5,676	10.7	798
1998	6,097	7.4	785
1999	Missing		Missing
2000	7,781		816
2001	10,650	36.9	847
2002	Missing		Missing
2003	16,689		825

Source: American Business Information (1986–2002); InfoUSA (2003).
[a]About 90 percent of these listings are CCOs in Illinois.

1,016 active payday lender offices. ABI, however, reported 941 CCO listings in that state in early 2003. Undoubtedly, its list includes many payday loan offices that list themselves under "check cashing" in the yellow pages.

Tables 2.5 and 2.6 provide additional evidence supporting the conclusion that the recent rapid growth in yellow page listed CCOs largely reflects the boom in payday lending, not a boom in traditional CCOs. Table 2.5 provides ABI's 1993 and 2003 counts of the number of CCOs in seventeen states in which payday lending was common as of late 2002. Table 2.6 presents the same data for four states where payday lending was rare as of late 2002.[18] The difference in growth rates across the two groups of states is striking.

As indicated in table 2.6, even in these four states where payday lending had not gained a foothold by late 2002, check cashing grew significantly over the past decade. Undoubtedly, this was largely due to the strong economic expansion between 1992 and 2000. National employment in 1992 was 118.2 million. By 2000, it was 137.6 million. Because traditional CCOs gain most of their revenue from

Table 2.5   Listings of CCOs in States Where Payday Lending Was
Common in Late 2002

State	ABI List of CCOs, Early 1993	ABI List of CCOs, Early 2003	Percentage Increase
Alabama	33	388	1,076%
Arizona	71	446	528
California	1,089	2,293	111
Colorado	85	314	269
Florida	343	1,116	225
Georgia	143	531	271
Kentucky	19	409	2,053
Louisiana	47	326	594
Mississippi	8	714	8,825
Missouri	50	314	528
North Carolina	84	673	701
Ohio	98	817	734
South Carolina	46	638	1,287
Tennessee	38	941	2,376
Texas	560	1,309	134
Utah	6	169	2,717
Washington	69	310	349

Source: American Business Information (1993) and InfoUSA (2003).

cashing people's paychecks, increased employment raises the demand for their services.[19]

The large returns to check cashers from entering the payday loan business were reflected in the rapid increase in the percentage of CCOs offering payday loans. As noted earlier, in the early 1990s only a small share of CCOs offered payday loans. By 2002, available evidence suggests that a strong majority of CCOs did so in states

Table 2.6   Listings of CCOs in States Where Payday Lending Was Rare in
Late 2002

State	ABI List of CCOs, Early 1993	ABI List of CCOs, Early 2003	Percentage Increase
Connecticut	31	67	116%
Massachusetts	57	87	53
New Jersey	84	295	251
New York	420	647	54

Source: American Business Information (1993) and InfoUSA (2003).

Table 2.7   Data for ACE Cash Express, Incorporated

Fiscal Year (Ends July 31)	Number of Company-Owned Stores	Total Revenue (Thousands of Dollars)	Revenue per Average Number of Stores (Thousands of Dollars)	Check-Cashing Fees as Percentage of Revenue	Loan Fees and Interest as Percentage of Revenue
1992	220	$26,001	$130	84.2%	0.0%
1993	276	32,666	132	82.4	0.2
1994	343	39,902	129	79.8	0.4
1995	452	47,790	120	78.4	1.2
1996	544	68,959	138	74.4	3.6
1997	617	87,392	151	71.9	6.5
1998	683	100,194	154	68.9	10.1
1999	798	122,314	165	64.5	11.7
2000	915	140,636	164	63.7	12.7
2001	988	196,775	207	53.6	27.8
2002	1,003	229,266	230	51.9	32.4

Source: ACE Cash Express, Inc. (1992–2002).

where the laws permitted payday lenders to charge 15 percent or more for a two-week loan.[20]

Financial data from ACE Cash Express, Inc., a publicly held company with 1,189 CCOs in 35 states and Washington, D.C., provide further evidence of the importance of payday loan revenue to CCOs. ACE began to make payday loans from a few of its stores in the mid-1990s. In states where laws permitted payday lending to be profitable, ACE expanded this program through mid-1999. In 1999, ACE formed a partnership with a bank in California and used this relationship to offer payday loans in the vast majority of its stores. As shown in table 2.7, in fiscal year 1998 payday lending accounted for 10 percent of ACE's overall revenue and check-cashing fees accounted for 69 percent. Total revenue per average number of open stores was $154,000.[21] By fiscal year 2002, payday lending revenues accounted for 32 percent of ACE's overall revenue and check-cashing fees accounted for 52 percent. Total revenue per average number of open stores had risen to $230,000.

Although CCOs benefited financially from moving into payday lending, many check cashers worry about the long run health of their traditional business—cashing people's paychecks. One threat to the future of this business is the marked decline in the use of checks for paying wages and for making government transfer payments. The *Federal Reserve Bulletin* (Gerdes and Walton 2002, 369), for example, reported that "the proportion of payroll payments made via direct deposit rather than paper check increased from close to zero in 1979 to about 50 percent in 2000." Similarly, the National Automated Clearing House Association (2001) reports that 51 percent of social security recipients used direct deposit in 1991. By 2001, 79 percent did so. Data indicate that lower-income households and households headed by younger adults or less-well-educated adults are less likely to use direct deposit, but even within these categories there is a growing use (Mester 2001). Assuming that these trends continue, CCOs may see a persistent decline in their revenues from check-cashing fees.

A traditional limitation to direct deposit has been that employees without bank accounts could not participate. But, in recent years, numerous firms have developed "payroll cards" that enable all employees to receive electronic transfers of their wages. There is much variation in the details of these cards but most have the following features. An employer gives its participating employees an ATM-type card. A participating bank creates "virtual" deposit accounts for all workers receiving the card. The account is an accounting entry that is credited when an employer pays wages electronically. The employee can remove funds from the account using the employer-issued payroll card at an ATM machine or as a debit card at a merchant. The employee cannot overdraw the account so it can be offered to those with bad credit histories or a history of mismanaging a checking account. The fees that employees pay for using the payroll cards vary widely depending on the company that issued the card, the participating bank's fees, and the willingness of an employer to shoulder some of the cost.

To date, there are no reliable reports on the success of the payroll cards. The promoters report that many employers like the cards because they reduce the employers' payroll processing and distribution costs. To comply with state labor laws, however, employers cannot generally mandate that employees switch to the cards. Celent Communications, a commercial research firm, estimated that 6 percent of unbanked workers were using the cards in 2002. The *American Banker* newspaper quoted Celent's report as saying that "convincing . . . [unbanked employees] to accept a piece of plastic as their paycheck is quite difficult" (David Breitkopf, "Celent: Adoption Barriers Persist for Payroll Cards," *American Banker*, December 24, 2002, p. 6). Nevertheless, these cards may find growing acceptance if unbanked employees begin to see other unbanked workers using the cards and hear favorable reports. Such a development would clearly threaten the traditional check-cashing business.

A second threat is the automated check-cashing machine. Marketed by several companies, they resemble traditional ATMs. Customers insert their paychecks into the machines. The machine uses a personal identification number or some other method to identify the customer, it reads information from the check and uses a software algorithm to determine whether it should cash the check. If the check is approved, the machine dispenses the cash. If it is not, the machine returns the check to the customer. Frequently, the machines are equipped with telephones linked to a processing center. A customer can use the telephone connection to get or give information that the machine does not handle or for person-to-person guidance.

The most prominent firm to develop such machines was InnoVentry, a joint venture capitalized with hundreds of millions of dollars from Wells Fargo Bank, Capital One, Cash America, and Diebold. InnoVentry began deploying check-cashing machines in the late 1990s and by early 2001 had placed more than 1,000 in department stores, supermarkets, and convenience stores in numerous states. By September of 2001, InnoVentry stopped operations and began to liquidate its assets ("Check Cashing at ATMs Faces an Uncertain Future," *ATM & Debit News*, October 4, 2001, p. 1). The company provided no explanation for its failure, but rumors indicate that many check-cashing customers simply preferred the human interaction at traditional CCOs. In addition, InnoVentry's machines cost more than $45,000 each and the company had to pay retailers to place the machines in their stores, so the machines had to achieve a high volume of business to cover the associated costs. Finally, it is reported that servicing costs on the machines were high.

Despite this experience, a few firms are continuing to develop and deploy automated check-cashing machines. The major actor after InnoVentry's failure is the convenience chain 7-Eleven Incorporated. It first installed automated check-cashing kiosks in several of its stores in 1998. Since then, it has worked to refine the technology. Its Vcom kiosks can cash paychecks, handle money order purchases and money transfers, and pay bills through Western Union's Quick Collect payment service. As of January 2003, 7-Eleven had placed kiosks in 389 of its 5,800 stores across the United States (7-Eleven news release, February 5, 2003). If such machines prove cost effective and significant numbers of check-cashing customers begin to use them, it would obviously threaten the survival of traditional CCOs.

Conclusions

Two strong conclusions emerge. First, the regulatory environment and trends in electronic payments are likely to be the most important factors over the next several years shaping payday lending, pawnbroking, and commercial check cashing. Second, the explosive growth in payday lending reinforces the fact that many people are willing to pay very high short-term interest rates in order to get or maintain relatively small cash loans.[22] As indicated in the Wisconsin data, a state with no limits on customers' loan renewals, the typical long-term payday loan customer had about nineteen loan originations or renewals over the course of a year. Based on an average cash advance of $245 and an average finance charge of $49, this implies that the typical long-term customer paid $931 in finance charges over the course of a year, more than three times the average loan balance outstanding. This is remarkable. Does this behavior reflect a conscious decision? Or is it the unconscious result of a series of simple transactions, each of which was understood by the customer, but the cumulative effect of which was not understood? Would these long-term customers, using hindsight, explain their actions as resulting from a lack of self-control? Or would they view them as resulting from a series of reasonable decisions which they would wish to repeat again given the same circumstances? These are questions for future research.

Notes

1.   This section draws extensively on an earlier paper that I wrote on payday lending (Caskey 2002b).
2.   According to a recent survey of 521 banks across the country, banks' bounced check fees average $26 for "big" banks and $22 for "small" banks (Mierzwinski et al. 2001).
3.   If the borrower fails to pay the NSF charges, the bank may report her

to "ChexSystem," a business that maintains records of individuals' deposit account management histories. Since most banks subscribe to this service, an adverse report with ChexSystem can make it difficult for someone to open an account at another bank.

4. My earlier study on payday lending (Caskey 2002b) includes references to the state reports and brief summaries of the key data. The strength of these data is that they come from the official records of the payday loan offices themselves and do not rely on the memory of customers. A disadvantage is that they underestimate the number of transactions among customers who patronize more than one loan office, and this practice is common. A telephone survey of payday loan customers asked about their use of different payday advance companies within the previous year. About half reported using more than one (Ellihausen and Lawrence 2001).

5. Using data provided by the North Carolina Commissioner of Banks, Michael Stegman and Robert Faris (2003) estimated that a 1 percent increase in the percentage of payday loan customers who borrow at least monthly raised the revenue of a typical payday loan outlet by $1,060.

6. Just as the data from active loans files at a point in time can understate the frequency with which a typical customer borrows over the course of a year due to the inclusion of many new customers, the data from the long-term customers selected from among the active customers at a point in time could also be a misleading indicator of a typical customer's experience. Selecting customers who borrowed 10 months or more prior to the survey date and who are still active customers may well over sample the heavy users of payday loans.

7. According to the list of "best practices" for members of the trade association for the payday advance industry (Community Financial Services Association of America 2003), in states where rollovers are permitted, "a member will limit rollovers to four or the State limit, whichever is less."

8. Jean Ann Fox and Edmund Mierzwinski (2001) provide an overview of state laws, as of 2001, governing payday lending.

9. Another way that some payday lenders try to avoid state usury laws is by structuring the loans as "prepaid product" agreements. There are many variations in the details, but typically the customer agrees to make a series of fixed biweekly payments for a particular product, such as Internet service, long-distance telephone calls, and so forth. At the moment the customer enters into the agreement, the lender provides the customer with a cash payment.

10. Although a bank might permit the account to remain in negative balance for thirty days, any incoming deposits that return the account to a positive balance effectively repay the implicit loan. Thus anyone who uses the overdraft privilege and deposits biweekly paychecks receives only a two-week implicit loan.

11. Truth-in-Lending Regulations of the Federal Reserve state that some

bank charges are not finance charges, including "Charges imposed by a financial institution for paying items that overdraw an account, unless the payment of such items and the imposition of the charge were previously agreed upon in writing" (Regulation Z of Federal Reserve Regulations, 12 CFR 226.4 [c] [3]). The banks offering overdraft coverage typically state that they will pay the overdrafts as a favor to the customer but that they are not obligated to do so. By stating that they are not obligated to pay overdrafts, the banks hope to avoid having the overdraft fees categorized as finance charges with the associated Truth-in-Lending disclosures. At the time of this writing, the Federal Reserve Board is reviewing these payday-loan-like overdraft programs to decide whether or not they should comply with Truth-in-Lending regulations. Presumably, these programs may also raise bank safety issues for regulators, as have bank/payday lender partnerships.

12. The broad reliability of ABI's listings is suggested by the following. State regulatory agencies in Illinois, Indiana, Louisiana, Mississippi, and Oklahoma report that they had 221, 144, 209, 296, and 363 pawnshops respectively in 2001 or 2002. ABI's early 2003 listings show these states as having 256, 151, 220, 378, and 379 pawnshops respectively.

13. Based on a 1996 survey of lower-income households, Caskey (1997) estimated that about 64 percent of people who borrowed from a pawnshop within the previous year had a deposit account of some type. From a 1998 survey of pawnshop loan customers, Robert Johnson and Dixie Johnson (1998) also found that 64 percent had deposit accounts, and 47 percent had checking accounts.

14. The sharp decline in gold prices between 1996 and 1997 likely played a smaller role in the stagnation of the pawnbroking industry. In 1996, gold averaged $369 an ounce. In 1997 it averaged $287, and it generally remained close to this level through 2001. A low gold price has two adverse effects on pawnshops. First, it reduces the value of their inventory held for sale since a significant share of the collateral at most pawnshops consists of jewelry. Second, it reduces the size of the loans that pawnshops can make on newly pledged jewelry. This, in turn, hurts their interest earnings and discourages potential customers from borrowing from pawnshops.

15. In approximately thirty states, there are no legal limits on the fees that CCOs can charge. Connecticut, Illinois, New Jersey, and New York are the most populous states that have low legal fee ceilings.

16. The data in the table use the weights that the OCC supplies to convert the sample responses into responses representative of the 2.6 million adults living in the low- and moderate-income census tracts of the two cities.

17. Stegman and Faris (2001) found that 61 percent of the lower-income families they surveyed bought a money order in the previous year. Among those buying money orders, the mean number purchased in a

year was forty-six. Data from the OCC survey indicate that 81 percent of unbanked individuals reported purchasing twelve or more money orders over the previous year, 37 percent reported purchasing twenty-four or more. A survey of check-cashing outlets in four cities conducted for the U.S. Treasury Department by Dove Consulting (2000) in early 2000 found that the average fee for purchasing a money order at a CCO in these cities varied between $0.40 and $0.80. Unfortunately, I am not aware of any surveys of money order fees at banks, but my own 2002 survey of ten banks in the Philadelphia metropolitan area found them charging $2 to $5 per money order.

18. Payday lenders were not active in these states because state usury laws were too restrictive for them to be profitable. In addition, several payday lenders told me that they did not try to make payday loans in these states using an out-of-state bank because they expected that state regulators would challenge them aggressively, resulting in large litigation expenses.

19. Over the 1990s, two of these four states raised the check-cashing fees that they allowed CCOs to charge, a move that also would have increased the number of CCOs in the states. In 1992, New York permitted CCOs to charge 1.1 percent. New York raised its fee ceilings in 1999 to 1.4 percent for all checks. In 1992, New Jersey permitted CCOs to charge 1.0 percent for checks issued by in-state banks and 1.5 percent for checks issued by out-of-state banks. In late 1998, New Jersey raised the fees that CCOs could charge to 1.0 percent for welfare checks, 1.5 percent for social security checks, and 2 percent for all other checks.

20. I noted above that 68 of 233 CCO license holders in North Carolina did not make payday loans in 2000. A large percentage of these, however, are grocery stores and other businesses that cash checks as a sideline to their main business. The 114 CCOs that offered payday loans were mainly dedicated CCOs. As noted earlier, the remaining 51 CCO license holders were actually monoline payday lenders.

21. Because ACE was opening new stores over this period, I assumed that the average number of stores open in any one year was the number of stores open at the end of the previous year plus the number open at the end of the current year, divided by two.

22. Shane Frederick, George Loewenstein, and Ted O'Donoghue (2002) made this point in a more general context and explored a variety of reasons that might explain the phenomenon.

References

ACE Cash Express, Inc. 1992–2002. Form 10-K filings with the U.S. Securities and Exchange Commission, 1992–2002. Available at: http://www .sec.gov/cgi-bin/browse-edgar?type=10-K&dateb=&owner=include&

action=getcompany&CIK=0000849116 (1996–2004 only) (accessed January 25, 2005).

American Business Information. 1986–2002. *American Business Lists.* Catalogs. Omaha: InfoUSA, Inc.

———. 1993. *American Business Lists.* Catalog. Omaha: InfoUSA, Inc.

Caskey, John P. 1994. *Fringe Banking: Check-Cashing Outlets, Pawnshops, and the Poor.* New York: Russell Sage Foundation.

———. 1997. "Lower Income Americans, Higher Cost Financial Services." Monograph. Madison, Wisc.: Filene Research Institute.

———. 2002a. "Check-Cashing Outlets in a Changing Financial System" Working Paper #02-4. Federal Reserve Bank of Philadelphia.

———. 2002b. "The Economics of Payday Lending." Monograph. Madison, Wisc.: Filene Research Institute.

Community Financial Services Association of America. 2003. "Best Practices for the Payday Advance Industry." Alexandria, Va.: CFSA. Available at: www.cfsa.net/genfo/egeninf.html (accessed January 25, 2005).

Dove Consulting. 2000. "Survey of Non-Bank Financial Institutions for Department of the Treasury." Boston: Dove Consulting. Available at: www.treas.gov/press/releases/reports/nbfirpt.pdf?IMAGE.x=28\&IMAGE.y=11 (accessed January 25, 2005).

Elliehausen, Gregory, and Edward Lawrence. 2001. "Payday Advance Credit in America: An Analysis of Customer Demand." Monograph #35. Washington, D.C.: Credit Research Center, McDonough School of Business, Georgetown University.

Fox, Jean Ann, and Edmund Mierzwinski. 2001. "Rent-A-Bank Payday Lending: How Banks Help Payday Lenders Evade State Consumer Protections." The 2001 Payday Lender Survey and Report. Washington, D.C.: Consumer Federation of America and the U.S. Public Interest Research Group.

Frederick, Shane, George Loewenstein, and Ted O'Donoghue. 2002. "Time Discounting and Time Preference: A Critical Review." *Journal of Economic Literature* 40(2): 351–401.

Gerdes, Geoffrey, and Jack Walton. 2002. "The Use of Checks and Other Noncash Payment Instruments in the United States." *Federal Reserve Bulletin* 88(8): 360–74.

InfoUSA. 2003. General information. Available at: http://list.infousa.com/cgi-bin/abicgi/abicgi.pl?cca_username=DEMO&cca_password=DEMO&bas_session=S83480590824426&bas_elements=4&bas_vendor=190000&bas_page=999&bas_type=BLB&bas_action=new (accessed February 2, 2005).

Johnson, Robert, and Dixie Johnson. 1998. "Pawnbroking in the U.S.: A Profile of Customers." Monograph. Washington, D.C.: Georgetown School of Business Credit Research Center.

Kennickell, Arthur B., Martha Starr-McCluer, and Brian J. Surett. 2000. "Recent Changes in U.S. Family Finances: Results from the 1998 Survey of Consumer Finances." *Federal Reserve Bulletin* 86(1): 1–29.

Mester, Loretta J. 2001. "Changes in the Use of Electronic Means of Payment." *Federal Reserve Bank of Philadelphia Business Review* (3rd Quarter): 10–12.

Mierzwinski, Edmund, Richard Butler, Andrew Harnik, Kristen Keran, and the State PIRG Consumer Team. 2001. "Big Banks, Bigger Fees 2001: PIRG National Bank Fee Survey, November 2001." Washington, D.C.: U.S. PIRG. Available at:www.uspirg.org/reports/bigbanks2001/banks2001final.PDF (accessed January 25, 2005).

National Automated Clearing House Association. 2001. "ACH Statistics: 1991–2001." Unpublished report. Available at: www.nacha.org/news/Stats/ACH_Statistics_Fact_Sheet_2001.pdf (accessed January 25, 2005).

Neifeld, Morris R. 1939. *Personal Finance Comes of Age*. New York: Harper and Brothers.

North Carolina Office of the Commissioner of Banks. 2001a. "2000 Annual Report of Check Cashing Businesses, Fact Sheet." Available at: www.nccdo.org/NR/rdonlyres/5F7F31CF-2645-4CD2-8EE1-EE349F9F6AE8/0/cccon00.pdf (accessed January 25, 2005).

——. 2001b. "Report to the General Assembly on Payday Lending." Available at: http://www.nccob.org/NR/rdonlyres/2A95D7DA-75C0-49F3-B896-CAC45D947727/0/ccfinal.pdf (accessed January 25, 2005).

Robinson, Jerry. 2001. "The Deferred Deposit Industry/Payday Advance Product Overview." Unpublished report presented at the annual meeting of the Financial Service Centers of America. San Diego (October 6–8, 2001).

Stegman, Michael, and Robert Faris. 2001. *"Welfare, Work, and Banking: The North Carolina Financial Services Survey."* Monograph. Chapel Hill: Center for Community Capitalism, University of North Carolina.

——. 2003. "Payday Lending: A Business Model that Encourages Chronic Borrowing." *Economic Development Quarterly* 17(1): 8–32.

Tennessee Department of Financial Institutions. 2001. *Annual Report*. Nashville: Tennessee Department of Financial Institutions.

Wilson, Dean. 2002. "Payday Lending in Victoria—A Research Report." Monograph. Melbourne, Australia: Consumer Law Centre Victoria Ltd.

Wisconsin Department of Financial Institutions. 2001. "Review of Payday Lending in Wisconsin." Unpublished report.

Wolf, Irving J. 1975. "The Licensed Check-Cashing Industry in New York City," M.B.A. Thesis, Pace University.

Chapter 3

Online Banking and the Poor

Lisa J. Servon, Robert Kaestner, and
Antwuan Wallace

In recent years, poverty research has shifted from focusing exclusively on strategies to increase the income of the poor to attempts to enable low-income people to generate assets (Oliver and Shapiro 1997). Asset creation strategies tend to encourage saving among the poor, targeting the saving for assets such as education and home ownership. During the same period in which asset creation strategies have grown in popularity, other researchers and practitioners have focused on the digital divide—the lack of access to information technology (IT) among low-income people. A few attempts have been made to use technology to increase economic and financial literacy among low-income people, thereby bridging these two movements. Here we review one such attempt by a major bank (the Bank), which created a program (the Program) in order to understand whether access to IT, combined with training on how to use the Internet and appropriate content, has an effect on the savings patterns of low- and moderate-income individuals.

Through its examination of the Program, we examine more deeply the ways in which the Internet may aid the unbanked to join the ranks of the banked.[1] We look at the ways in which information technology has changed banking processes, and what evidence exists about access to electronic banking. More important, how can IT encourage low-income groups to increase their attachment to the economic mainstream, if at all?

The Nexus of Technology and Banking

Economic development initiatives to stimulate wealth creation through greater access to online and electronic financial services in low- and moderate-income communities continue to generate increased policy consideration and political capital. The Debt Collection Improvement Act of 1996, also known as EFT 99, included a provision that all federal payments be made by electronic funds transfer to garner some $100 million in administrative savings (U.S. Department of Treasury 1997). EFT 99 intended that all recipients would have access to an account at a financial institution at a reasonable cost with the same consumer protections as other account holders. The merits of EFT 99 remain hotly debated. However, for our purposes, EFT 99 pinpoints the federal government's position of incorporating previously unbanked populations into the economic and financial mainstream.

Access for many low- and moderate-income families to financial mainstream institutions such as banks, credit unions and Community Development Financial Institutions (CDFIs) are tenuous because of what are often poor credit histories, inadequate and inconsistent cash flows, and lack of economic literacy. James Carr and Jenny Schuetz (2001) maintain that lower-income families' non-use of traditional financial services occurs for complex reasons including unfamiliarity with banking and savings services, not writing enough checks to justify an account, and distrust of mainstream financial services providers.

Although there is a generally accepted recognition among community technology practitioners and experts in the field that the digital divide consists of access, training, and content issues, this message has reached few policymakers and corporate actors. Training and content are equally important dimensions of the digital divide; consequently, researchers and policymakers now recognize that access-only solutions are flawed (Servon 2002; Lazarus and Mora 2000; Kirschenbaum and Kunamneni 2001). Issues facing the unbanked and those who have only a tenuous connection to financial services require a strategy that addresses all three components of the digital divide.

Expanding Access Through Technology

An Internet and online banking alternative has emerged to offer new products, retail delivery mechanisms, staff training and incentives, organizational structures, and other innovative approaches to answer questions about the future of traditional banking and financial services. Banks are now exploring the potential of IT banking tools to serve low-income customers and to attract the unbanked. At this point, we know less how information technology has changed banking processes for low- and moderate-income families than we do about higher income households' experiences and use of electronic banking. We know even less about whether and how electronic banking has encouraged low-income groups to fall in step with the economic mainstream. We therefore outline research to assess how current online banking, e-banking and Internet choices have affected low and moderate-income families' access to the financial mainstream and to wealth accumulation.

One thing we do know is that low-income people and nonwhites tend to have less access (in terms of quantity and quality) to information technology than whites and the more affluent. Overall, access to IT is increasing rapidly. Although some groups of people, namely African Americans, Latinos, and the disabled remain persistently and disproportionately on the wrong side of the digital divide, the gaps between those who have access and those who do not are rapidly closing. Gaps between rural and nonrural households and between seniors and younger people have begun to narrow. Some divides, such as that between women and men, have disappeared altogether.

And yet the larger problem persists. Deep divides remain between those who have the resources, education, and skills to reap the benefits of the information society and those who do not. Persistent gaps remain between different racial and ethnic groups, people with and without disabilities, single and dual parent families, the old and the young, and people with different levels of income and education. Low-income persons and people of color, particularly those in inner cities, are among the groups being left behind.

With respect to online banking, the data show that in 1994 there were only 150,000 people banking from home computers; by 1999 that number had grown to 3.2 million paying bills online (J. Scott

Orr and Sam Ali, "Online Banking is Earning More Interest, Consumers Are Shedding Their Fears," *The Star Ledger,* November 8, 1999). In response to increased demand, banks are creating and expanding their online and e-banking presence (Furst, Lang, and Nolle 2001). The American Bankers Association states that some 450 U.S. banks offer Internet banking services (J. Scott Orr and Sam Ali, "Online Banking is Earning More Interest, Consumers Are Shedding Their Fears," *The Star Ledger,* November 8, 1999). The most essential components are the ability to see one's account balances, pay bills, and transfer funds among accounts (Goldfield 1998). Banks are strongly encouraging customers to conduct transactions online because electronic banking lowers costs for the institution. The Booz-Allen Hamilton study (1998) finds that the average transaction for banks over the Internet is one cent, compared to $.27 via ATM, $.54 by telephone and $1.07 at a full-service branch.

If predictions about online banking, e-banking, and other Internet-based financial services become reality, these services will remain a sphere reserved only for well-educated, high-income customers. Public policy research has not produced any empirical data on how e-banking, online banking, or Internet services have shaped low- and moderate-income households' economic fortunes. However, current proposals suggest that information technology can expand access to greater financial freedom and less expensive banking alternatives for low- and moderate-income household users and poor inner-city communities.

The Program

In its materials, the Bank describes the Program as "a comprehensive community economic development initiative to stimulate wealth creation through digital inclusion and greater access to online financial services in low- and moderate-income (LMI) communities." LMI communities face serious challenges in: gaining access to and benefiting from information technology and in accessing and using financial services. The Program is innovative because it jointly addresses both the digital divide and the financial literacy issue. Broadly, the goals of the Program are to increase the economic literacy of participants, enhance the ability of participants to obtain assets, and help bridge the digital divide. The stakeholders of the program are somewhat diverse, however, which has created a set of overlapping, but not entirely consistent goals.

Clearly, the Bank had other goals as well. These included getting people to move from tellers and ATMs to online banking, which is much less expensive for the banks, customer retention, and converting customers with savings or checking accounts to users of other investment products and loans. The Program was originally launched with the intention of being tested in five inner-city communities in the Northeast.

Unlike many programs designed to bridge the digital divide, which focus primarily on access to computers and the Internet, the Program intended to address all three components of the digital divide: access, training, and content. The Bank has addressed the access component by providing all Program participants with free computers and one year of Internet access. Comfort consists of training and technical assistance both with respect to computer and Internet skills, and economic literacy. Computer classes are mandatory for beginners and optional for those who have had some experience with computers. The Program has attempted to address the content aspect of the digital divide problem by creating websites for the communities the program targets.

To be eligible to participate in the Program, applicants had to meet certain criteria:

- Bank customer for at least six months,

- be low to moderate income (self-reported),

- live in the target area served by the branch, and

- not have a computer at home.

The Bank changed these requirements somewhat for Site 5 because the bank was opening a new branch there. Therefore, the Bank allowed people to apply for the program and open an account at the same time; these applicants had to wait six months before receiving their computers. The Bank hoped to recruit 200 participants for the Program in Site 5, and did so very quickly.

Methodology

Given that the Program is a pilot, the evaluation was designed to document both processes and outcomes of the program, to provide ongoing feedback to the Bank on how well the program is working and what changes can be made during the course of the program and built into a replicable model. Quantitative data from baseline telephone surveys creates the bones of the story to be told from participants' background and experiences in this program. Qualitative data from interviews and focus groups helps to put flesh on the bones.

The first two sites to host the Program were initiated before the evaluation began, and were therefore ineligible for quantitative study. For Site 3 and Site 4, we employed a random sample control group methodology. Half of all applicants at each site were randomly assigned to either the participant or the control group. Controls were told that they would receive their computers nine months after becoming eligible. The baseline survey was conducted by telephone and was administered by the Center for Survey Research and Analysis (CSRA) at the University of Connecticut.

We also conducted telephone interviews with key staff at the Bank, relevant staff at Program partner community-based organizations (CBOs), and other partners. We also held focus groups with program participants at all five sites. In December, we attended a meeting called by the Bank's Foundation which brought together all of the CBO partners for the first time. Finally, we conducted an extensive literature review and drafted a paper that focuses on electronic banking and LMI communities.

The Bank would not allow us to use the random control group survey methodology in Site 5. This, combined with the difference in the structure of this site, keeps us from combining Site 5 data with that of other sites.

Baseline Survey Findings

The Bank originally hoped to enroll 3,000 participants in the Program. Given the numbers from the launches at the first two sites, the evaluation proposal assumed 400 participants at each of the re-

Table 3.1   Interviews Attempted and Completed

	Site 3		Site 4	
	Participants	Controls	Participants	Controls
Total called	182	98	40	36
Interviews completed	134	62	25	22
Percentage of total completed	73.6%	63.3%	62.5%	61.1%

Source: Authors' compilation.

maining sites. In reality, the numbers have been much lower. These low numbers compromise our ability to analyze anything more than differences between participants and controls. Table 3.1 documents numbers of participants and controls at Site 3 and Site 4, along with response rates for the baseline survey.

We do not believe that the low numbers reflect lack of interest in the program; they are more likely to result from early decisions made regarding how to market it. The Program budget did not allow for extensive marketing. In addition, given that this was the first program of its kind, Bank staff had no way to gauge the potential response. Believing that giving away free computers could be a huge draw, staff understandably wanted to avoid a situation in which the Bank was flooded with applicants who would need to be turned away. The Bank therefore conducted outreach only through its branches. Most of the participants we spoke with heard about the program from friends or family members. In addition, the window of time during which people could apply for the program was relatively small. Finally, the fact that the Bank restricted the program to current clients also restricted the potential pool. The Bank opened the applicant pool to those without a Bank account in Site 5, and quickly had more applicants than it could take.

Sample Descriptive Statistics

Table 3.2 presents sample means of baseline survey responses. The table is divided by experimental group status (treatment versus control), by neighborhood (Site 3 and Site 4), and by experimental status within neighborhood. We begin with a description of the complete sample. Survey participants are mostly female (80 percent), unmarried (80 percent), and African American (70 percent).

Single parents make up approximately half of the sample, and approximately half of the sample has twelve or fewer years of education. The labor market attachment and earnings of the sample are consistent with the research objective of focusing on low-income populations. A nontrivial portion of the sample, 20 percent, did not work at all in the last year, and only 46 percent worked full-time and full-year. The average earnings of the sample were approximately $20,000 per year and 15 percent of the sample received public assistance. In general, the sample population is unsophisticated when it comes to banking and finances. About one-quarter have a checking and savings account, but few (12 percent) own stocks or bonds. Slightly more than half (52 percent) has a credit card. Participants' financial knowledge is also limited; only 32 percent of the sample understand that mutual funds are risky investments. Finally, approximately 40 percent use the Internet sometimes or often, but only 17 percent bank online.

From a research perspective, one of the most important issues is whether the random assignment of study participants resulted in similar treatment and control groups. To investigate this, we show sample means by experimental group status in columns two (treatment group) and three (control group). Surprisingly, there are some statistically significant differences between the groups. Members of the treatment group are less educated, more likely to be female, more likely to bank by phone or online, and more likely to use the Internet than members of the control group. These differences are most likely due to the relatively small sample sizes of the treatment (N = 159) and control (N = 84) groups. They do not necessarily indicate a non-random assignment.

There are also some significant differences by neighborhood. Survey participants from Site 4 tend to have larger families and are more likely to be a single parent than survey participants from Site 3. Participants in Site 4 also have fewer financial accounts such as checking and savings, and are less likely to bank online or by phone than participants from Site 3 are.

Within neighborhood, there are some differences by experimental group status. In Site 3, members of the treatment group are less educated, more likely to be female, more likely to bank by phone or online, and more likely to use the Internet than members of the control group. This finding is similar to that for the full sample of which participants from Site 3 make up 81 percent. In Site 4, members of the treatment group are less likely to be single parents and more likely to use the Internet than members of the control group. Other differences between the treatment and control groups in Site 4 are sometimes large, but because of the small sample sizes, these differences are not statistically significant. For example, 40 percent of the treatment group worked full time, full year, but 60 percent of the control group did so.

Because of unanticipated delays in program implementation, it is too soon to report findings from follow-up surveys. We have, however, conducted focus groups with participants at all five sites. We split the population at each site into those that had used the Bank's online banking site and those who had done no banking online.

Findings from Focus Groups and Interviews

At each site, we held one focus group for participants who have used the Bank's electronic banking website, and one for those who have not. At each group, we held a drawing for $100, which we used as an incentive for people to participate. We also conducted interviews with staff from the Bank, relevant staff from the CBOs, and representatives of other organizations that the Bank partnered with. The findings below are separated into two sections—one related to the program and another that concerns participants.

Program-Related Findings

Our findings regarding the Program concern the mechanics and implementation of the program. We wanted to understand the extent to which program design was sound, whether it reached the target population, and what could be done to better facilitate its use. Challenges that kept the Program from achieving its potential included insufficient marketing, inadequate resources for supporting participants, logistical problems, and the cost of maintaining their computers. We believe these challenges could be overcome quite easily.

Marketing

Initial marketing decisions led to much smaller numbers than the Bank anticipated. All marketing of the Program was done through

Table 3.2 Descriptive Statistics by Experimental Group Status, Facility, and Experimental Group Status Within Facility

Variable	Total (N = 243)[a]	Total Sample		Facilities		Site 3		Site 4	
		Treat (N = 159)	Control (N = 84)	Site 3 (N = 196)	Site 4 (N = 47)	Treat (N = 134)	Control (N = 62)	Treat (N = 25)	Control (N = 22)
Female	0.80	0.83	0.74*	0.81	0.74	0.84	0.74*	0.76	0.73
Hispanic	0.12	0.11	0.15	0.11	0.17	0.10	0.13	0.16	0.18
Non-Hispanic white	0.02	0.03	0.01	0.02	0.02	0.03	0.00	0.00	0.05
Non-Hispanic black	0.70	0.68	0.74	0.70	0.70	0.68	0.75	0.68	0.73
Married	0.20	0.20	0.20	0.22	0.13	0.20	0.26	0.20	0.05
Number of adults in household	1.74	1.75	1.73	1.65	2.13**	1.64	1.67	2.32	1.91
Number of children in household	1.37	1.31	1.49	1.25	1.85**	1.24	1.28	1.68	2.05
Single parent	0.52	0.51	0.52	0.50	0.60	0.52	0.45	0.48	0.73*
Less than twelve years of education	0.08	0.09	0.07	0.08	0.09	0.09	0.07	0.08	0.09
Twelve years of education	0.38	0.33	0.48**	0.38	0.36	0.33	0.50**	0.32	0.41
Did not work last year	0.20	0.22	0.16	0.21	0.15	0.22	0.18	0.20	0.09
Worked full time, full year	0.46	0.46	0.45	0.45	0.49	0.48	0.40	0.40	0.59
Annual earnings[b]	$19,966	$20,037	$19,838	$20,248	$19,163	$20,666	$19,378	$17,874	$20,811

(Table continues on p. 56.)

Table 3.2 Continued

Variable	Total (N = 243)[a]	Total Sample Treat (N = 159)	Total Sample Control (N = 84)	Facilities Site 3 (N = 196)	Facilities Site 4 (N = 47)	Site 3 Treat (N = 134)	Site 3 Control (N = 62)	Site 4 Treat (N = 25)	Site 4 Control (N = 22)
Missing earnings information	0.35	0.36	0.33	0.40	0.13**	0.41	0.39	0.08	0.18
Total household income[b]	$29,582	$29,577	$29,590	$29,815	$28,839	$30,482	$28,538	$26,118	$32,143
Received public assistance	0.15	0.14	0.15	0.15	0.15	0.15	0.15	0.12	0.18
Has checking account	0.23	0.25	0.19	0.25	0.13*	0.28	0.19	0.08	0.18
Has savings account	0.25	0.27	0.21	0.27	0.17	0.29	0.24	0.20	0.14
Has stocks, bonds, mutual funds	0.12	0.11	0.12	0.12	0.11	0.12	0.11	0.08	0.14
Has credit card	0.52	0.50	0.56	0.53	0.47	0.51	0.58	0.44	0.50
Banks online	0.17	0.21	0.10**	0.19	0.09*	0.23	0.11*	0.12	0.05
Banks by phone	0.15	0.18	0.09**	0.16	0.09	0.20	0.10	0.12	0.05
Uses debit card	0.16	0.19	0.10*	0.17	0.09	0.20	0.11	0.12	0.05
Saves money each month	0.65	0.66	0.63	0.62	0.77*	0.65	0.54	0.68	0.86

Always uses monthly budget	0.39	0.37	0.42	0.40	0.36	0.39	0.41	0.28	0.45
Always pays bills on time	0.59	0.60	0.58	0.59	0.60	0.61	0.55	0.52	0.68
Pays credit card balance each month[c]	0.12	0.12	0.13	0.13	0.09	0.12	0.14	0.09	0.09
Knows mutual funds have risk	0.32	0.30	0.35	0.31	0.34	0.29	0.35	0.36	0.32
Knows how to minimize credit card interest	0.87	0.88	0.86	0.88	0.85	0.89	0.84	0.80	0.91
Uses Internet often	0.21	0.24	0.14*	0.21	0.20	0.26	0.10**	0.16	0.24
Uses Internet sometimes	0.22	0.28	0.10**	0.23	0.17	0.28	0.12**	0.28	0.05**

Source: Authors' intake survey data.

[a]Sample sizes listed in column headings represent number of interviews and not number of valid responses. The number of valid responses differs for each item.

[b]Calculated for those with valid earnings and income.

[c]Calculated for those with credit cards.

*0.10 < p < 0.05, **0.05 < p; asterisks indicate that difference in means is statistically significant at specified level. Difference in means is within columns as labeled in first row of table.

the branches and it was uneven. According to one Bank staffer, "the program wasn't marketed actively enough at the branches—they weren't doing a real sales pitch." Another commented, "we were unable to get out into the community as much as we would have liked." Word of mouth worked well but takes time. By the time word got out about the program, the six-month sign-up windows were closing.

CBO partners also believed that the program was limited because of the criteria that participants had to have an existing account with the Bank. Several recognized that it would have been possible to recruit many more participants if people could have signed up for an account and applied for the program at the same time. However, the Bank understandably wanted to avoid a situation in which many applicants would be turned away, given that funding for the program was limited.

Some CBO partners were disappointed by the brevity of the program. One explained, "this program really needs multi-year funding. If we could do this for two or three years, the impacts would be much deeper. We would get much more bang for the buck." This is a common problem for CBOs, and they expressed their frustration at putting together the infrastructure only to have to dismantle it in a year. One executive director explained that it would be difficult for her to let go of the trainer she had hired to help implement the Program. "We all know it's people that make an organization work well. It would be great to have [Mary] keep doing this. It's a shame to just find them, train them, and then have to let them go." At the same time, demonstration programs are just that—limited tests to gauge the potential of a program idea.

Representatives of all of the CBOs interviewed expressed a desire that they could have been more involved in outreach from the beginning of the program. They believed that they have a better understanding of the community they serve than does the Bank. Said one CBO representative, "we can hustle here—we have organizers." One interviewee offered the following explanation: "There has been an overall concern about the possibility of negative PR that has resulted in the project being more low-key than I would have liked it to be. . . . I understand the concern, but the program was promoted very passively."

When asked how they had heard about the Program, many mentioned that it had been poorly publicized and that they heard about it from a friend. One mentioned that she had asked the bank repre-sentative at her local branch about it, but that the rep did not have any information. Most participants did not feel that the program had been publicized in the community.

Differences Among the Sites

Because implementation of the program at the five sites was done sequentially, the program differed somewhat from site to site. To some extent, these differences are the logical result of the incorpora-tion of learning that occurs in any demonstration program. Other dif-ferences stem from differences in the neighborhoods themselves and the ways in which the Bank did, or did not, address these differences.

One site in particular seems not to have been incorporated fully into the Program. The branch at this site "didn't have much busi-ness. . . . It was interesting but there were not enough customers and research to make it work." The primary language of a significant portion of residents at this site is Portuguese. Program materials were not translated into Portuguese, making it difficult for those res-idents to fully access the program.

Program Resources

It was the perception of many community actors that the Program budget was not large enough to realize the full potential of the Pro-gram. Bank staff generally agreed with this assessment. As one staff member said, "we have only two people to implement this—there is so much more we believe we could be doing. [Our primary staff per-son] makes house calls if we can't solve problems over the phone. I just know the impact of that is so great. If we could replicate that across even 50 percent of participants our impact would be that much greater." A CBO executive director explained, "there needs to be at least one dedicated person to focus on managing this and really be up on what's going on. There are only a couple of people [at the Bank] working on this, and they are working on other things. [The Program] needs a champion, someone to go to community meetings and keep in better touch with the stakeholders."

Logistical Problems

Logistical problems, which arise during any demonstration program, compromised the potential success of the program. The Bank initiated the Program before all of the necessary pieces were in place. For example, participants in the first site received their computers a few months before the curriculum was completed, which delayed their training. At another site, a CBO executive director (ED) complained that only two participants had received their computers when training began. The others therefore could not go home and practice between classes. From this ED's point of view, it was "essential that they have their computers when they are going through the training." Another believed that "logistics were very poor. There were people who had already started and completed the program when they received letters from the Bank saying they were now eligible to participate. And they still had no computers." In addition, some CBOs complained that the Bank repeatedly postponed events and changed dates. These included training sessions for the CBOs and dates by which computers would be delivered to participants. Clearly, these are problems that any startup program could encounter. They key is to learn from these early problems and incorporate them into ongoing work; early evidence is that the Bank has done this at Site 5.

Bank and CBO Relations

CBO staff believed that, overall, the Program was a good one. However, they believed it could have been better implemented, and that their input along the way would have improved that process. As one staff member put it, "we should have had much stronger relationships with the CBOs. We'll take that learning to [our fifth site] and have much more constant interaction with them." The Bank did bring CBO stakeholders together in December 2003, but it was too late for some of the partners to benefit.

Several CBO staffers felt that the Bank had been too controlling in administering the program. One staffer felt that "they [the Bank] keep wanting to control things and they don't have the capacity. We could have done some of this work much more effectively." There is no way to test whether this is true. Another wanted "better communication between [the Bank] and the CBOs. It's great that they are involving CBOs, but they need to use us better and use us more." Examples of pieces of the program that CBOs thought they could manage better than the Bank included outreach, distribution of computers, and communicating with participants.

Cost

The LMI individuals the Program targeted are very sensitive to cost. One participant said she has not replaced her printer cartridge because they are too expensive ($30 to $40). Another said that she could not find the cartridges in her neighborhood, and that it was hard for her to get a ride to a store that carried them. This story begins to reveal the complexity of the lives of low-income urbanites and how comprehensive a program must be to be effective. We confronted the transportation issue ourselves on one of the days we held our focus groups. The weather was very cold with freezing rain, and snow was predicted. As we made calls the morning of the focus groups to remind people to attend, several told us they were unable to make it out because of the weather and their lack of transportation options.

Other participants have come to the end of their year of free Internet service and do not know if they can afford to pay for it themselves. Some expressed concern about the fees they would have to pay to continue banking online (as part of the program they received free access to the Bank's online banking site for only one year). Although online banking is inexpensive for banks, it is relatively expensive for consumers who may not otherwise use high-speed Internet services because of the associated fees. Sophisticated online banking software is cumbersome with a dial-up connection. One participant noted that there were other computer classes available at the CBO, but that they cost money, and she could not afford them— she believed she would have benefited from more free training.

Participant-Related Findings

We also endeavored to understand the Program at the participant perspective—were there differences between participants who used their computers more and achieved economic literacy and those who did not? What elements of the Program did participants most respond to?

Availability of Other Resources

One clear difference between those who were using the Bank's electronic banking website and those who were not was that those who were had some prior experience with computers or a friend or family member who could help them navigate the Internet and answer questions when they got stuck. Inexperience and fear of being taken advantage of were two factors that came across clearly in the groups of participants who did not use electronic banking. One said, "I'm afraid to do it [bank online]. You hear about all of these scams, and people getting your number. I would have to make sure I had it down pat in order to put my info in there." Another was fearful of banking online "because you're dealing with bills and dealing with money and I don't want to mess it up." With respect to inexperience, one participant said that the first several times she tried to connect to the Internet, the computer "made a funny noise, so I just shut it down because I thought I was breaking it." Upon telling her instructor about her "problem," she learned that the noise was her modem connecting to the Internet. Stories such as this one illustrate the basic level at which IT neophytes must be addressed. Even those who are using electronic banking expressed some trepidation about doing business online. One participant explained, "if I want to do something and I find out it's not a secure line, I'm out of there."

When asked why they were interested in applying for the Program, participants spoke mostly about feeling the need to learn about technology. Responses were varied. One person said, "it's something that you need to know to keep up." Another said that she had "been told that it's something you need to know to get jobs," and that she had been asked whether she was computer literate. Said another, "I felt like, 'Wow, I can really learn this.' I don't have to feel funny now." Another echoed this sentiment, saying, "now I know what it's like to have a computer in my home—it's like not being left out."

Content

The original idea behind the local website was to create a web application that would enable low-income residents of the community to use IT in ways that would improve their lives. The content of the site was to come from organizations and individuals within the neighborhood. Reactions to the website were largely negative. Many participants had not heard of it. Others had visited it once or twice but found it "not useful" or "two months out of date." One participant explained, "it's always the same thing on that site, so it made no sense for me to go back."

Comfort

One general finding that held across all groups was that most participants wanted more training—longer classes and more classes. Several spoke of having forgotten what they learned in class and wishing they could return for a refresher course. One explained that "if you've never done computers, it's like someone hitting you over the head with a block. The information goes over my head, like there's so much coming at you and bombarding you that you start to tune it out." Participants were perhaps less comfortable with technology than Bank staff anticipated. One staff member said that "many of the customers were needy; they had a lot of questions and concerns that needed to be addressed." Another recognized that "ten hours of free training was not quite enough, especially for those with no experience. We stretched it from ten to fifteen because we didn't hit the numbers we wanted."

Both Bank staff and CBO staff believed that the surveys used to identify the technology level of participants could have been better. The surveys used consisted of subjective questions. In hindsight, a Bank staff member thought that perhaps participants "may not have been truthful but rather told us what we wanted to hear." As a result, classes consisted of participants with widely varying levels of expertise, making the experience frustrating both for students and for the instructors. An in-person diagnostic would be more effective.

Reactions to the curriculum were mixed. As one participant explained, "the budgeting information was helpful but I don't use it. The spreadsheets were more in depth and more complicated than I need." When asked whether and how the financial literacy information helped them to keep track of their expenses, another said, "the computer won't help you if you don't have the discipline yourself." In some classes, apparently, there were problems with the electronic banking website, making it impossible for the instructors to show it to participants at class time. In general, CBO staffers felt that the materials provided by the Bank were good. One CBO executive director felt that the curriculum was geared toward more advanced students—at that CBO, they incorporated their own curriculum into what the Bank provided. This ED believed that a more basic curriculum was needed, and that the Bank should do a more precise screening to separate participants with no computer experience from those with limited experience.

The Bank had some problems with the contractor used to create the curriculum, and some staff were unhappy with the result. One explained that "there were not enough visuals, it wasn't portable enough, and it was not good for people who have trouble reading."

Another staffer said that Program participants get interested in the computer training quickly, even if they are new users. "Once they get to the second lesson, they want to keep going—that sort of locks them in."

With respect to technical assistance, participants were generally unhappy with the computer manufacturer's customer service line. One participant said, "it's hard for me to get help because I only have one phone line, and they can't really help you unless you're logged on." Another echoed that the manufacturer was "really unhelpful—you have to figure it out on your own." A third said that when she called the manufacturer and was asked to provide her computer's identification number, the company had no record of her computer.

Financial Literacy

Those who are using the Bank's electronic banking website find that electronic banking helps them pay their bills on time. One participant said that it "keeps me organized." Another noted that it "made it easier for me to look at my spending by seeing my statements online." Others echoed this sentiment that the visual aspect of electronic banking was key. For example, "I feel like I have more control of my money because I can see it." "Now I know where my money is, and how much I have to play with. I don't carry cash anymore." Yet another liked that she "could easily tell when a bill was paid" although she "didn't realize it might take five days to get to the payee and it would help if they could speed that up." A few participants are very happy with the enhanced website, which they find easier to use. There is some anecdotal evidence that learning the budgeting software is enabling participants to think differently about money and to begin to save. One participant explained, "I do have money. I save more now because I can see it." One of the CBO trainers said that in the classes on financial literacy she saw, "lightbulbs going off. They were seeing how they could make adjustments and begin to save. These tools are helping them to make better choices, and nobody else is giving them these tools. They are learning that saving even $25 a month will make a difference." This trainer told us she could see the value added of this target group having computers and using them for their finances.

Others said that being able to transfer money from one account to another online enabled them to avoid costly fees and because it helped them avoid bouncing checks. Going through the program has generally made participants more comfortable with technology, and particularly with online banking. Said one CBO staff member, "everyone was so afraid of it, and now they realize there's nothing to it."

At the same time, some participants had had negative experiences that made them even more reticent about trusting the technology. For example, one participant relayed that she had tried to set up her account to pay bills while she was on vacation; she returned to find that several checks had bounced. Although she was able to negotiate with the Bank to get the fees reduced, she is now "scared to go back and try it again."

Spillover Effects

In addition to direct program effects, we are also looking for spillover effects of the program. One we anticipated was that the computers would be used by other family members and friends, and that participants themselves would use the computers for a range of activities. Indeed, even those who are not using electronic banking are using their computers for other purposes, such as doing research, working with digital photos, burning CDs, getting news, and writing letters. It is also clear that these computers are becoming household resources, enabling children and grandchildren to benefit from the technology. One participant told us that her seventeen-year-old son uses the computer to help him with school. Another participant, who clearly had had quite a bit of experience with computers, uses his computer to assist him with his community work. One woman, who is from Liberia where the mail system is completely unreliable, is using her computer to keep in touch with friends and relatives back home. Another told us, "I really needed a computer because I'm back in school and needed a computer to do my work." A second participant who is also a student said, "the computer itself saves me time because I don't always have to go to the library now and wait for a free terminal."

We also thought that there might be some spillover effects to the participating CBOs. Thus far, it is difficult to tell whether participants are going to the CBOs for other purposes. Several participants at our focus groups claimed that they did not even know about the partner CBO until they began to take classes there, and that they had not been back since training ended. One participant said that she had tried to hook up with other students but that it didn't work out. On the other hand an executive director of one of the CBOs told us that more people were coming to the CBO because of the program, and that they then began to use other programs of the CBO.

Finally, we believed that there might be some broader benefit from participants learning to use computers and the Internet. There does appear to be some evidence of this happening. A trainer at one CBO told us that one reason people are interested in the Program is that they recognize the value of a computer, and training, to their ability to advance their skills and get better jobs. According to this staffer, "at least nine people from the program have upped their skills and gotten better jobs. Now they are coming back for intermediate and advanced classes."

Overall Findings

Thus far, we can report the following findings:

- Participants require significant support in the form of training and technical assistance.

- The content piece is weak, but potentially not that important as defined by the Bank. The curriculum appears to be more important.

- Administrative capacity and resources limit the Program.

We hope to be able to say more about the incidence of other findings for which there is currently only anecdotal evidence, such as:

changes in savings patterns; increases in financial literacy; and increased facility with IT.

Recommendations for Future Programs

If the Bank or another institution were to continue the Program, it would be important to incorporate changes based on the learning from this demonstration. The changes we would recommend include the following.

- Produce materials in other languages to meet the needs of the people who live in the targeted neighborhoods.

- Create options for follow-up help and/or refresher courses.

- Conduct more comprehensive outreach.

- Extend the sign-up time to accommodate the many who hear about the program by word of mouth.

- Create a group-building dynamic among stakeholders, allowing key players to get together, connect with each other, and share learning.

- Address marketing issues by extending marketing beyond the branch, or using new branches, which are already getting a lot of publicity, as in Site 5.

- Conduct more precise screening of technology level for participants.

- Consider partnerships with actors that are experienced with technology and financial issues, such as OneEconomy.

Conclusions

Clearly, it is too soon to draw any definitive conclusions about the effectiveness of the Program. At present, however, we can say a few things that are relevant for future policy and programs.

First, technology does appear to be a draw for this population. Participants who had had little or no experience with computers prior to this program felt that they were being "left behind" by not having access to technology. Participants not only appear to be using their computers for a variety of purposes, but these computers have also become household resources for other family members. Programs of this sort therefore do have the potential to help close the digital divide.

Second, making a program of this kind work requires significant investment and maintenance. Many of the participants wanted more training, both on how to use their computers and the Internet, and on how to use the electronic banking website. Programs of this sort need to incorporate ongoing training and resources to help those who become easily frustrated and may give up, as some of the stories we have told illustrate. It remains to be seen to what extent Program participants have shifted to online banking, and what this shift represents in terms of cost savings to the Bank.

Third, it will likely be a long time before we see any significant asset accumulation among this population. To put it simply, low-income people do not have much money to save. What we hope to see when we compare participants and controls is some difference in the pattern of saving. In our focus groups, participants indicated that they had learned about how and where to save during the budgeting portion of the curriculum. This knowledge could lead to a new pattern of saving, which in itself would be significant.

All demonstration programs need the space to try out new ideas and incorporate the learning from initial tests into later models. Although the Program set out to address access, content, and training issues, it fell somewhat short on the content and training fronts. Participants clearly wanted more training, and the website created to address content did not meet participants' needs. The key is to use evaluation to, first, decide whether the idea was viable and, if it is, to use the learning from the evaluation to improve upon the model. Too often, evaluation is used to kill programs rather than to improve them. We believe that the idea behind the Program is viable. At the end of the demonstration, we will have learned enough to make significant improvements in the program that could very well lead to better outcomes.

Note

1.   "Banked" and "unbanked" are standard terms in the community development finance field. They refer to people who have formal relationships with banks, and those who do not, respectively.

References

Booz-Allen Hamilton. 1998. "Internet Banking Survey Revealed a Huge Perception Gap." Available at: http://www.bah.com/bahng/SilverDemo? PID=Home.html&contType=TABLE&dispType=HTML&Region=& Geography=&language=English&Taxonomy1=&Taxonomy2=35& Taxonomy3=178187,185116,3523,3553,3583,3613,3643&SortBy= dateline+DESC&GroupBy=dateline+by+year&FORM_ACTION=BROWSE& style=item&sCacheID=&sNumHits=0&sNumJobHits=0&sNumVideo Hits=0&Area=&ITID=2627 (accessed December 12, 2004).

Carr, James H., and Jenny Schuetz. 2001. *Financial Services in Distressed Communities: Framing the Issue, Finding Solutions. Financial Services in Distressed Communities: Issues and Answers.* Report. Fannie Mae Foundation (August).

Furst, Karen, William W. Lang, and Daniel E. Nolle. 2001. "Internet Banking Developments and Prospects, Economic and Policy Analysis." Working paper 2000-9, Office of the Comptroller of Currency.

Goldfield, Robert. 1998. "Banking on the Web." *The Business Journal of Portland* (July): n.p. Available at: http://www.bizjournals.com/portland/stories/1998/07/13/focus1.html (accessed January 25, 2005).

Kirschenbaum, Joshua, and Radhika Kunamneni. 2001. "Bridging the Organizational Divide Toward a Comprehensive Approach to the Digital Divide." Report. Oakland, Calif.: PolicyLink. Available at: http://www.policylink.org/publicationsArchives.html (accessed January 25, 2005).

Lazarus, Wendy, and Francisco Mora. 2000. *Online Content for Low-Income and Underserved American: The Digital Divide's New Frontier.* Santa Monica, Calif.: The Children's Partnership.

Oliver, Melvin L., and Thomas M. Shapiro. 1997. *Black Wealth, White Wealth.* New York: Routledge.

Servon, Lisa. 2002. *Bridging the Digital Divide: Technology, Community and Public Policy.* Malden, Mass.: Blackwell Publishers.

U.S. Department of Treasury. 1997. *Debt Collection Improvement Act of 1996.* 62 Fed. Reg. 48714, 48721. Washington: U.S. Government Printing Office.

Part II

Borrowing with Collateral:
Legal Institutions and Default

Chapter 4

Mortgage Debt, Bankruptcy, and the Sustainability of Homeownership

Raisa Bahchieva, Susan M. Wachter, and
Elizabeth Warren

The family home continues to hold iconic status for most Americans—a tangible indication that they are solidly middle class, a sign of their guaranteed membership in a neighborhood, a defining characteristic for who they are and how they will raise their children. The home is also a family's bulwark against economic reversals and a hedge against rent increases in the neighborhood. With each monthly payment, families who buy, rather than rent or live with relatives, protect themselves against the risk of rising rents. Traditionally, they also build wealth in their home, securing an appreciating asset that can provide them rent-free housing in their old age, a source of funds in an emergency, and possibly an inheritance for their children.

But there are increasing signs that homeownership has become less a financial safe haven for at-risk householders. We approach the changing economics of homeownership for these households from two perspectives. We begin by examining rising mortgage debt levels for homeowners generally. We develop evidence of the reasons for the rise in mortgage debt, including the effects of tax incentives, lower interest rates, and marketing to lower income homeowners.

Our focus is on homeowners in bankruptcy. The major issues we address are the increasing use of mortgage debt and the implications of this for these families' ability to remain homeowners and to attain a "fresh start" after bankruptcy. We explore the effects that changes in the levels of mortgage debt have on the vulnerability of home-owners to losing their homes. Our results also suggest that rising mortgage debt has important consequences for federal bankruptcy policy.

Over the past two decades, the number of filings for bankruptcy has increased five-fold, rising to more than 1.6 million households by 2003 (Administrative Office of the United States Court 2004, table F-2). A number of commentators have linked the rise in bank-ruptcy filings to the rapid (and well-publicized) increase in credit card and other consumer debt. Less well understood is that in recent years, Americans have also borrowed more money secured by their homes. We explore this phenomenon and its implications for the continued utility of bankruptcy as a workable option for financial relief.

The bankruptcy code is designed to give people a second chance after a catastrophe, permitting the family a chance to right itself fi-nancially, and, if possible, to hold on to its home. As households substitute mortgage debt for consumer debt, however, the protec-tion provided by bankruptcy erodes. If most of a household's debt is mortgage rather than general unsecured debt, filing for bankruptcy may not help unless the family is willing to give up its home. Even after bankruptcy, homeowners with substantial mortgage debt may continue to fail. High mortgage debt leaves post-bankruptcy home-owners tied to high and unsustainable payment obligations that may ultimately place their homes at risk and undercut their at-tempts at financial stability.

To establish the context for the analysis, we will describe the trends in overall debt and in mortgage debt for U.S. households. Our findings demonstrate the substantial increase in mortgage debt that homeowners have incurred over the past two decades. This increase is reflected in higher ratios of mortgage debt-to-total debt for home-owners on average and mortgage payments-to-income for low-income homeowners. We also find that mortgage indebtedness, as reflected by these indicators, expanded most quickly among low-income families. We will also examine the relationship between mortgage debt and bankruptcy, using data from a new survey of homeowners in bankruptcy. These data show that a substantial num-ber of bankrupt households have mortgage debt in excess of the value of their homes at the time of filing. These debt burdens are likely at-

tributable both to high loan-to-value ratios at origination and subsequent increases in borrowing or refinancing to consolidate consumer debt. We also explore how bankruptcy law itself may contribute to putting homes at risk. Regardless of the reason, high
loan-to-value ratios at the time of bankruptcy filing are likely to reduce a household's prospects for continued homeownership and in-
hibit the family's ability to emerge as a stable economic unit once
the bankruptcy is resolved.

Mortgage Debt on the Rise

Over the past twenty years, American households have substantially increased their indebtedness. As shown in table 4.1, from the
end of World War II, total value of all forms of outstanding household debt as a percentage of disposable income rose from 33 percent
to 36 percent in 1979. By 2001, this figure had risen to 109 percent.[1]
As a percentage of total assets, debt also rose from 6.1 percent in
1949, to 13.7 percent in 1979, and to 16.7 percent in 2001. The
overall increases in debt for average households have dramatically
outpaced the average increases in stock holdings and other assets
(Federal Reserve Board 2000).

Our focus is on home mortgage debt. While growing credit card
debt receives substantial attention in the popular press, the growth
in mortgage debt has also been dramatic. As a share of disposable
personal income, mortgage debt has increased from 19.6 percent in
1949, to 27 percent in 1979, and to 73.2 percent in 2001, and as a
share of assets, mortgage debt has increased from 15.0 percent in
1949, to 27.5 percent in 1979, and to 40.9 percent in 2001 (Mishel,
Bernstein, and Boushey 2003). Thus in the last two decades, the
growth in mortgage debt as a share of assets and disposable income
has exceeded the growth in consumer debt.

While debt has increased sharply, the increase in the overall debt
service burden has been modest, and the mortgage burden has declined slightly. These data are provided in table 4.2. The aggregate
statistics, however, conceal a significant part of the story. The increase in total debt has been accompanied by a rise in financial distress—for families of modest means. The number of households in
the $25,000 to $49,999 income bracket who were late in paying
their bills nearly doubled from 1989 to 1998, from 4.8 percent to 9.2

Table 4.1   Changes in Debt, Income, and Assets, 1949 to 2001

	1949	1979	2001
Household debt-income	33.0%	73.2%	109.0%
Household debt-assets	6.1	13.7	16.7
Mortgage debt-income	19.6	46.1	73.2
Mortgage debt-assets	15.0	27.5	40.9

Source: Mishel, Bernstein, and Boushey (2003).
Note: All debt as a share of all assets; mortgage debt as a share of real estate assets.

percent. This 4.4 percentage point change was more than fourteen times higher than the next highest change of 0.3 percentage points among households with income over $100,000. In addition, bankruptcies per 1,000 adults steadily increased from 1980 to 2001; these bankrupt families had incomes well below the national median income (Sullivan, Warren, and Westbrook 2000; American Bankruptcy Institute 2002).

For homeowners, the picture was much the same. Low-income homeowners, unlike their high-income counterparts, have seen an increase in the mortgage debt burden. Moreover, changes in debt payment relative to income occurred in a period when household income increased substantially as a rapidly growing number of married couples sent both adults into the workforce. In other words, the proportion of total family income dedicated to debt repayment was not reduced for households in the aggregate and increased for low-income households despite the fact that more families had a second income to spend.

While the lower debt service burden would seem to provide a dose of good news in the financial picture for these families, the overall level of household indebtedness continues to exert a crucial impact on household financial stability because high overall levels of

Table 4.2   Income Committed to Debt Service, by Type, 1980 to 2001

	All Debt Percentage	Mortgage Percentage	Consumer Percentage
1980	12.9%	8.4%	4.5%
1989	13.6	7.6	6.0
1995	12.7	6.8	5.9
2001	14.1	7.9	6.3

Source: Mishel, Bernstein, and Boushey (2003).

debt increase the vulnerability of households to events associated with loss of income. Households with high overall debt do not have the financial flexibility to respond to household crises such as a loss of a job, time off from work following a medical problem, or family breakup. The family that can squeeze out payments month by month may survive financially so long as no other events disrupt the household, but any interruptions in income or sudden increases in expenses will push the family with high debt burdens into financial collapse.

It is the debt that homeowners have, rather than the absolute value of their homes, that is crucial to a household's economic survival or failure. So long as homeowners can meet their monthly obligations, they can steer clear of the bankruptcy courts, whether the value of their homes rises or falls. Homeowners always have the option to sell, of course, and if they are having trouble meeting their monthly obligations, there are reasons to turn to bankruptcy in either rising or falling housing markets. A rising market gives homeowners the chance to sell off and pay some of their debts outside bankruptcy, but bankruptcy gives them the option to preserve any equity they have built up in the house. It also permits them to stay in a home when rising prices might deny them a home if they sold. A falling house market gives a homeowner a reason to walk away from the house, with or without a discharge in bankruptcy to eliminate any deficiency judgment or to wipe out nonmortgage debts. With so many possible incentives working in so many directions, it is unsurprising that no obvious link to rising or falling home prices and the likelihood of filing for bankruptcy is evident. Instead, the interview data suggest that homeowners in financial trouble are extremely reluctant to give up their homes even when it is financially rational to do so; many homeowners in bankruptcy describe themselves as trying to save their homes even when their own description of the value and the mortgage amounts would suggest they should abandon it.

The increasing vulnerability of homeowners is in part due to a change in the way Americans borrow (Warren and Tyagi 2003; Sullivan, Warren, and Westbrook 1989, 2000). Because a refinancing boom has taken hold, many homeowners have taken on larger loan balances after their initial purchases, so that even families with a single mortgage may carry a mortgage debt. Filtering through this is the sharp increase in subprime loans and the greater use of risk-based price in mortgage lending (Calem, Gillen, and Wachter 2004). These changes have affected the likelihood that a family will lose its home to a foreclosure, not only because they cannot manage the debts but also because increases in mortgage debt affect the reorganization options through bankruptcy available to the troubled debtor. As the proportion of debt shifts over time from consumer debt to mortgage debt, the role of bankruptcy to discharge debts becomes more deeply entangled with issues of home ownership.

To further the understanding of the sources of the growth of mortgage debt, we use micro household data from the Survey of Consumer Finances (SCF) for portions of the past two decades that allow us to disaggregate outcomes by income group and to perform regression analysis to test competing hypotheses for why debt has grown. Our outcomes are based on an analysis of SCF data derived for a weighted population of homeowners for the years 1983, 1989, 1992, 1995, and 1998. The SCF is sponsored by the Federal Reserve Board every three years to provide detailed information on the finances of American families and contains data on income and debt, mortgage loans, and a variety of demographic characteristics. We combine five years of SCF data to create a time-series cross-section database. For purposes of this analysis, low-income, middle-income, and high-income households are defined for each survey year relative to the weighted sample median in that year as below 70 percent of median, between 70 percent and 140 percent of median, and above 140 percent of median, respectively. We first report trends in mortgage debt ratios by income group. We then report results of regression analyses that allow us to confirm and to throw some light on their likely source.

Figure 4.1 shows the average mortgage payment to income ratio for homeowners with outstanding mortgage debt from 1989 to 1998.[2] The ratio grew between 1989 and 1995 and then slightly decreased between 1995 and 1998. Disaggregating the data by income, however, reveals a different picture. Most of the increase in the aggregate ratio is attributable to increases in payment burdens among low-income households. Figure 4.2 shows that the ratio increased only slightly among middle- and high-income households after 1989 and remained constant after 1992. Among low-income house-

Figure 4.1   Mean Payments-to-Income Ratio, Weighted

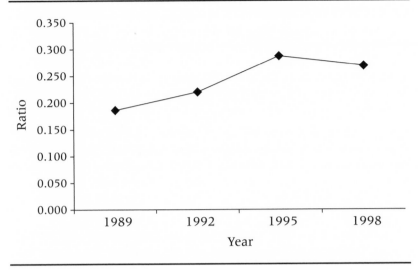

Source: Survey of Consumer Finances 1989, 1992, 1995, 1998, and authors' calculations.

Figure 4.2   Mean of Mortgage Payments, Weighted

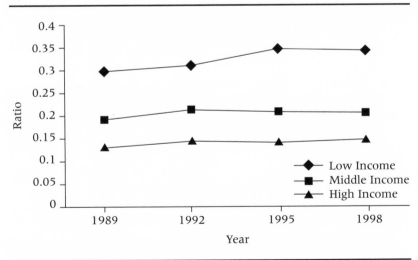

Source: Survey of Consumer Finances 1989, 1992, 1995, 1998, and authors' calculations.

holds, the payment to income ratio almost tripled between 1989 and 1995, and stabilized thereafter.

It is also possible to examine the growth of mortgage debt relative to consumer debt by income group. Figure 4.3 displays average values of the mortgage to total debt ratios for homeowners with home-secured debt. The ratio increased substantially between 1989 and 1992 and declined only slightly thereafter.

When these data are disaggregated by income group, once again a different picture emerges. While the ratio of mortgage debt to overall debt increased for all income levels, the increase was most pronounced for lower income households. High-income households, as illustrated in figure 4.4, showed sharp increases in mortgage debt to total debt ratios between 1989 and 1992, with the ratios declining slightly from 1992 on. For middle- and low-income households there was a similar sharp increase in mortgage debt ratios to 1992. From 1992 onward, however, ratios for low-income households continued to rise, while ratios for middle-income households remained relatively flat.

The cumulative effect of these changes is powerful. In 1988, middle-income families had the highest mortgage-to-debt ratios, with low-income and high-income households trailing. By 1998, mortgage-to-debt ratios for all families were higher, but the relative positions were reversed. Middle-income families now had the lowest ratios, closely followed by high-income families. The biggest change was for low-income debtors. In less than a decade, low-income families moved to the worst position, reaching mortgage-to-debt ratios substantially higher than their counterparts.

To determine whether other factors that are correlated with income are spuriously producing these results, we use regression analysis to isolate the role of income by holding other factors, such as age, constant. Table 4.3 lists the variables included in the estimations.[3] We first specify a model to estimate changing income elasticities over time; we then introduce time dummies to interact with income groups to illustrate relative shifts in the growth of mortgage debt by income group over time. The results of the first model are displayed in table 4.4, where the dependent variable is the log of mortgage payments. In this regression, as expected, income growth is shown to have a major role in explaining the growth in mortgage payments. The coefficient of income indicates that for a 1 percent

Figure 4.3   Mean Mortgage-to-Debt Ratio, Weighted

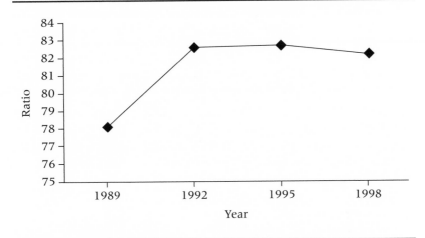

Source: Survey of Consumer Finances 1989, 1992, 1995, 1998, and authors' calculations.

increase in income, mortgage debt payments increase by 3 percent in 1989, 5 percent in 1992, 6 percent in 1995, and 7 percent in 1998, ceteris paribus. Thus the income elasticity of mortgage payments has increased over time. The Wald tests of coefficient differ-

Figure 4.4   Mortgage-to-Debt Ratio, Weighted

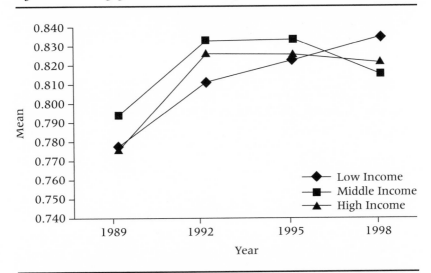

Source: Survey of Consumer Finances 1989, 1992, 1995, 1998, and authors' calculations.

Table 4.3   List of Independent Variables Compiled from the Survey of
Consumer Finances

Variables	Time-Series Sample Distribution over Observed Characteristics[a]	Mean (Standard Deviation)
Race		
White (omitted)	86.8	
Black	6.3	
Hispanic	3.4	
Other race	3.5	
Education		
Less than high school (omitted)	26.1	
High school	17.4	
Some college or college degree	34.7	
Graduate school	21.8	
Family type		
Couple, no children (omitted)	33.3	
Couple with children	46.1	
Single parent	5.7	
Single male	7.6	
Single female	7.3	
Age		
Young (below thirty-five years old; omitted)	16.9	
Middle-aged (thirty-five to sixty-four years old)	75.0	
Elderly (over sixty-four years old)	8.1	
Income sources (dummies)		
Income from wages only (omitted)	5.6	
Supplementary income from business, interest, dividends, rents, trusts, royalties, sales gains	67.9	
Income from alimonies, welfare, unemployment compensation	11.2	
Income from pensions	15.1	
Debt and payments		
Whether household pays alimonies	8.4	
Whether household has consumer debt	78.6	

Table 4.3   Continued

Variables	Time-Series Sample Distribution over Observed Characteristics[a]	Mean (Standard Deviation)
Income group interactions with the survey years		
Low income 1983 (omitted)	1.9	
Middle income 1983	5.2	
High income 1983	12.4	
Low income 1989	1.3	
Middle income 1989	3.1	
High income 1989	11.9	
Low income 1992	1.7	
Middle income 1992	3.1	
High income 1992	14.6	
Low income 1995	2.1	
Middle income 1995	4.5	
High income 1995	16.1	
Low income 1998	1.8	
Middle income 1998	4.1	
High income 1998	16.2	
Interactions of the log of itemization probability with the survey years		
Ln_probitemize 1983		0.135 (0.291)
Ln_probitemize 1989		0.132 (0.309)
Ln_probitemize 1992		0.158 (0.336)
Ln_probitemize 1995		0.180 (0.347)
Ln_probitemize 1998		0.181 (0.351)

Source: Survey of Consumer Finances 1983, 1989, 1992, 1995, 1998, and authors' calculations.
[a]8,075 observations used in the estimation of payments-to-income ratio.

ences show that this increase is significant. Moreover, the positive coefficient on the log of income square shows that income elasticity of payments has increased at an increasing rate.

The other control variables have coefficients consistent with the literature. Education variables, which are correlated with wealth and permanent income, have positive coefficients. Household type indicates that families with children and single parents have more mortgage debt than those without children. Age group variables indicate that mortgage payment size significantly decreases with age. The variables indicating whether the household head is a minority

Table 4.4   Regression Results, Dependent Variable: Log of Mortgage
Payments

Model 1

Variable	Parameter Estimate	Standard Error	t Value
Intercept	4.32423****	0.04177	103.52
Log of income square	0.17341****	0.00196	88.54
Log of income 1989	0.03242****	0.00175	18.57
Log of income 1992	0.05228****	0.00175	29.94
Log of income 1995	0.06165****	0.00172	35.87
Log of income 1998	0.07016****	0.00173	40.45
Black	−0.12653****	0.01564	−8.09
Hispanic	0.1389****	0.02071	6.71
Other race	0.17786****	0.02	8.89
High school	0.08169****	0.01713	4.77
Some or completed college	0.26827****	0.01655	16.21
Graduate school	0.38344****	0.01809	21.19
Couple with children	0.10285****	0.00887	11.59
Single parent	0.08471****	0.01785	4.75
Single male	0.01031	0.01511	0.68
Single female	0.02814*	0.01559	1.8
Middle-aged	−0.09465****	0.01039	−9.11
Elderly	−0.11086****	0.01903	−5.82
Paying alimony	0.07005****	0.01364	5.13
Supplementary income	0.1049****	0.00895	11.72
Support income	-0.06372****	0.01237	−5.15
Pension income	-0.08445****	0.01251	−6.75
Consumer debt	0.02696****	0.00921	2.93
Adjusted R-square		0.510	

Model 2

Variable	Parameter Estimate	Standard Error	t Value
Intercept	3.81414****	0.0482	79.14
Log of gross income	0.40854****	0.00427	95.78
Black	−0.12504****	0.01563	−8.0
Hispanic	0.13993****	0.02066	6.77
Other race	0.18082****	0.01994	9.07
High school	0.08945****	0.01739	5.14
Some or completed college	0.27968****	0.01685	16.6
Graduate school	0.39692****	0.0183	21.69
Couple with children	0.10704****	0.00885	12.1
Single parent	0.07987****	0.018	4.44
Single male	0.00508	0.01512	0.34
Single female	0.01257	0.01573	0.8
Middle-aged	−0.10238****	0.01039	−9.86

Table 4.4   Continued

Variable	Model 2		
	Parameter Estimate	Standard Error	t Value
Elderly	−0.13583****	0.01908	−7.12
Paying alimony	0.05818****	0.01361	4.28
Supplementary income	0.10394****	0.00899	11.56
Support income	−0.06584****	0.01238	−5.32
Pension income	−0.09026****	0.01248	−7.23
Consumer debt	0.03006****	0.00922	3.26
Middle income 1983	-0.19524****	0.03037	-6.43
High income 1983	−0.14245****	0.0292	−4.88
Low income 1989	0.23127****	0.04178	5.54
Middle income 1989	0.12599****	0.03586	3.51
High income 1989	0.17761****	0.03316	5.36
Low income 1992	0.55159****	0.04004	13.78
Middle income 1992	0.36045****	0.03575	10.08
High income 1992	0.39635****	0.03311	11.97
Low income 1995	0.73165****	0.03773	19.39
Middle income 1995	0.4816****	0.03401	14.16
High income 1995	0.48862****	0.03298	14.82
Low income 1998	0.84362****	0.03942	21.4
Middle income 1998	0.56788****	0.03454	16.44
High income 1998	0.59415****	0.03324	17.88
Adjusted R-square		0.514	

Source: Survey of Consumer Finances 1983, 1989, 1992, 1995, 1998, and authors' calculations.
****Coefficient significant at 1 percent level. *Coefficient significant at 10 percent level.

(black, Hispanic, or other) are also significant with a negative coefficient for black. Households paying alimonies and those receiving supplemental income, as well as those having consumer debt, make higher mortgage payments, while households with support income sources or pension make lower payments.

Another version, model 2, is estimated to test changes in the income elasticity of mortgage payments over time. This model includes interactions of the log of income with year dummies, as well as log of square of income. Table 4.4 reports the results. The income group and year interactions over time are the variables of particular interest. These coefficients are displayed graphically in figure 4.5. In each case, the time dummy variables for lower income households are greater than for other groups. For example, the coefficient on the low-income group in 1989 is 0.29 versus only 0.13 for the

Figure 4.5   Size of Mortgage Payment, Regression Results

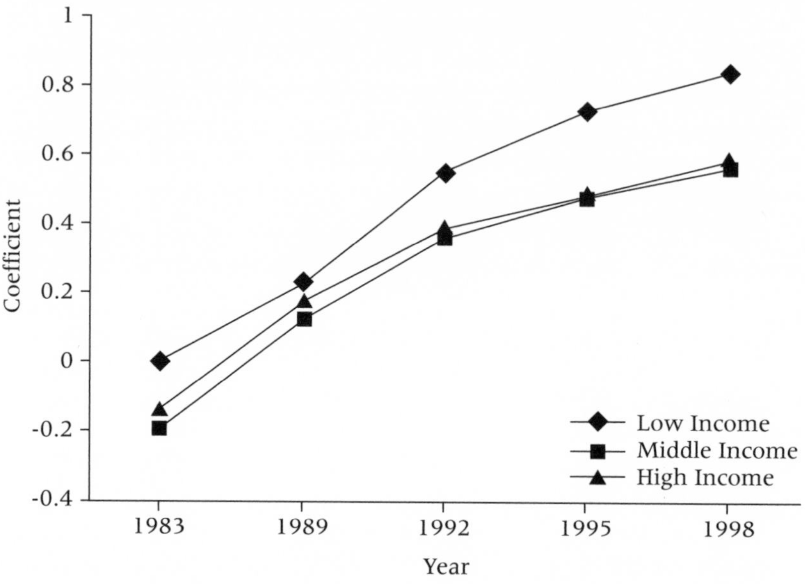

Source: Survey of Consumer Finances 1983, 1989, 1992, 1995, 1998, and authors' calculations.

middle-income and 0.18 for the high-income groups; in 1998, the coefficient on the low-income group is 0.84 versus 0.57 and 0.59 for the middle- and high-income, respectively. The data show that increases in mortgage payments are greatest for low-income households. Indeed, the difference between the low-income and other two groups is substantial throughout the study period.[4] Thus, the uncontrolled results on the relatively large increase in mortgage debt for low-income households are confirmed.

We also separately model two relevant mortgage ratios, mortgage payment-to-income and mortgage debt-to-total debt with income group-year interactions with substantially similar results, reported in table 4.5.

Two possible causes have been suggested to explain the growth of mortgage debt in the last two decades: tax laws and credit marketing. One is the passage of the Tax Reform Act (TRA) of 1986.[5] Prior to TRA, the Internal Revenue Code allowed for the deduction of interest on all debt, whether the debt was unsecured or secured by a

Table 4.5 Regression Results

Variable	Model 3: Log of the Ratio of Home-Secured Debt to Total Debt			Model 4: Log of the Ratio of Mortgage Payments to Income		
	Parameter Estimate	Standard Error	t Value	Parameter Estimate	Standard Error	t Value
Intercept	−0.213****	0.022	−9.780	−1.536****	0.035	−43.770
Black	−0.108****	0.011	−9.360	−0.052****	0.019	−2.730
Hispanic	0.004	0.015	0.280	0.221****	0.025	8.810
Other race	0.011	0.015	0.720	0.177****	0.024	7.290
High school	−0.011	0.011	−1.070	0.112****	0.021	5.280
Some or completed college	0.021**	0.011	2.020	0.174****	0.020	8.510
Graduate school	0.017*	0.011	1.470	0.050	0.022	2.290
Couple with children	0.109****	0.006	16.730	0.163****	0.011	15.170
Single parent	0.125****	0.013	9.450	0.202****	0.022	9.240
Single male	0.041****	0.011	3.700	0.113****	0.018	6.170
Single female	0.174****	0.011	15.380	0.255****	0.019	13.440
Middle-aged	−0.088****	0.008	−11.490	−0.257****	0.013	−20.500
Elderly	−0.123****	0.014	−8.960	−0.392****	0.023	−16.990
Paying alimony	−0.047****	0.010	−4.720	−0.090****	0.016	−5.440
Supplementary income	−0.033****	0.007	−5.030	−0.127****	0.011	−11.840
Support income	0.039****	0.009	4.250	−0.006	0.015	−0.380
Pension income	0.027****	0.009	3.010	0.037	0.015	2.480
Consumer debt				0.151****	0.011	13.550
Middle income 1983	−0.054***	0.022	−2.420	−0.685****	0.037	−18.680
High income 1983	−0.236****	0.021	−11.15	−1.196****	0.034	−34.920
Low income 1989	−0.150****	0.029	−5.220	0.098	0.051	1.920
Middle income 1989	−0.127****	0.025	−5.170	−0.442****	0.043	−10.210
High income 1989	−0.199****	0.021	−9.370	−1.043****	0.039	−26.840
Low income 1992	−0.095****	0.027	−3.490	0.397****	0.049	8.160
Middle income 1992	−0.026	0.024	−1.050	−0.264****	0.043	−6.130
High income 1992	−0.102****	0.021	−4.880	−0.891****	0.039	−23.060
Low income 1995	−0.071****	0.026	−2.750	0.617****	0.046	13.460
Middle income 1995	−0.033	0.023	−1.420	−0.252****	0.041	−6.180
High income 1995	−0.070****	0.021	−3.350	−0.837****	0.038	−21.820
Low income 1998	−0.032	0.026	−1.220	0.658****	0.048	13.750
Middle income 1998	−0.050	0.023	−2.140	−0.192****	0.041	−4.640
High income 1998	−0.024	0.021	−1.160	−0.814****	0.038	−21.150

(*Table continues on p. 88.*)

Table 4.5   Continued

Variable	Model 3: Log of the Ratio of Home-Secured Debt to Total Debt			Model 4: Log of the Ratio of Mortgage Payments to Income		
	Parameter Estimate	Standard Error	t Value	Parameter Estimate	Standard Error	t Value
Adjusted R-square	0.038			0.255		
Intercept	−0.244****	0.017	−14.320	−1.016****	0.028	−35.960
Black	−0.089****	0.013	−7.020	0.100****	0.021	4.780
Hispanic	0.007	0.015	0.460	0.281****	0.025	11.270
Other race	0.020	0.015	1.350	0.186****	0.024	7.650
High school	−0.013	0.011	−1.150	0.334****	0.015	22.280
Some or completed college	0.025***	0.011	2.310	0.386****	0.013	29.920
Graduate school	0.018*	0.012	1.550	0.262****	0.015	17.980
Couple with children	0.099****	0.006	15.270	0.148****	0.011	13.800
Single parent	0.131****	0.013	9.860	0.195****	0.022	8.920
Single male	0.050****	0.011	4.570	0.109****	0.018	5.930
Single female	0.178****	0.011	15.620	0.245****	0.019	12.850
Middle-aged	−0.084****	0.008	−10.740	−0.284****	0.013	−22.230
Elderly	−0.108****	0.014	−7.820	−0.398****	0.023	−17.190
Paying alimony	−0.078****	0.010	−7.880	−0.101****	0.016	−6.150
Supplementary income	−0.054****	0.007	−8.130	−0.209****	0.011	−19.020
Support income	0.039****	0.009	4.190	0.035	0.015	2.290
Pension income	0.017*	0.009	1.850	0.050****	0.015	3.300
Consumer debt				0.138****	0.011	12.340
Middle income	0.001	0.011	0.080	−0.868****	0.019	−44.750
High income	−0.064****	0.012	−5.570	−1.509****	0.020	−75.320

Ln probability
  of itemization
  1983
	0.018**	0.009	2.030	0.256****	0.015	17.040

Ln probability
  of itemization
  1989
	0.071****	0.013	5.470	0.305****	0.021	14.520

Ln probability
  of itemization
  1992
	0.003	0.010	0.310	0.137****	0.016	8.400

Ln probability
  of itemization
  1995
	0.054****	0.010	5.590	0.149****	0.016	9.230

Ln probability
  of itemization
  1998
	−0.001	0.011	−0.130	0.149****	0.021	7.030

Adjusted R-square	0.026				0.250	

Source: Survey of Consumer Finances 1983, 1989, 1992, 1995, 1998, and authors' calculations.
**** Coefficient significant at 1 percent level.
*** Coefficient significant at 2 percent level.
** Coefficient significant at 5 percent level.
* Coefficient significant at 10 percent level.

home. The TRA, however, restricted the deductibility of interest only to mortgage debt secured by a "qualified residence,"[6] in effect offering a tax subsidy for those families that take on mortgage debt, but not those who take on credit card and other consumer debt.

The TRA is likely to have affected taxpayers differently depending on whether they itemize or instead take the standard deduction. Among households that itemize, the elimination of the deductibility of personal interest while home mortgage interest remained deductible should have increased the incentive to borrow money secured by a mortgage on their primary or secondary residences. Thus, it might be expected that the total debt secured by homes for this group would increase and the total debt secured by homes would also have grown. All else equal, we would not expect these same changes among households that claimed the standard deduction.

A second explanation for the growth in mortgage debt is the change in behavior after 1993, as financial institutions sought to increase their lending to low and moderate income households. Because these two groups would be likely to take the standard deduction, a marketing outreach, rather than a tax, hypothesis would more likely explain the increase in mortgage debt.

To test directly for the role of the TRA, it is possible to model the probability of itemization. Tax benefits for mortgage debt are available only to families that itemize on their tax returns. To test whether households are responding to incentives to move debt from tax-neutral debt (credit card and other consumer debt) to tax-preferred debt (mortgage debt), we examine proxies for the likelihood a family will itemize. Models 5 and 6 seek to capture differences among itemizers and non-itemizers by substituting a variable for the probability that a household will itemize its deduction in place of the income group proxies of models 3 to 4.[7] The results are depicted graphically in figure 4.6. The coefficients on each of these variables represent the percentage change in the value of the dependent variable associated with a 1 percent increase in the probability of itemizing in a given year.

In the estimation of the ratio of mortgage-to-total-debt model (model 5), the coefficient for 1983 is 0.018 indicating that a 1 percent higher probability of itemization would lead to a 1.8 percent greater mortgage-to-total-debt ratio. In 1989, this coefficient increased to 0.07. Thereafter, the coefficient declines. In the estima-

Figure 4.6   Regression Coefficients on Itemization Probability

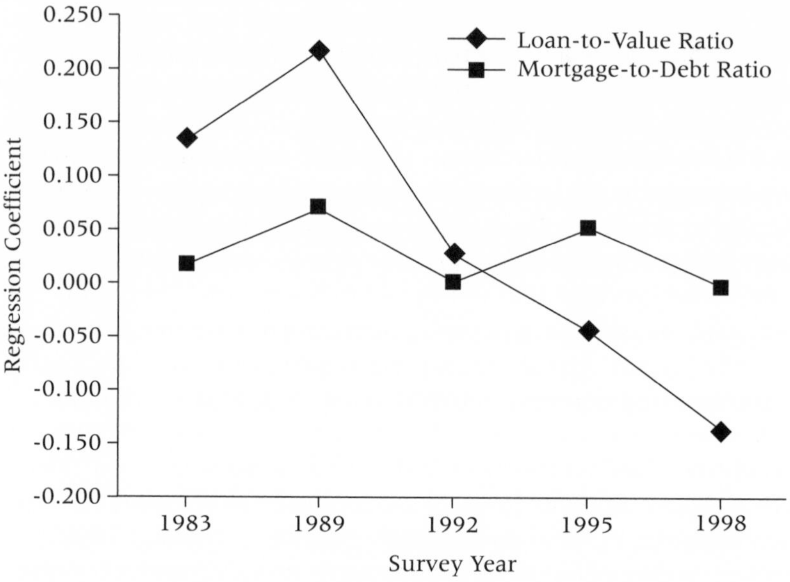

Source: Survey of Consumer Finances 1983, 1989, 1992, 1995, 1998, and authors' calculations.

tion of the mortgage payments-to-income ratio (model 6), the coefficient again increases between 1983 and 1989 and then falls substantially in 1992.

The results of these models suggest that between 1983 and 1989, households with higher probabilities of itemization tended to experience increased mortgage debt-to-total-debt ratios and mortgage payment-to-income ratios. This is consistent with the hypothesis that the households responded to the incentive contained in TRA 86 to borrow money secured by their primary or secondary residences. After 1989, however, differences among households with high and low probabilities of itemization tended to dissipate, suggesting that other factors must have been at work as well.

The other factors relate to changes in the mortgage market in general. Until recently, many potential homeowners whose incomes are too low to justify itemization were unable to obtain mortgage financing either because of poor credit histories or because their incomes and assets were too low to qualify under typical underwriting standards. Access to home mortgage credit has expanded as a number of factors have combined to make it possible for these marginal homebuyers to obtain credit. First, the federal government, through the Community Reinvestment Act and the affordable housing mandates for Fannie Mae and Freddie Mac, has substantially increased the incentives for regulated banks and secondary mortgage market agencies to make loans to low- and moderate-income people and people living in low- and moderate-income neighborhoods. To compete for these borrowers, loan products have been created that effectively loosen underwriting standards and require less borrower equity.

A large part of this outreach was undoubtedly attributable to the efforts of the Clinton administration to enforce the Community Reinvestment Act of 1977 (Belsky, Schill, and Yezer 2001). At the same time, attitudes among lenders began to shift, and subprime and risk-based mortgage lending developed as a business strategy for many lenders, particularly in the mortgage refinance market. Mortgage companies, attracted by the low wholesale cost of borrowing and the willingness of marginal borrowers to pay high rates of interest, began to market home loans to these marginal borrowers.

In the past few years, the country has experienced an explosion in subprime lending and risk-based pricing for loans. According to a recent report issued by the Harvard University Joint Center for Housing Studies (2002), the proportion of all loans made by subprime lenders jumped from less than 5 percent in 1994 to almost 13 percent in 1999. These loans typically carry higher interest rates in return for higher risk. Again, many are obtained by marginal borrowers who would otherwise be shut out of the prime market (Calem, Gillen, and Wachter 2004). A subset of the subprime market has also been accused of predatory practices. The federal government has sought to reduce the level of predatory lending and a number of states have increased their regulatory supervision in response to such practices.

While it appears from our analysis that changes in tax law may have contributed to the increase in mortgage debt shouldered by American homeowners, such changes cannot explain the increase in mortgage lending to lower-income households. The greater increase in lending to lower-income households that could not gain from the TRA suggests the weakness of the tax incentive explanation. The data are consistent with current changes in the mortgage market that make credit more easily available to marginal borrowers and allow homeowners to borrow more as a proportion of the total value of their homes. In particular, after 1989, factors other than those related to tax incentive effects appear to be responsible for the increases in mortgage debt.

Bankruptcy and Mortgage Indebtedness

As we document, overall debt is on the rise, and mortgage debt, especially among lower-income households, constitutes an increasing proportion of overall indebtedness for American families. In this part, we concentrate on the most financially distressed homeowners, those who file for bankruptcy. We examine the increasing rates of bankruptcy and the debt characteristics of these households, particularly the loan-to-value (LTV) ratios for their home mortgages. As a substantial body of research indicates, LTV ratios are the major determinant of whether financially distressed homeowners are at risk of ultimately losing their homes to foreclosure; they provide an important perspective on the financial problems facing these families.

The rate at which homeowners are declaring bankruptcy has risen substantially over the past two decades. In 1981, the number was approximately 165,000. By 1991, it had grown to about 380,000. In 2001, it was an estimated 760,000—about 52.5 percent of all families in bankruptcy.[8] To be sure, bankruptcy filings increased for homeowners and nonhomeowners alike, but the rate for homeowners showed a significant rise. In 1981, about 2.8 per thousand filed for bankruptcy.[9] By 2001, that number had climbed to 10.9 per thousand.[10]

The depth of the problems facing homeowners may be even more pervasive than these data suggest. The data reported here capture the number of families who owned homes at the time of their bankruptcy filings. But the bankrupt population is in severe financial distress, and some of the nonhomeowners may have lost their homes prior to bankruptcy.

In calculating the number of families in bankruptcy that had been homeowners and lost a home before bankruptcy, it is necessary to go beyond loss of home due to formal foreclosure. Many people do not lose a home through a formal foreclosure process. When they have fallen behind on their payments, some borrowers will deed the property back to the mortgage lenders to satisfy the outstanding mortgages. Looking only for debtors who lost their homes through formal legal proceedings will understate the number of families in bankruptcy that lost their homes during their financial collapse.

The 2001 questionnaire and telephone survey posed a broad question to the debtors, "Within the past five years, have you owned a home that you lost or sold for financial reasons?" This identified those who, until fairly recently, had been homeowners and who had been squeezed out of their homes for financial reasons. One in every seventeen families in bankruptcy—5.8 percent—indicated that they were no longer homeowners and had lost their homes for financial reasons within five years preceding the bankruptcy. Among the nonhomeowners in the sample, the proportion is even higher, one in eight, or 12.2 percent.

When the current homeowners and the past homeowners are combined, the homeownership rate among the debtors in bankruptcy climbs to 58.3 percent, or about 850,000 current and former homeowners in 2001 alone. This combination is not strictly comparable to the population generally because the proportion of nonbankrupt families who lost homes for financial reasons within the past five years is unknown, nor do we have comparable data about the homeowners from 1981 or 1991. Even so, the high proportion of former homeowners in the bankruptcy sample raises the possibility that a larger number of families in bankruptcy may share—or may have once shared—more characteristics with homeowners in the population generally.

These data show that homeowners have not been immune to the financial pressures on families, and that their prized assets—their homes—are not saving them from financial collapse. Surveys of the homeowners who filed for bankruptcy in 1991[11] and 2001 provide more insight into their financial stress. We can use these data to document the large share of bankrupt households with LTV ratios greater than 90 percent and the substantial increase in such households since 1991. We examine factors correlated with LTV ratios using cross-tabulations and regression analysis. Once again, we examine the data to see if it is consistent with different hypotheses explaining family borrowing. High and rising LTV ratios may be attributable to the incentives created by the Tax Reform Act of 1986 and to the changes in the mortgage market we have described, or these LTV ratios may also reflect some of the incentives created by the bankruptcy law itself, as indicated, among other things, by regression results.

This analysis of bankrupt homeowners is based primarily on a new survey of a subsample of 400 petitioners who filed for bankruptcy in 2001. These cases are part of the first phase of a recently completed study of 1,771 households that filed for bankruptcy in 2001. The study includes an extensive written questionnaire, a detailed analysis of court records, and intensive follow-up telephone surveys.[12] This subsample is drawn from a total sample of cases of bankrupt homeowners from five states. The subset includes all those cases in which both mortgage debt and house value were known both at the time of home purchase and at the time of bankruptcy; those for whom this information was not available were excluded. Table 4.6 presents the size of LTV, house value, and mortgage debt in the sample at the time of purchase and at the time of filing. We also use data for comparative purposes from a more limited survey of homeowner households who petitioned for bankruptcy in 1991.

Our findings document that a large and growing proportion of bankrupt homeowners had high LTV ratios when they filed for bankruptcy. For almost the entire sample financial distress was coupled with increased mortgage borrowing. Mean size of mortgage debt increased from nearly $88,000 at home purchase to nearly $103,000 at bankruptcy filing, or 17 percent. Moreover for the majority of bankrupt homeowners, mortgage borrowing at the point of filing came close to or exceeded the value of their homes. One-third of the petitioners had mortgage debt equal to or in excess of home value at the time of filing.

A high LTV ratio can affect a family in three ways. First, a high LTV is associated with an increased likelihood of eventual foreclosure. Second, if these families lose their homes through sale or foreclosure, those with high LTV ratios will have little or no equity for a down payment for another home. With credit ruined, high LTV debtors may not only lose their homes, but may also remain closed out of homeownership for some time. Third, because bankruptcy laws distinguish mortgage debt from all other kinds of debt, homeowners who try to keep their homes must make payments in full and on time and pay off any arrearages, so that those with high LTV ratios are making substantial—often higher—payments after bankruptcy.

Table 4.6   Families in Bankruptcy, 2001: Summary Statistics

	Mean	Median	Standard Deviation
Purchase price	92,864	85,000	56,467
House value at filing	125,367	113,000	69,805
Debt at purchase	87,816	80,000	51,136
Debt at filing	102,893	89,152	62,094
LTV at purchase	0.966	1.000	0.197
LTV at filing	0.905	0.918	0.257

Source: Survey of Bankruptcy Petitioners (2001).
Note: Unweighted N = 400.

Foreclosure risk rises with a rise in LTV ratios, but the relationship is nonlinear. Transaction costs associated with the sale of a house are likely to be as high as 10 percent. After payment of transaction costs, there is little or no equity left for the homeowner, thus increasing the likelihood of foreclosure. Thus, LTV ratios greater than 90 percent are associated with heightened risks for foreclosure and wipeout of equity (Quercia and Stegman 1992). Table 4.6 shows the average LTV ratio for the 2001 sample of bankrupt homeowners. Despite gains in the value of homes and years in the residence to pay down the mortgage, in 2001 LTV ratios at filing were still on average slightly above 90 percent for the sample as a whole. In table 4.7 we disaggregate the 400 bankrupt homeowners in 2001 into two con-

Table 4.7   Bankrupt Homeowners, 2001: Summary Statistics

	LTV at Filing Less than 0.9 (Unweighted N = 157)			LTV at Filing Greater than or Equal to 0.9 (Unweighted N = 243)		
	Mean	Median	Standard Deviation	Mean	Median	Standard Deviation
Purchase price	85,051	78,000	59,139	99,360	90,000	53,282
House value at filing	140,061	130,000	72,556	113,152	100,000	64,951
Debt at purchase	76,714	72,300	48,733	97,046	88,000	51,254
Debt at filing	94,422	84,196	56,694	109,935	94,000	65,422

Source: Survey of Bankruptcy Petitioners (2001).

Table 4.8   LTV at Filing Among Bankrupt Homeowners, 1991 and 2001

	Mean LTV at Filing	Percentage with LTV 90 Percent and over
1991	0.78	43%
2001	0.91	60*

Source: Surveys of Bankruptcy Petitioners (1991 and 2001).
*Difference significant at 1 percent level.

stituent groups of lower LTV ratios, those with LTV ratios of less than 90 percent, and higher LTV ratios, those with LTV ratios greater than or equal to 90 percent. Somewhat more than 60 percent of the homeowners in the 2001 bankruptcy sample fall into the higher LTV group.

As table 4.8 indicates, the proportion of higher LTV homeowners in bankruptcy has increased over time. The 60 percent of bankrupt homeowners with LTV ratios greater than 90 percent in 2001 is 50 percent higher than the 40 percent with higher LTV ratios in 1991. To probe for the factors that may explain higher LTV ratios, we first focus on how the 2001 high and low LTV subsamples differ.

The 2001 bankruptcy data suggest that among higher LTV bankrupt homeowners, refinancing and home equity loans are likely to have played a key role in increased leverage and reduced equity in the years preceding bankruptcy.[13] For the 60 percent of all homeowners in bankruptcy with high mortgage debt burdens relative to the value of their homes, during their tenure in the home, mortgage debt increased rather than decreased over time. For this higher LTV group the average LTV exceeded one by the time they filed for bankruptcy—that is, the average higher LTV debtor owed more on the mortgage than the full market value of the house.

As table 4.9 shows, the differences between the two groups for the most part are not surprising: higher LTV homeowners in bankruptcy tend to be younger on average than their lower LTV counterparts. In addition, they are slightly less well educated. Higher LTV homeowners are also more likely to be couples with children. The homes of higher LTV households appreciated less between the time of purchase and the time of filing. The lower LTV homeowners stayed in their homes nearly twice as long before filing for bankruptcy.

This last finding in particular suggests that higher LTV ratios at filing could be an artifact of recent home purchase and higher LTV ra-

Table 4.9   Variable Differences Between Higher and Lower LTV Groups
Among Bankrupt Homeowners, 2001

	LTV Less than 0.9 N = 149	LTV Greater than or Equal to 0.9 N = 231
Age		
Young (thirty-four years old or younger)	13.8	37.5
Middle-aged (thirty-five to forty-four years old)	59.3	54.0
Old (fifty-five years and older)	26.9	8.4
Education		
High school or less	34.2	41.1
Some college or higher	64.0	44.6
Family type		
Single male	12.3	8.2
Single female	19.6	10.2
Single parent	19.8	25
Couple with children	30.6	41.5
Couple with no children	17.8	15.1
State		
Low-exemption states	0.441	0.509
Pennsylvania	0.221	0.260
High-exemption states	0.338	0.231
Consumer debt in dollars	41,811	19,037
Change in house value between purchase and filing	2.12	1.40
Income	35,103	33,720
Tenure in home	11.8	6.7

Source: Survey of Bankruptcy Petitioners (2001).

tios at origination. To explore whether this is the case, as shown in
table 4.10, we divide the group of higher LTV households into two
subgroups —those who had lived in their current homes for less
than five years and those who have lived in their homes for more
than five years. The data show that both groups experienced increases in their LTV ratios. Indeed, contrary to expectations, rather
than having smaller LTV ratios, the more than five years group had
marginally higher LTV ratios than those in the more recent homeowner group (1.08 percent versus 1.05 percent). These data imply
that high LTV ratios among the homeowners in bankruptcy are not
attributable to high LTVs at the onset or to brief tenure. These homeowners have refinanced and increased the outstanding principal on

Table 4.10   LTV Among Bankrupt Homeowners, by Tenure, 2001

	LTV at Purchase		LTV at Filing	
	Mean	Median	Mean	Median
Total sample	.96	1.0	.90	.92
LTV at filing less than 0.9	.94	.99	.72	.77
Five years or less in house	.97	.96	.78	.80
More than five years in house	.93	1.0	.70	.74
LTV at filing greater				
than or equal to 0.9	.99	1.0	1.06	1.0
Five years or less in house	1.01	1.0	1.04	1.0
More than five years in house	.95	1.0	1.08	1.02

Source: Survey of Bankruptcy Petitioners (2001).

their mortgages before they filed for bankruptcy, although the analysis thus far does not identify attributes associated with their doing so.

One explanation may be the role consumer debt plays in the overall financial picture for these families. Consumer debt is noticeably lower for the higher LTV group by almost $20,000. This difference implies a role for substitution of mortgage debt for consumer debt in high LTV outcomes. A second source of information about why homeowners at bankruptcy have higher LTV ratios that come from the homeowners themselves supports this finding.

Each debtor reports on the reasons for bankruptcy filing, giving some glimpse into the financial problems facing the household before the filing. Table 4.11 reports the reasons homeowners gave for why they filed for bankruptcy. Interestingly, the only major difference between higher and lower LTV homeowners was over whether their filing was attributable to "credit card debt out of control." According to the debtors' responses, this was a significantly bigger problem among the lower LTV homeowners. This is consistent with the inference that the higher LTV group substituted mortgage debt for credit card debt. By the time of the bankruptcy filing, the higher LTV group may have seen itself as dealing with other problems, while the lower LTV group was more likely to be battling the credit card companies. This result supports the differences in average consumer debt that we found for the two subsamples.

An additional factor that may explain differences among LTV ra-

Table 4.11   Reasons for Filing by Bankrupt Homeowners, 2001

	LTV Less than 0.9	LTV Greater than or Equal to 0.9
May lose home (eviction or foreclosure)	0.90	0.92
Job problems	0.68	0.73
Medical problems	47.8	48.1
Credit card debt out of control	0.41*	0.27
Trouble managing money	0.34	0.31
Aggressive collection efforts by creditors	0.23	0.24
Car accident	0.04	0.05
Divorce or family breakup	0.13	0.18
Addition of a family member	0.06	0.09
Victim of fraud or crime	0.07	0.03
Victim of disaster (flood, fire)	0.02	0.00
Gambling	0.03	0.01
Alcoholism or drug addiction	0.02	0.02
Other reasons	0.02	0.04

Source: Survey of Bankruptcy Petitioners (2001).

*Difference significant at 1 percent level.

tios is the state in which the bankrupt homeowner lives. When a home is sold either in mortgage foreclosure or by a trustee in bankruptcy, the mortgage lender will get first call on the proceeds from the sale. If any money remains, the debtor is permitted a "homestead exemption." If there is any equity after the mortgage and the exemption have been satisfied, it is distributed to the remaining creditors. By statute, federal bankruptcy law yields to state law to determine the amount of property a debtor may keep free from general creditor collection following a bankruptcy. Such exemption laws vary widely by state. In particular, the homestead exemption or the amount of equity that bankrupt households are allowed to keep is quite different among the states. In seven—Arkansas, Florida, Iowa, Kansas, Oklahoma, South Dakota, and Texas—the amount of equity protected is unlimited; in twenty-five it is $20,000 or less. This means that in the first seven states, once the mortgage lender is paid off, a homeowner in bankruptcy can keep the home (or the proceeds from the sale of the home) regardless of its value. In the twenty-five, the homeowner can retain only that $20,000 or less; any additional proceeds must go to the general unsecured creditors on a pro rata basis.

Our sample included a diverse group. One, Texas, is among the seven states that permit homeowners to retain an unlimited amount of equity in a home. Next most generous is California with its $75,000 exemption, placing it near the highest of the capped states. Pennsylvania is next, allowing $17,425 for an individual and $34,850 for a couple in bankruptcy. Illinois and Tennessee permit exemptions of only $7,500, placing them near the bottom.

To examine the effect of these caps, we combine the two high-exemption states (California and Texas) and the two low-exemption (Illinois and Tennessee), and compare the LTV for these groups to the state with the mid-level exemption, Pennsylvania. All other things being equal, a higher exemption should permit homeowners with lower LTV ratios to file for bankruptcy without fear of losing their homes, and a lower state exemption should discourage homeowners with much equity from turning to bankruptcy. The data for the LTV comparisons based on simple averages are shown in table 4.12.[14]

We can probe the effect of homestead exemptions on debt-taking by including state exemption status in a multivariable regression analysis along with other factors that may drive higher LTV ratios. The regression analysis permits testing for the significance of each factor in higher LTV outcomes. It is also possible to determine whether there has been an increase in LTV among bankrupt households over time and, if so, to measure the estimated extent of this rise.

To proceed, we estimate a binomial logit model with the probability of LTV at filing being 0.9 or higher as the dependent variable. We use the factors discussed above, as right-hand side variables, along with demographic and housing characteristics of bankrupt households as controls, as listed in table 4.9. To analyze changes in LTV over time, we use the subset of these data for which we have information in 1991 as well as 2001. We combine the 2001 data set with the similar though not as complete data set with information about bankrupt homeowners collected ten years earlier, in 1991, to form a time-series cross-section database. We use these data to estimate a binomial logit model that includes a year dummy on the right-hand side. Table 4.13 shows means of variables used in the time-series cross-section regression.[15]

Table 4.12   LTV in States

Exemption Level	N	Mean	Median
Low-exemption states (Illinois, Tennessee)	191	0.94	0.96
Middle-exemption state (Pennsylvania)	97	0.95	0.95
High-exemption states (California, Texas)	109	0.87	0.88

Source: Survey of Bankruptcy Petitioners (2001).

LTV Regression Results

The results of the first regression are listed in table 4.14. The fit of the regression is quite good and the signs of the variables are all reasonable. As expected, the change in house value between the time

Table 4.13   Demographic Differences between Lower-LTV and Higher-LTV Groups of Bankrupt Homeowners in the Time-Series Cross-Section (1991 and 2001)

	LTV Less than 0.9 N = 276	LTV Greater than or Equal to 0.9 N = 325
Year		
1991	0.478	0.311
2001	0.522	0.689
Age group		
Young (thirty-four or younger)	0.200	0.366
Thirty-five to forty-four	0.746	0.625
Old (fifty-five and older)	0.054	0.009
Education		
High school or less	0.609	0.532
Some college or higher	0.391	0.468
Family type		
Single male	0.152	0.135
Single female	0.261	0.302
Couple	0.587	0.563
Exemption status		
High-exemption	0.362	0.265
Low-exemption	0.254	0.243
Middle-exemption		
Log (income)	10.201	10.257
Log (consumer credit)	9.372	9.224

Source: Survey of Bankruptcy Petitioners (1991 and 2001).

Table 4.14   The Logistic Procedure (Binomial)

Parameter	Parameter Estimate	Standard Error	Wald Chi-Square
Intercept	3.8241	3.2451	1.3887
Log (consumer debt)	−0.155*	0.0975	2.5305
High-exemption states	−0.5853**	0.282	4.3088
Pennsylvania (middle exemption)	−0.0202	0.2986	0.0046
Log (change in house value)	−0.781***	0.3369	5.3754
Log (income)	−0.0843	0.3076	0.0751
Middle-aged	−0.4105*	0.2742	2.2418
Old	−0.7709	1.0044	0.5891
Some college or higher education	0.1197	0.2464	0.236
Single parent	−0.1126	0.3961	0.0809
Single male	−0.4619	0.4803	0.9251
Single female	−0.0937	0.4598	0.0415
Couple with children	−0.0793	0.3693	0.0462
Duration of tenure in the home	−0.0342*	0.0221	2.3989
ROC (measure of fit)	0.711		

Source: Survey of Bankruptcy Petitioners (2001), and authors' calculations.
Note: Dependent variable: probability of LTV is greater than or equal to 0.9, 2001 sample.
***Coefficient significant at 2 percent level.
**Coefficient significant at 5 percent level.
**Coefficient significant at 10 percent level.

of purchase and the time of filing is a significant and negative predictor of a higher LTV as is the duration of tenure in the home. In other words, lower LTV homeowners tended to experience both appreciation in the value of their homes and paid down the principal balance of their mortgages. Also as expected, middle-aged debtors, compared with a young age group, were also less likely (at a 10 percent level) to have a higher LTV at filing. For the two variables of policy interest, all else being equal, high exemption states are significantly and negatively related to the probability of higher LTV at filing. That is, families living in states with high homestead exemptions are likely to have a lower LTV when they file for bankruptcy. This confirms predictions suggesting that the exemption status of the state of residence matters for LTV outcomes. The size of consumer credit is also significantly (at 10 percent) and negatively related to a higher LTV at filing, a finding consistent with the substitution of mortgage debt for consumer debt.[16]

The time-series cross-section results displayed in table 4.15 support the previous results. Strong and negative predictors of higher

Table 4.15   The Logistic Procedure (Binomial) with 2001 Year Dummy

Parameter	Parameter Estimate	Standard Error	Wald Chi-Square
Intercept	0.8631	2.0677	0.1742
Year 2001	0.657****	0.2098	9.8059
Log (consumer debt)	−0.0795	0.072	1.2183
High-exemption states	−0.3933**	0.2038	3.7235
Pennsylvania (middle exemption)	−0.2782	0.2209	1.5863
Log (income)	0.0408	0.2025	0.0406
Middle-aged	−0.761****	0.196	15.0757
Old	−2.1688****	0.6711	10.4443
Some college or higher education	0.0131	0.203	0.0042
Single male	−0.1118	0.2566	0.1899
Single female	0.0358	0.2179	0.0269
ROC (measure of fit)	0.666		

Source: Surveys of Bankruptcy Petitioners (1991 and 2001), and authors' calculations.
Note: Dependent variable: probability of LTV greater than or equal to 0.9, 1991 and 2001 samples.
****Coefficient significant at 1 percent level.
** Coefficient significant at 5 percent level.

LTV are middle and old ages, compared to the left-out young age cohort. The high exemption state variable retains a significant and negative effect on the probability of higher LTV at filing compared to low exemption states. We include a year dummy in this regression to test for whether and how much LTV ratios have increased over time. We would like to determine whether otherwise similar households will be predicted to have a higher LTV in 2001 than in 1991. The year 2001 dummy variable is positive and significant. That is, the 2001 homeowners who filed for bankruptcy had more mortgage debt relative to house value at the time of filing than their counterparts in 1991, all else being equal.

While we know the shift over time is statistically significant, we can also determine whether the size of the measured increase is economically significant. To do so, we simulate the importance of the shift in LTV over the decade by calculating predicted probabilities of higher LTV for each of the two survey years (keeping all the dependent variables except the survey year dummy at their mean level). The predicted probability of having a higher LTV in 1991 is 43.7 percent, and in 2001 it is 60.0 percent. Thus, predicted LTV ratios at filing have increased by almost 50 percent, an outcome similar to the actually observed shift in the two samples.

This implies that higher LTV ratios at filing over time are not an artifact of the respective household compositions of the 1991 and 2001 samples. Rather the data suggest that there is an underlying trend to more mortgage debt and as a result to greater LTV ratios among bankrupt homeowners over time. While we do not know the underlying source of this increase, the institutional shifts toward risk-based pricing, subprime debt, and marketing of mortgage debt to consolidate consumer credit over time are fully consistent with these results.

Homeowner Protection Under Bankruptcy Law

Homeowners overwhelmed by their debt burdens may turn to bankruptcy for relief. Often desperate to save their homes, many file in the hopes that they can forestall a mortgage foreclosure and get current on payments. The bankruptcy system, as it is now structured, is oriented to providing relief for debtors with extensive consumer debt, but more than half the families seeking bankruptcy relief are homeowners, most of whom face substantial mortgage debts.

Debtors have a choice of chapters when they file for bankruptcy. About 70 percent choose Chapter 7, in part because it is less complicated and less expensive, typically providing a discharge from consumer debts within a few weeks. The 30 percent who choose Chapter 13 must propose a repayment plan, agreeing to turn over to a trustee all of their disposable income for a three- to five-year period. They receive a discharge of their remaining debt only at the end of their agreed payments. In fact, only about a third of those who attempt a Chapter 13 discharge manage to complete their payments and discharge their debts. About a third convert to Chapter 7 for an immediate discharge of debt, and about a third are dismissed from the bankruptcy system altogether with no discharge of debt.

Homeowners, however, disproportionately choose Chapter 13— 37.4 percent of the core sample versus 55.3 percent of the homeowners. This suggests that a bankrupt homeowner is nearly 50 percent more likely to file for Chapter 13 than Chapter 7. The reason is straightforward: Chapter 7 provides no special protection to homeowners. If a homeowner is in default on mortgage payments, Chapter 7 will permit him or her to discharge personal liability for the debt, thus escaping any deficiency judgment if the property is ultimately sold for less than the outstanding mortgage, but the mortgage remains firmly attached to the property. The homeowner must continue to make all the payments in full and on time, or the lender can continue foreclosure proceedings as soon as the Chapter 7 proceeding is concluded—usually a matter of weeks.

Chapter 7 also has a major drawback for some homeowners: if the homeowner has built up equity in the home, there is some risk that the trustee will sell the home for the benefit of all the creditors. As noted earlier, the mortgage lender will get first call on the proceeds from the sale, the debtor will then be permitted a "homestead exemption," and the remainder of the equity will then be distributed to the remaining creditors. Whether such a sale will take place depends on two factors: the amount of equity and the amount of the "homestead exemption." The latter, in turn, depends on the state in which the homeowner resides. Whether the amount of the homestead exemption is an issue for a particular homeowner, of course, depends first on whether the homeowner has substantial equity in the home. Higher LTV debtors may have to struggle with their mortgage companies, but can file for bankruptcy without fear that a trustee will sell the home for the benefit of other creditors because there is no excess equity for those creditors to claim. If the homeowner does not have more equity than state law exemptions will protect, then he or she can file for Chapter 7, receive a discharge of consumer debt, and reestablish some financial balance while keeping both home and equity.

In Chapter 13, homeowners have two opportunities to save their homes that they would not have in Chapter 7. First, if they are in default on their mortgages, they will be permitted to confirm a repayment plan in which they cure and reinstate their mortgages. That is, the law will give them a grace period to catch up on late mortgage payments. But the protection is modest. The homeowner must pay off all the debt within a fairly constrained period of time, making current mortgage payments as they come due and making regular payments (with interest) to cure the arrearage promptly. In effect, the homeowner in bankruptcy trying to catch up on late payments must make a larger—not a smaller—payment, which can be problematic. Nonetheless, the homeowner can force the recalcitrant lender to accept both current payments and arrearages, which can give a homeowner a chance at saving the home even when the lender has decided to foreclose.

Second, if the homeowner has equity in excess of state-permitted levels, the Chapter 7 homeowner would have lost the home to a trustee sale. In Chapter 13, however, he or she may make payments over time to its nonmortgage creditors that are equal to the outstanding equity (plus interest). For example, in a state with a homestead exemption of $10,000, a homeowner with a house valued at $100,000 with a $75,000 mortgage, would lose the property in Chapter 7; the trustee would sell it and distribute the proceeds first to the mortgage lender. The remaining $25,000 in equity would first cover the expenses of sale, second the homeowner's exemption ($10,000 in this example), and the remainder would be distributed pro rata to all the unsecured creditors. In Chapter 13, the homeowner could instead make payments (plus interest) equal to the $15,000 distribution that would have been made to the creditors after a trustee sale. But, as this example makes clear, the homeowner with substantial equity does not lose the home immediately to sale, but to save it must make more payments. If he or she is unable to make these payments, the Chapter 13 filing is dismissed and the mortgage lender may proceed to foreclose on the property or the other creditors may have the house seized and sold by the sheriff.

The protected position enjoyed by home mortgage lenders unifies their incentives across states with a spectrum of varying homestead exemptions. The law in all fifty jurisdictions is the same: a mortgage lender's mortgage takes precedence over a state's homestead exemption. In other words, whether the mortgage lender is in Florida (unlimited homestead) or Delaware (no homestead), the mortgage lender's right remain the same—pay the mortgage or the lender can foreclose on the home. The same is true whether the mortgage is a purchase money mortgage or added later as a second mortgage or home equity line of credit. General unsecured creditors, such as credit card companies, will be treated differently in the two states—unable to file a lien against the home in Florida but able to do so in Delaware—but mortgage lenders' right remain paramount in bankruptcy.

Nonetheless, differences in homestead exemptions may affect

whether and how financially troubled debtors use bankruptcy. Current bankruptcy laws may actually create an incentive for homeowners to become higher LTV borrowers. The states from which our sample of bankrupt homeowners was drawn illustrate the problem. Homestead exemptions among the five sample states vary widely. One, Texas, permits an unlimited amount of equity. The rest are capped: $75,000 in California (placing it near the highest of the capped states), $17,425 for an individual and $34,850 for a couple in Pennsylvania, and $7,500 in both Illinois and Tennessee. This means that a homeowner who had home equity worth $20,000 or more would lose the home immediately in Chapter 7 in three of the five states or would have to come up with payments equal to the amount of equity in a Chapter 13 plan. To put this in context, in twenty-four states in the country, the same would happen: a homeowner with $20,001 in equity would either lose the home immediately or lose it if he or she could not come up with payments equal to the amount of equity.

For those high LTV homeowners whose equity is less than the exemption amount, however, bankruptcy provides much greater relief. The homeowner's only concern will be to make all mortgage payments on time. If that can be done, there will be no foreclosure. Thus the combination of federal bankruptcy law and state exemption law may create an incentive for financially strapped households to become higher LTV borrowers. By borrowing against their homes before they file for bankruptcy, these homeowners can protect themselves in low-exemption states from having their homes seized and sold. In effect, they receive protection if they load up on mortgage debt. Of course, the difficulty with encouraging higher LTV ratios for families in financial trouble is that the borrowers must still pay off their mortgages. With higher LTV ratios the home is at greater risk of foreclosure, and homeowners will have more debt to pay (higher mortgage rates), and those payments must be made on time and in full even after a bankruptcy filing.

The increase in the number of homeowners in bankruptcy and the distribution of higher LTV ratios observed among those homeowners is consistent with the hypothesis that the current laws encourage some homeowners to load up on mortgage debt as they get into financial trouble.

Implications

More than 60 percent of the homeowners we examined have little or no equity cushion. Most have borrowed against the home to the point that their mortgages are now as large as, or larger than, the full value of their property. If they cannot manage their mortgage payments, they are at great risk of losing their current homes. By the time they pay closing expenses for a voluntary sale or foreclosure expenses are added to their outstanding mortgage, there will be nothing left for a down payment on another home. While filing for bankruptcy provides substantial assistance to those with high credit card debt, current law provides little help for the higher LTV homeowners who want to keep their homes.

We have presented some suggestive evidence on the phenomenon of increasing mortgage debt over time. Families' borrowing behaviors are likely to be influenced by a variety of factors. Those of modest income seem to be caught between intensive mortgage marketing and a willingness to turn to the equity in their homes in times of financial stress. Mortgage debt may be high for those in bankruptcy because these families saw their financial troubles as temporary and borrowed against their homes in an effort to stabilize themselves financially. That strategy may have worked for many troubled families—that is, prevented them from ending up in bankruptcy. But for hundreds of thousands of other families who are in bankruptcy, the effort to borrow one's way out of trouble backfired. Moreover, given their increased mortgage debt relative to the house value, they are at heightened risk of losing their homes.

The data reported here suggest that low homestead exemptions in many states may play a role in high mortgages for financially troubled households. They may provide some incentive for households to obtain high LTV loans in an effort to hold on to their homes as they spiral into bankruptcy. When added to the other incentives homeowners have to mortgage their residences—the tax incentives created by the TRA and the increased availability of high risk debt—the result is high and increasing levels of mortgage debt relative to home values for homeowners in bankruptcy. The data presented here suggest that the increase in the number of bankrupt homeowners over time has been accompanied by a substantial increase in their use of mortgage debt, which cannot be reduced or eliminated at filing and which may substantially reduce their prospects for continued homeownership.

We are particularly indebted to Michael H. Schill, professor of law and urban planning at New York University, who made important contributions both to the development of this study and to the ideas in this paper. The 2001 Consumer Bankruptcy Project was made possible through generous funding from The Ford Foundation, as well as grants from Harvard Law School and New York University Law School. We offer our special thanks to Dr. George McCarthy, program officer of The Ford Foundation, who offered many helpful comments in the design of this study. The enthusiastic support and assistance of many bankruptcy judges, bankruptcy clerks, Chapter 7 and Chapter 13 trustees, and attorneys also contributed significantly to this work. The principal investigators express our sincere gratitude to the organizations that provided financial support and to each of the judges, clerks, trustees, and lawyers who made this research possible. No project of this kind could be put together without the contribution of a number of people. Consumer Bankruptcy Project I, in 1981, and Consumer Bankruptcy Project II, in 1991, were the work of Professors Teresa A. Sullivan, Elizabeth Warren, and Jay Lawrence Westbrook, all of whom have continued their work into Consumer Bankruptcy Project III, in 2001. In addition, Professors David Himmelstein, Robert Lawless, Bruce Markell, Michael Schill, Susan Wachter, and Steffie Woolhandler have shared in the design and development of the 2001 study. Ms. Katherine Porter, Professor John Pottow, and Professor Deborah Thorne served as project directors at different times, participating in the design of the study and managing much of the data collection. Alexander Warren designed and managed all the coding databases. We are collectively grateful for the contributions of each person.

Notes

1. These statistics and the following discussion are derived from an excellent discussion of changing patterns of indebtedness in *The State of Working America* (Mishel, Bernstein, and Boushey 2003).
2. Because the growth of home-equity and second mortgages is a phenomenon of the last decade and because of a small sample problem in

earlier years, in our cross-tabulations we focus on the past decade only.

3. The time-series sample used in estimating the payment regression and payment-to-income ratio (8,075 household-level observations) includes all homeowners who reported having outstanding home-secured debt at the time of survey, except those homeowners with debt who had a negative or zero income and/or reported having zero annual mortgage payments. This led to a small loss of 361 observations. The proportion of homeowners with outstanding home-secured debt in the total sample of homeowners in the SCF data increased over the study period from 57.8 percent in 1983 to 65.1 percent in 1998. The sample is dominated by white couples with children who have some college education or a college degree and who are middle-aged and high-income (as defined earlier).

    The time-series sample used in estimating the LTV and mortgage-to-total-debt ratios includes all homeowners who reported having outstanding home-secured debt at the time of the survey (8,436 household-level observations). The sample distribution by the observed characteristics is identical to the one used in the estimation of payment-to-income data.

4. Wald tests were performed to test differences between coefficients.

5. Although the new law became effective for the fiscal year 1987, it was subject to a phase-in rule. For the years from 1987 through 1990, deductions of personal interest were disallowed according to the following proportions: 35 percent in 1987, 60 percent in 1988, 80 percent in 1989, 90 percent in 1990, and 100 percent in 1991. Whether a household will deduct home mortgage interest depends upon whether its total deductions exceed the standard deduction. The standard deduction increased throughout the 1980s and 1990s, with a considerable increase in 1988.

6. Under the statute, a "qualified residence" is the principal residence of the taxpayer and one other residence selected by the taxpayer for purposes of the deduction. To qualify as a second residence, the taxpayer must have used the dwelling as a residence for part of the year if the home was rented to others. If the dwelling is neither rented nor used as a dwelling unit, it is still eligible for treatment as a qualified residence.

7. The construction of this variable is described in Raisa Bahchieva, Michael Schill, Susan Wachter, and Elizabeth Warren (2002).

8. The 1981 data are calculated from Sullivan, Warren, and Westbrook (1989) (reporting 52 percent homeownership rate among families filing for bankruptcy in 1981) and data from the Administrative Office of the United States Courts (reporting 315,818 nonbusiness bankruptcy filings). The 1991 data are calculated from Sullivan, Warren, and Westbrook (1989), (reporting 43.9 percent) and data from the AO (reporting 872,438 nonbusiness bankruptcy filings). The 2001 data

are from the 2001 Consumer Bankruptcy Project. For a more detailed discussion of the relative filing rates in 1981, 1991, and 2001, see Warren (2003).

9. Calculated from data reported in Sullivan, Warren, and Westbrook (1989).

10. Calculated from 2001 Consumer Bankruptcy Project and census data reported earlier.

11. For a detailed discussion of the 1991 database and survey instruments, see Sullivan, Warren, and Westbrook (2000). The 1991 study was based on a sample of debtors filing for bankruptcy during 1991 in sixteen judicial districts in five states—the same five states as the 2001 study. The survey sample was 2,400 debtors, with additional court record data for 450 of those families.

12. For a detailed explanation of the survey instrument, see Bahchieva, Schill, Wachter, and Warren (2002).

13. A second reason for the increased LTV ratios could be that the homeowners kept their borrowing constant but defaulted on payments. Because past due amounts are typically added to principal, this could also account for the increase in LTV ratios. According to our survey, more than three-quarters (77.5 percent) of all high LTV homeowners did indeed fail to make at least one payment. The magnitude of the effect of penalty payments compared with additional borrowing is, however, likely to be small. It is possible to get an indirect look at the effects of missed payments by comparing the lower LTV households with the high LTV households; the two groups report defaults at similar rates, suggesting that increases in the LTV are not driven largely by penalties and other late charges for missed payments.

14. Exploring the impact of exemptions controlling for other factors would also be of interest.

15. A higher proportion of the high-LTV group comprised the 2001 sample than the 1991 one. As in the 2001 sample, high-LTV homeowners are younger. Unlike in the 2001 sample, they are somewhat better educated than their low-LTV counterparts.

16. Andreas Lehnert and Dean Maki (2003) provide evidence on the role of exemptions in determining household debt and asset positions that are consistent with our results. However, unlike our analysis they do not present findings on secured debt.

References

Administrative Office of the United States Court. 2004. Table F-2, "Business and Nonbusiness Bankruptcy Cases Commenced, By Chapter of the Bankruptcy Code, During the 12-Month Period Ended December 31, 2003."

American Bankruptcy Institute. 2002. *U.S. Bankruptcy Filings 1980–2001.*

Alexandria, Va.: American Bankruptcy Institute. Available at: www .abiworld.org (accessed February 2, 2005).

Bahchieva, Raisa, Michael H. Schill, Susan M. Wachter, and Elizabeth Warren. 2002. "Homeownership and Financial Distress: The Interplay of Tax, Real Estate and Bankruptcy Laws." Grant Report to the Ford Foundation.

Belsky, Eric S., Michael Schill, and Anthony Yezer. 2001. "The Effect of the Community Reinvestment Act of Bank and Thrift Home Purchase Lending," *Proceedings, Federal Reserve Bank of Chicago* (April): 271–300.

Calem, Paul, Kevin Gillen, and Susan Wachter, 2004. "The Neighborhood Distribution of Subprime Mortgage Lending." *Journal of Real Estate Finance and Economics* 29(4): 393–410.

Federal Reserve Board. 2000. "Recent Changes in U.S. Family Finances: Results from the 1998 Survey of Consumer Finances." *Federal Reserve Bulletin* 86(1): 1–29.

Harvard University, Joint Center for Housing Studies. 2002. *The 25th Anniversary of the Community Reinvestment Act: Access to Capital in an Evolving Financial Services System.* Cambridge, Mass.: Harvard University, Joint Center for Housing Studies.

Lehnert, Andreas, and Dean M. Maki. 2003. "Consumption, Debt and Portfolio Choice." Working Paper. Washington: Federal Reserve System.

Mishel, Lawrence, Jared Bernstein, and Heather Boushey. 2003. *The State of Working America 2002/2003.* Ithaca, N.Y.: Cornell University Press, Economic Policy Institute.

Quercia, Roberto, and Michael Stegman. 1992. "Residential Mortgage Default: Review of the Literature." *Journal of Housing Research* 3(2): 341–79.

Sullivan, Teresa, Elizabeth Warren, and Jay Westbrook. 1989. *As We Forgive Our Debtors: Bankruptcy and Consumer Credit in America.* New York: Oxford University Press.

———. 2000. *The Fragile Middle Class: Americans in Debt.* New Haven, Conn.: Yale University Press.

Survey of Bankruptcy Petitioners. 1999 and 2001. The Consumer Bankruptcy Project.

Survey of Consumer Finances. 1983, 1989, 1992, 1995, 1998. Washington: Board of Governors of the Federal Reserve System.

Warren, Elizabeth. 2003. "Financial Collapse and Class Status: Who Goes Bankrupt?" Lewtas Lecture. *Osgoode Hall Law Journal* 41(1): 115–46.

Warren, Elizabeth, and Amelia Warren Tyagi. 2003. *The Two-Income Trap: Why Middle Class Mothers and Fathers Are Going Broke.* New York: Basic Books.

Chapter 5

Legal Institutions, Credit Markets, and Poverty in Italy

Daniela Fabbri and Mario Padula

In investigating the distortions generated by Italy's ill-functioning legal system in the credit allocation to households, it is especially important to analyze whether how poorly loan contracts are enforced affects credit constraints and volume of debt and how this effect varies with household characteristics such as income or wealth.

Low-income and low-wealth households are the most affected for two reasons. First, they are more likely to be credit constrained. Second, poor legal enforcement reduces the amount of debt of low-income households but has no significant effects on high-income households. This evidence suggests that a reform of the Italian judicial system is likely to have both allocative and redistributive consequences.

The underlying economic mechanism, through which the performance of courts is assumed to affect the credit allocation, is formalized in Daniela Fabbri and Mario Padula (2004). They start with the observation that most of the loan contracts signed by Italian households are secured with collateral.[1] Generally, the collateral is a physical asset, like the residence. Thus, they assume that the enforcement of the right to repossess the collateral is costly for the creditor and that the cost depends on the performance of the judicial system.

For example, one might assume that the judicial system sets the time when the transfer of the asset takes place. Because a consumer also benefits from keeping the asset, it might be that he or she prefers to default on the contract rather than repay the loan, whenever courts are slow enough in enforcing the creditor's rights. Consumers are more likely to be credit constrained when judicial costs are high, which means that the quality of enforcement is poor (Fabbri and Padula 2004). The reason for this is that the borrowers' incentive to repay decreases and banks respond by increasing the minimum collateral (rationing credit). Second, the higher the judicial costs, the less the credit provided, because banks compensate for the lower revenues from liquidation by charging higher interest rates.

For an empirical analysis along the lines of this idea, one needs a proxy for the performance of courts. We use data on the backlog of trials pending across judicial districts in Italy. Given that our focus is on the effect of legal enforcement rather than the content of laws, this data set is particularly well suited for the problem under scrutiny. In fact, legal rules on credit contracts are the same nationwide, while law enforcement, measured by the backlog of trials pending, differs considerably across judicial districts. Italy thus offers a useful natural experiment that allows us to disentangle the enforcement effect from the legislative.

Information on households credit is taken from the Survey of Household Income and Wealth. We focus on two variables: the information on credit constraints and the amount of debt. Unlike many other data sets, this survey allows us to identify credit-constrained households through self-reported information, without relying on implausible and often endogenous identification restrictions.[2] We define a household as credit constrained if it responds positively to the question: "during the year did you or a member of your household apply for a loan to a bank or other financial intermediary and have the application partially or totally rejected?"

The use of micro-economic data is motivated by the fact that macro-data do not allow us to disentangle the effect of the legal enforcement from the one of the economic development. As we will explain, there is a strong positive correlation among credit availability, legal enforcement and economic development. The share of credit-constrained households is higher and the debt-to-income ratio is lower in regions with a lower per capita gross domestic product and weaker law enforcement. Moreover, the strength of enforcement, which varies widely across Italian regions, improves with per capita gross domestic product. Beyond all this, micro data also allow us to control for unobserved heterogeneity at the regional level by using a full set of judicial district dummies.[3] Finally, these data make our analysis more robust to endogeneity problems since both the probability that a given household is credit constrained, and its amount of debt are likely to have negligible effects on overall regional economy and court activity.

We document that a decline in legal enforcement increases a household's probability of being credit constrained. This effect is found to decrease with income or wealth. The probability that a given household in the bottom quartile of the income distribution is credit constrained ranges from 55 percent in the worst judicial district to 9 percent in the best. If we consider households in the top quartile, we find that this probability ranges from 24 percent in the worst judicial district to 6 percent in the best.

We also look at the effect of legal enforcement on the availability of credit. We find that it varies in magnitude across income and wealth quartiles. A decline in legal enforcement reduces the amount of debt of poor households but does not affect the rich. This effect is found to be economically significant. Computing the semi-elasticity of household debt with respect to the legal variable, we find that a 1 percent increase in the legal costs[4] is associated to a reduction of €1,600 in the debt volume of low-income households.

Our findings parallel the evidence provided by Reint Gropp, John Karl Scholz, and Michelle White (1997) for the household credit market in the United States. However, our focus on the quality of the enforcement rather than on the content of law distinguishes our work from their analysis. Using the Survey on Consumer Finances, they document that the size of asset bankruptcy exemptions positively affects the probability that a household is turned down for credit in United States. In their analysis, they do not control for possible differences in the enforcement of laws. The effect is found to be larger for low-asset households. They also show that an increase in the asset bankruptcy exemptions reduces the volume of credit for households in the lower half of the asset distribution, while it increases it for those in the upper half.

The other existing work on this topic focuses on the effects of differences in the content of laws (see, for example, Gropp, Scholz, and White 1997). Moreover, this literature does not consider explicitly the effects on credit availability. For example, Richard Hynes (1997) provides evidence that the generosity in the asset bankruptcy exemptions across U.S. states is positively correlated with bankruptcy filing rates of consumers. Mark Meador (1982) and Austin Jaffee (1985) focus on the impact on lending rates. They provide evidence suggesting that mortgage interest rates were generally higher in U.S. states where the content of laws extends the length and the expenses of the foreclosure process.

More broadly, we link the literature on liquidity constraints with the more recent interest in institutions. Although the role and the design of institutions have always attracted the attention of researchers, recently there has been a revival of this interest in political science as well as in economics. We will discuss how our analysis is related to this literature.

Related Literature

Here we link two strands of the economics literature: the empirical that investigates the determinants of households' liquidity constraints and a more recent line of research focusing on the role of institutions in economic activity.

Our contribution to the first line consists in emphasizing the role of institutional determinants of credit constraints rather than focusing only on household characteristics. From previous empirical works (see, for example, Hall and Mishkin 1982; Hayashi 1985; Zeldes 1989; Jappelli 1990; and more recently Duca and Rosenthal 1993), we have a clear picture on the individual characteristics of credit-constrained households in United States. Younger and single consumers with lower wealth and lower income are more likely to be credit rationed. Level of schooling, employment status, and sex are not significant, while marital status and race are: being married or white decreases the probability of being credit constrained. Moreover, regional dummies accounting for different regulations and characteristics in the credit markets also seem to be relevant.

Similarly for the Italian case, Tullio Jappelli and Marco Pagano (1989) find that borrowing constraints are tighter for young households, nonhomeowners, the unemployed, and residents of southern Italian regions. Our main goal is to explore more deeply the significance of the regional or area dummies arising from this evidence and to relate it to the performance of legal institutions. We argue that individuals are more likely to be credit constrained in southern Italy because banks compensate for higher legal costs arising from an inefficient legal system by increasing the collateral requirement or the interest rate and by denying credit to some applicants. Most of the available evidence on the role of legal institutions in financial markets comes from the corporate governance literature. The research in this field is based on the idea that the degree of legal protection of investor rights affects the allocation of incentives across parties and that through this mechanism, it may have effects on corporate ownership and firm financing decisions (see among others La Porta et al. 1997a). Two channels are identified: the content of laws and the quality of enforcement provided by the judicial system (see, for example, Cristini, Moya, and Powell 2001 for Argentina; Jappelli, Pagano, and Bianco, forthcoming, for Italy; and Fabbri 2001 for Spain).

One important feature distinguishes this analysis from the literature. We investigate the effects of legal institutions, but focus on the allocation of credit to households, rather than to firms. In doing that, we look at legal enforcement rather than at the content of laws. Moreover, as opposed to most of these works (see, for example, Jappelli, Pagano, and Bianco, forthcoming; and Cristini, Moya, and Powell 2001), we use micro-data (at the household level) instead of aggregate data (at the provincial level). This has two primary advantages. First, we obtain more robust results, as potential problems of endogeneity in our estimates are less likely to arise. Second, we are able to test a larger set of predictions and to control for compositional effects. In particular, the use of this data set allows us to investigate how the effect of the quality of legal enforcement on the probability of being credit constrained and on the volume of debt depends on household characteristics.

While the economics literature focuses mostly on the allocative effects of different institutions, recently political scientists have also started investigating the determinants of institutions. An important contribution to this line of research is the seminal work of Robert Putnam (1993), who uses regional Italian data to investigate the relation among economic development, performance of local public institutions, and degree of civicness. It is interesting that he finds that economically advanced Italian regions appear to have more successful regional governments merely because they happen to be more civic. Regions with many civic associations, many newspaper readers, high participations in referenda and few patron-client networks seem to have more effective governments. He also argues that the root of civicness must be found in the concept of social capital or trust defined as a propensity toward cooperation.[5]

If the level of social capital turns out to be a determinant of the performance of legal institutions, this would have implications for our empirical analysis, because our estimates could be biased. We focus on the degree of legal enforcement without presuming any relation between this variable and social capital because the evidence provided by Putnam (1993) and later on also documented by Raphael La Porta et al. (1997b)[6] is a simple correlation between two aggregate variables—social capital and performance of institutions— and the direction of the causality is not clear. It seems to us that it would be equally reasonable to think that people trust each other because they learned to trust in institutions. In this case, it would be the performance of legal institutions that shapes the degree of social capital and not vice versa.

It has also been argued that the level of social capital could directly affect economic activity (as in Knack and Keefer 1997; or Knack and Zak 2001) and the allocation of credit (as in Guiso, Sapienza, and Zingales 2004). In this case, to estimate the effect of the legal enforcement correctly, we should control for differences in the level of social capital across regions. Even though we do not include any measure of social capital in our analysis, we are able to control for differences in this variable, because all our estimates include a full set of judicial district dummies. Moreover, it is not clear from the literature how the level of social capital could affect the performance of the judicial system or the behavior of economic agents. Conversely, we do clearly understand the mechanisms through which legal institutions might have economic implications. For example, a well-accepted theory shows that the degree of legal protection of creditors can modify the outcome of the contracting activity between individuals by affecting the incentives of both debtors to engage in opportunistic behavior and creditors to monitor the borrower (see, among others, Bebchuk and Fried 1996; Bebchuk and Picker 1993; Berkovitch, Israel, and Zender 1997; Posner 1992; or Fabbri and Padula 2004).[7]

Credit, Economic Performance, and Legal Enforcement: A Look at the Data

In providing some preliminary evidence on the relation between credit availability, legal enforcement, and economic development based on aggregate data at the regional level, we use three different sources of information. First is data on credit allocation to households. Second is that on the activity of the legal system by judicial district. Third is that on the degree of economic development by region.

Data on households are drawn from three survey years (1989, 1995, and 1998) of the Survey of Household Income and Wealth (SHIW), which the Bank of Italy has conducted every other year since 1984. The SHIW has a structure similar to the Survey of Consumer Finances (SCF) and is a representative national household survey providing data on income, consumption, and household characteristics.[8] A summary of that data is reported in table 5.1. The numbers in the first column correspond to the average taken over the three sample years and deflated to 1998 euro prices. We use information on family disposable income (€25,763), wealth (€142,570),[9] and real assets (€128,128). This last variable is used as a proxy for the collateral and includes houses, land, valuables and the business, if any, owned by the households. We also report the value of the house of residence for homeowners (64 percent of the sample), which is on average €122,574 and represents the most important component of real assets for most households.

The survey also provides information on liabilities and distinguishes the amount borrowed to finance the purchase of houses, real goods such as valuables and jewelry, cars, other durable goods such as furniture and appliances, and nondurable consumption. Table 5.1 summarizes the information on households' liabilities. Conditional on being indebted, the average amount borrowed to finance these types of consumption is, respectively: €20,706 (house), €3,743 (real goods), €5,744 (car), €2,477 (other durable goods), and €4,367 (nondurable goods). The proportion of households who are indebted to finance these purchases is, respectively: 10.74 percent, 0.26 percent, 6.28 percent, 3.12 percent, and 0.96 percent. These figures together show that households borrow almost entirely to purchase houses, cars, and other durables.[10]

Table 5.1   Summary Statistics

	Mean	Standard Deviation
Family disposable income	25,763	19,912
Wealth	142,570	282,613
Real assets	128,128	261,941
House of residence	122,574	101,124
Percentage of homeowners	0.64	0.48
Debt for house purchase	20,706	23,943
Debt for purchase of valuables	3,743	14,214
Debt for car purchase	5,744	5,778
Debt for other durables purchases	2,477	3,377
Debt for nondurable consumption	4,367	8,678
Percentage of households holding debt for house purchase	10.74	
Percentage of households holding debt for purchase of valuables	0.26	
Percentage of households holding debt for car purchase	6.28	
Percentage of households holding debt for other durables purchases	3.12	
Percentage of households holding debt for non-durables consumption	0.96	
Percentage of loan applicants	6.24	
Percentage of credit-constrained households	11.22	
Percentage of discouraged borrowers	1.65	

Source: Authors' calculations.
Note: Figures are in 1998 euros except for those that are explicitly cited as percentage. Debt is measured as the amount of end-of-year household liabilities. The figures for debt are computed including only those households that are actually indebted. For continuous variable the standard deviation is reported.

An important feature of the survey is that it allows us to identify credit-constrained households through self-reported measures, without relying on implausible and often endogenous identification restrictions. Households are credit constrained if they respond affirmatively to the question: "during the year did you or a member of your household apply for a loan to a bank or other financial intermediary and have the application partially or totally rejected?" The data show that around 11.22 percent of those who apply for a loan (6.24 percent of the sample) have their application rejected and are thus credit constrained. However, the percentage of rejected applications can underestimate the strength of credit constraints if some borrowers are discouraged; in other words, if they do not apply anticipating a rejection. In our data 1.65 percent of the households are discouraged borrowers. The proportion of loan-applicants, credit-constrained households, discouraged borrowers, and the availability of credit vary with the household's income and wealth.

The first column of table 5.2 displays the percentage of households who ask for a loan. This is 3.7 percent for households living in the first quartile of the income distribution and doubles for households in the third and in the fourth quartile of the income distribution. Table 5.2 also reports the share of credit-constrained households by income quartile. Each cell in the second column of the table can be interpreted as the probability of being credit constrained given the relative position in the income distribution. The share of credit-constrained households decreases with income. It ranges from about 21.56 percent in the first quartile to 5.95 percent in the last quartile. These findings are consistent with the evidence provided by Jappelli (1990) and Gropp, Scholz, and White (1997) for the household credit market in the United States. The third column of table 5.2 hosts the percentage of discouraged borrowers by income quartile. This is higher for households belonging to the first two quartiles of the income distribution. In the last column, the amount of debt increases with income, which means that less credit is available to low-income households.

A similar picture arises from table 5.3, which reports the same variables as in table 5.2, but by wealth quartiles. Again credit-market participation increases with wealth, though almost linearly.[11] The percentage of credit-constrained households decreases from 14.88 percent in the first wealth quartile to 7.3 percent in the last.[12] The percentage of discouraged borrowers is almost twice as large in the first as in the last quartile, varying from 2.1 percent to 1.26 percent. Finally, the amount of debt increases from €585 in the first quartile to €5,150 in the last. In summary, this descriptive evidence shows that the percentage of loan applicants, credit-constrained households, discouraged borrowers, and the amount of debt vary nonlinearly with income. Although these results are similar if one considers the wealth distribution, in our analysis we study how the effect of enforcement on the availability of credit varies across both the income and the wealth distribution, separately. We do so for two reasons. First, the income and the wealth distribution are not per-

Table 5.2   Income, Credit Constraints, and Household Debt

	Percentage of Households that Are:			
Income Quartiles	Loan Applicants in the Sample	Credit Constrained Among Applicants	Discouraged Borrowers Among Nonapplicants	Household Debt (1998 Euros)
First quartile	3.70 (0.31)**	21.56 (2.11)**	1.69 (0.17)**	1,247.0970 (137.3254)**
Second quartile	6.52 (0.31)**	13.54 (1.59)**	2.09 (0.17)**	2,069.5520 (137.3254)**
Third quartile	7.32 (0.31)**	9.28 (1.50)**	1.37 (0.17)**	3,316.6840 (137.3254)**
Fourth quartile	7.42 (0.31)**	5.95 (1.49)**	1.43 (0.17)**	4,220.4950 (137.3254)**
Observations	23,556	1,470	22,086	23,556

Source: Authors' calculations.
Note: Standard errors are reported in parentheses.
*significant at 5 percent level; **significant at 1 percent level.

fectly correlated. For instance, only 50 percent of those households belonging to the first quartile of the income distribution belong also to the first quartile of the wealth distribution. Similarly, only 32 percent of households in the second quartile of the income distribution are also in the second quartile of the wealth distribution. This percentage is equal to 34 percent if we consider the third quartile and becomes 60 percent in the fourth. Second, income and wealth are likely to be differently affected by measurement errors, as one can see from the standard deviations of income and wealth reported in the second column of table 5.1.

The illustration of our measure of legal enforcement requires that we first briefly discuss the working of the judicial system. Italy is a civil-law country. This implies that the main attribute of the judicial system is enforcing the law. Italian laws regulate criminal and civil offences separately. Correspondingly, separate branches of the judicial system deal with them.

Civil trials can undergo three degrees of judgment. The first degree (lower court), a second degree (appeals court), and a third degree that can only deal with formal aspects of the summon issued in the lower courts. Readers familiar with the American system will

Table 5.3   Wealth, Credit Constraints, and Household Debt

Wealth Quartiles	Percentage of Households that Are:			Household Debt (1998 Euros)
	Loan Applicants in the Sample	Credit Constrained Among Applicants	Discouraged Borrowers Among Nonapplicants	
First quartile	5.71	14.88	2.14	585.2543
	(0.32)**	(1.72)**	(0.17)**	(136.1341)**
Second quartile	5.60	13.33	1.78	1,473.1250
	(0.32)**	(1.73)**	(0.17)**	(136.1341)**
Third quartile	6.47	10.50	1.40	3,645.7280
	(0.32)**	(1.61)**	(0.17)**	(136.1341)**
Fourth quartile	7.18	7.33	1.26	5,149.7220
	(0.32)**	(1.53)**	(0.17)**	(136.1341)**
Observations	23,556	1,470	22,086	23,556

Source: Authors' calculations.
Note: Standard errors are reported in parentheses.
*significant at 5 percent level; **significant at 1 percent level

recognize some similarities. This work concentrates on civil trials in the lower and appeals courts, which are the most relevant when households fail to honor their debts.[13] By law, the competent court is that of the borrower's district of residence.

We draw data on trials from an annual survey conducted by the National Institute of Statistics (ISTAT), for the years 1989 to 1998. The primary sample units are the judicial districts. We measure the quality of legal enforcement by the backlog of trials pending. However, this variable depends on the size of the judicial district and does not necessarily reflect poor functioning. Accordingly, we normalize backlogs by using the number of incoming trials to create a variable we label "Justice."[14] The ratio of the backlog of pending to incoming trials is displayed in figure 5.1. Each of the four panels of figure 5.1 shows the evolution of this measure in four different areas of Italy: north, central, south, and the islands. The ratio of the backlog of pending to incoming trials is increasing in each area from 1989.

This means that the quality of judicial enforcement is worsening across the country during the time period we consider. However,

Figure 5.1   Backlog of Trials Pending Divided by Incoming Trials

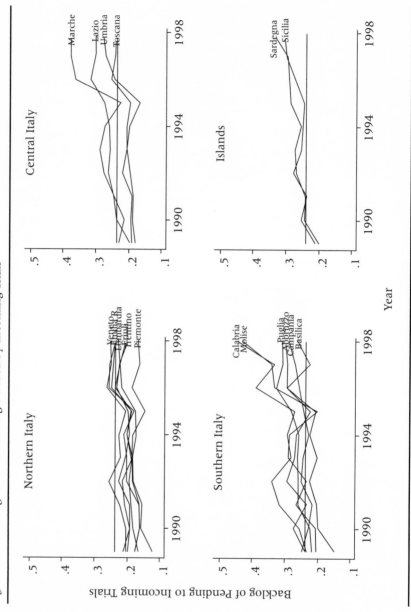

Source: Authors' calculations.

differences across regions persist and there seem to be common year effects, possibly due to the business cycle. The ratio is above the national average (horizontal line in the graph) in the south regions and in the islands of Sicily and Sardinia, while it is below the national average in the north.

Finally, the last piece of information used includes data on regional per capita GDP. These data come from the "Regional Accounts,"[15] and refer to the years 1989 to 1998. Before turning to the analysis of the micro-data, let us have a look at the relations among credit availability, legal enforcement and economic development, from a macroeconomic point of view. We do that by aggregating all the information at the regional level.

Figure 5.2 shows that the percentage of credit-constrained households within each region is higher in those with lower per capita gross domestic product. Figure 5.3 plots household debt on the regional per capita gross domestic product and shows that the availability of credit is higher in wealthier regions.[16] This preliminary ev-

Figure 5.2   Percentage of Credit-Constrained Households and Regional Per Capita Gross Domestic Product

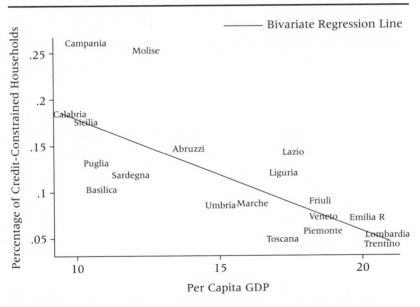

Source: Authors' calculations.

Figure 5.3   Ratio of Debt to Family Income and Regional Per Capita Gross
              Domestic Product

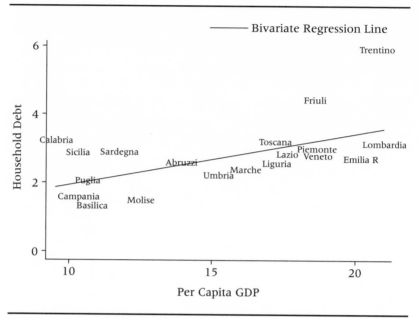

Source: Authors' calculations.

idence suggests that there is a positive correlation between credit channeled to households and economic development across Italy. Legal institutions are also related to credit availability. In figure 5.4 we plot the percentage of credit-constrained households against the quality of legal enforcement. The figure shows that the percentage is higher where the quality is weaker. In southern regions, such as Calabria and Molise, the backlog of trials pending is high, as is the percentage of credit-constrained households. Conversely, in northern regions, such as Piemonte, Lombardia, and Trentino-Alto Adige, the low share of credit-constrained households is associated with a low cost of enforcing credit contracts. Figure 5.5 parallels this evidence and shows that the availability of credit, proxied by the debt/family disposable income ratio, is lower the worse the quality of judicial enforcement. For example, the debt/family disposable income ratio is higher in regions such as Piemonte, where the quality of enforcement is better.

However, the cost of enforcement is also negatively correlated

Figure 5.4   Percentage of Credit-Constrained Households and Cost of Enforcement

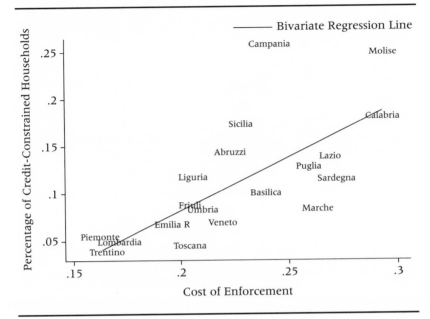

Source: Authors' calculations.

with the per-capita gross domestic product, as shown in figure 5.6. In the richer regions, such as Piemonte, Lombardia, and Trentino-Alto Adige, the backlog of pending trials is lower than in the regions with low per capita gross domestic product.

The evidence presented so far shows that credit availability, economic development, and legal enforcement are correlated across Italian regions. This implies that macro-data do not allow one to disentangle the effect of the legal enforcement from that of economic development on credit allocation.

To shed more light on the relation between the three variables and to remove any suspicion that differences in legal enforcement capture only differences in the degrees of economic development among regions, we perform an econometric analysis using micro-data. This allows us to achieve two important goals. First, it enables us to control for macro-effects, both observed and unobserved, which is quite crucial given the wide economic differences between northern and southern regions. Second, it makes our analysis more

Figure 5.5   Ratio of Debt to Family Income and Cost of Enforcement

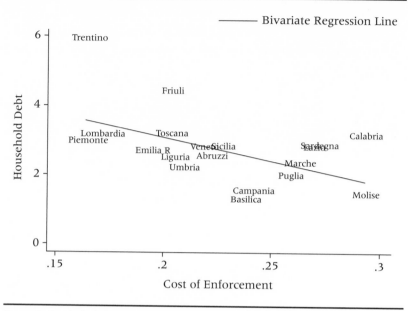

robust to endogeneity problems, because neither the probability of a household being credit constrained nor the household's amount of debt is likely to affect regional economic performance or enforcement cost.

In the econometric analysis, we focus on those households who apply for a loan and are credit constrained. We exclude the discouraged borrowers for two reasons. First, the focus of this chapter is on those who participate in the credit market. Second, our preliminary evidence reported in figures 5.7 and 5.8 shows that the share of discouraged borrowers is not strongly related to either the level of overall economic performance or the cost of enforcement.

Results

We analyze the effect of law enforcement on credit constraints and debt volumes and show how the relation between credit and enforcement varies within the wealth and income distribution.

Figure 5.6 Cost of Enforcement and Regional Per Capita Gross
Domestic Product

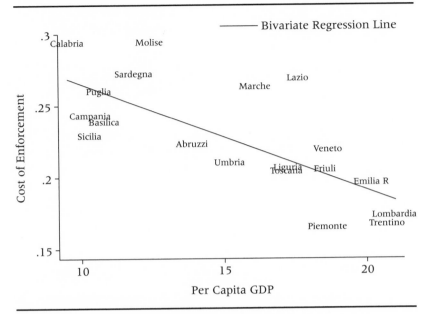

Source: Authors' calculations.
Note: Numbers are ratios.

Credit Constraints, Legal Enforcement, and Poverty

We test the hypothesis that the probability that a given household is credit constrained depends on the quality of legal enforcement provided by the judicial district where the household lives. In particular, we are interested in investigating whether and to what extent this effect varies with household characteristics such as income or wealth.

We control for household characteristics such as age, income, collateral, education, family size, employment status, and marital status, in line with previous analyses. We also control for observable macro-differences across Italian regions, by adding the regional per capita gross domestic product to all the specifications and for unobserved macro-factors by using district-level dummies. The correspondence across judicial districts, regions, and provinces is shown in table 5.4. Moreover, we add a full set of year dummies, because households coming from different survey years are pooled.

Figure 5.7   Percentage of Discouraged Households and Regional Per Capita
Gross Domestic Product

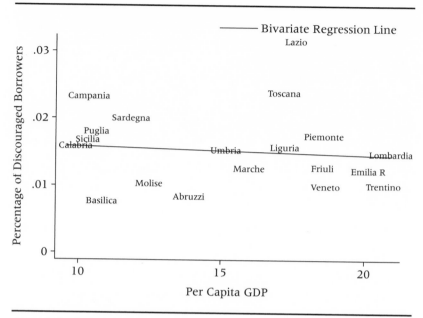

Source: Authors' calculations.

Table 5.5 shows the results of the probit estimation of the probability of being turned down for credit. The dependent variable is
a dummy variable that equals one if the household is credit
constrained. Each column of table 5.5 refers to a different measure
of collateral. We use the value of real assets held by the household,
the stock of land and houses, the value of the house of residence,
and the stock of land and houses less the value of the house of residence. We experiment with different measures because we cannot
observe the asset actually pledged as collateral.

The coefficients of the household variables are similar to what is
found elsewhere in the related literature (see, for example, the evidence provided by Jappelli 1990 and more recently by Gropp,
Scholz, and White 1997 for the United States). The probability that
a given household is credit constrained decreases with age, though
at a decreasing rate. It is lower for more educated people and for
households where the head is retired, married, and has a higher in-

Figure 5.8   Percentage of Discouraged Households and Cost of
Enforcement

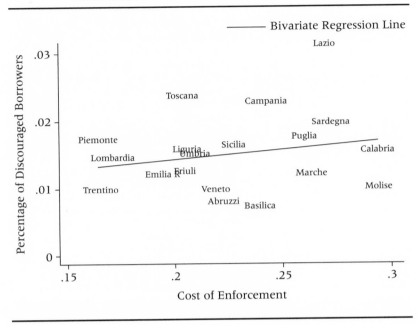

Source: Authors' calculations.

come. Conversely, larger families and households whose head is unemployed are more likely to be credit constrained.

To analyze how the effect of legal enforcement varies with household income, we split the sample into four income quartiles and we
interact the quartile dummies with the legal variable. Our reference
group is the households belonging to the first quartile (corresponding to the poorest ones in our sample).[17]

In each column of table 5.5, the coefficients of the second and
third quartile dummies are not significantly different from the
first. However, the coefficient of the fourth interacted variable is.
That is, the effect of the legal enforcement on credit constraints
depends on household income and it is much weaker for high-
income households.[18]

The pattern is similar if we consider the distribution of wealth,
as table 5.6 shows. Again, households in the upper tail of the
wealth distribution are generally less affected by weak legal en-

Table 5.4   Matching of Judicial Districts

Judicial Districts	Corresponding Regions and Provinces
Torino	Piemonte (all provinces), Valle d'Aosta (all provinces)
Genova	Liguria (all provinces) and Tuscany (Massa Carrara)
Milano	Lombardia (Milano, Como, Varese, Pavia, Sondrio, Lecco, Lodi)
Brescia	Lombardia (Brescia, Bergamo, Cremona, Mantova)
Trento	Trentino-Alto Adige (Trento)
Bolzano	Trentino-Alto Adige (Bolzano)
Venezia	Veneto (all provinces)
Trieste	Friuli-Venezia Giulia (all provinces)
Bologna	Emilia Romagna (all provinces)
Ancona	Marche (all provinces)
Firenze	Toscana (all provinces excluding Massa Carrara)
Perugia	Umbria (all provinces)
Roma	Lazio (all provinces)
Napoli	Campania (Napoli, Avellino, Benevento, Caserta)
Salerno	Campania (Salerno)
L'Aquila	Abruzzo (all provinces)
Campobasso	Molise (all provinces)
Bari	Puglia (Bari, Foggia)
Lecce	Puglia (Lecce, Brindisi)
Taranto	Puglia (Taranto)
Potenza	Basilicata (all provinces)
Catanzaro	Calabria (Catanzaro, Cosenza, Crotone, Vibo Valentia)
Reggio Calabria	Calabria (Reggio Calabria)
Palermo	Sicilia (Palermo, Agrigento, Trapani)
Messina	Sicilia (Messina)
Caltanissetta	Sicilia (Caltanissetta, Enna)
Catania	Sicilia (Catania, Ragusa, Siracusa)
Cagliari	Sardegna (Cagliari, Oristano)
Sassari	Sardegna (Sassari, Nuoro)

Source: ISTAT (1999).

Note: The table matches judicial districts with Italian regions and provinces. The names of provinces are in parentheses. Roughly, each district corresponds to a region. In a few regions (Lombardia, Campania, Puglia, Calabria, Sicilia and Sardegna) there is more than one judicial district. Provinces located in two different regions (Valle d'Aosta and Piemonte) belong to one judicial district, called Torino. Finally, the judicial district of Genova includes not only all the provinces located in Liguria but also one province in Toscana.

Table 5.5 Law Enforcement, Probability of Being Credit Constrained by Income Quartiles

	Real Assets	Estates	Residence	Estates–Residence
Age of the household's head	−0.0546 (0.0294)*	−0.0542 (0.0294)*	−0.0529 (0.0295)*	−0.0545 (0.0294)*
Age squared of the household's head	0.0609 (0.0314)*	0.0607 (0.0315)*	0.0594 (0.0316)*	0.0609 (0.0314)*
Collateral	0.0001 (0.0003)	−0.0002 (0.0004)	−0.0008 (0.0006)	0.0002 (0.0005)
Household disposable income	−0.0009 (0.0057)	0.0002 (0.0054)	0.0005 (0.0053)	−0.0010 (0.0056)
Years of schooling	−0.0388 (0.0137)**	−0.0386 (0.0136)**	−0.0381 (0.0136)**	−0.0386 (0.0137)**
Family size	0.1247 (0.0420)**	0.1237 (0.0420)**	0.1226 (0.0421)**	0.1248 (0.0420)**
Retiree	−0.1884 (0.1830)	−0.1854 (0.1829)	−0.1774 (0.1829)	−0.1914 (0.1831)
Unemployed	0.6187 (0.2457)**	0.6229 (0.2463)**	0.6264 (0.2468)**	0.6165 (0.2457)**
Marital status	−0.6164 (0.1414)**	−0.6180 (0.1414)**	−0.6156 (0.1417)**	−0.6149 (0.1415)**
Per capita gross domestic product	0.1771 (0.1005)*	0.1763 (0.1006)*	0.1769 (0.1009)*	0.1777 (0.1005)*
Justice × first income quartile dummy	4.7657 (1.5389)**	4.7329 (1.5408)**	4.6973 (1.5421)**	4.7847 (1.5400)**
Justice × second income quartile dummy	4.2821 (1.5280)**	4.2238 (1.5293)**	4.2027 (1.5291)**	4.3002 (1.5289)**
Justice × third income quartile dummy	3.5807 (1.5341)**	3.5246 (1.5340)*	3.5584 (1.5335)*	3.6064 (1.5359)**
Justice × fourth income quartile dummy	2.7748 (1.6218)*	2.7976 (1.6201)*	2.9041 (1.6216)*	2.7928 (1.6241)*
Constant	−4.5794 (2.1992)*	−4.5601 (2.2018)*	−4.5833 (2.2095)*	−4.5891 (2.1980)*
Observations	1470	1470	1470	1470

Source: Authors' calculations.
Note: The dependent variable is an indicator variable, credit rationing, that equals one if the household's head responds positively to the following question: "during the year did you or a member of your household apply for a loan to a bank or other financial intermediary and have the application partially or totally rejected?" Standard errors are reported in parentheses. Columns differ for the measure of collateral adopted. This is, in turn, real asset, estates, residence home and estates minus residence home. All the specifications include a full set of judicial district and year dummies.
*significant at 5 percent level; ** significant at 1 percent level

Table 5.6   Law Enforcement, Probability of Being Credit Constrained by Wealth Quartiles

	Real Assets	Estates	Residence	Estates–Residence
Age of the household's head	−0.0557 (0.0293)*	−0.0564 (0.0293)*	−0.0552 (0.0294)*	−0.0563 (0.0293)*
Age squared of the household's head	0.0625 (0.0313)*	0.0630 (0.0314)*	0.0617 (0.0315)*	0.0631 (0.0314)*
Collateral	0.0005 (0.0004)	−0.0001 (0.0004)	−0.0010 (0.0008)	0.0005 (0.0005)
Household disposable income	−0.0095 (0.0045)*	−0.0079 (0.0045)*	−0.0072 (0.0044)	−0.0090 (0.0046)*
Years of schooling	−0.0387 (0.0138)**	−0.0398 (0.0137)**	−0.0403 (0.0137)**	−0.0391 (0.0137)**
Family size	0.1182 (0.0420)**	0.1163 (0.0420)**	0.1159 (0.0420)**	0.1177 (0.0420)**
Retiree	−0.1952 (0.1836)	−0.1932 (0.1836)	−0.1814 (0.1834)	−0.2032 (0.1839)
Unemployed	0.6591 (0.2449)**	0.6613 (0.2452)**	0.6605 (0.2456)**	0.6523 (0.2449)**
Marital status	−0.6135 (0.1413)**	−0.6146 (0.1412)**	−0.6142 (0.1415)**	−0.6109 (0.1413)**
Per capita gross domestic product	0.1813 (0.1002)*	0.1773 (0.1001)*	0.1756 (0.1005)*	0.1802 (0.1000)*
Justice × first wealth quartile dummy	4.1862 (1.5610)**	3.9500 (1.5587)**	3.7318 (1.5628)**	4.0451 (1.5526)**
Justice × second wealth quartile dummy	4.4617 (1.5134)**	4.2763 (1.5113)**	4.1406 (1.5101)**	4.3791 (1.5091)**
Justice × third wealth quartile dummy	3.8647 (1.5119)**	3.7913 (1.5092)**	3.8348 (1.5080)**	3.8822 (1.5127)**
Justice × fourth wealth quartile dummy	3.2052 (1.5821)*	3.5981 (1.5617)*	3.8748 (1.5661)**	3.4923 (1.5517)*
Constant	−4.4490 (2.1906)*	−4.3064 (2.1863)*	−4.2677 (2.1968)*	−4.3740 (2.1838)*
Observations	1470	1470	1470	1470

Source: Authors' calculations.

Note: The dependent variable is an indicator variable, credit rationing, that equals one if the household's head responds positively to the following question: "during the year did you or a member of your household apply for a loan to a bank or other financial intermediary and have the application partially or totally rejected?" Standard errors are reported in parentheses. Columns differ for the measure of collateral adopted. This is, in turn, real asset, estates, residence home and estates home minus residence home. All specifications include a full set of judicial district and year dummies.

*significant at 5 percent level; **significant at 1 percent level forcement, though this difference is smaller than that across income quartiles.

Two figures help illustrate our main findings. Figures 5.9 and 5.10 plot the estimated probability of being credit constrained in three judicial districts (corresponding to the lowest, the average, and the highest degree of legal enforcement), after we split the sample into income and wealth quartiles, respectively.

In each income or wealth quartile, households located in the judicial district with the lowest degree of legal enforcement are more likely to be credit constrained than households located in other judicial districts. However, low-income people are the most affected by strong legal inefficiency. The probability that a household in the first quartile of the income distribution is credit constrained ranges from 55 percent in the worst judicial district to 9 percent in the best. This jump is strongly reduced in the last quartile where the probability ranges from 24 percent in the worst judicial district to 6 percent in the best. The evidence is similar if we consider the wealth distribution. The probability that a given household in the first wealth quartile is credit constrained ranges from 45 percent in the

Figure 5.9   Liquidity Constraints and Enforcement, by Income

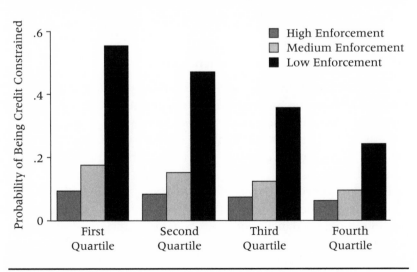

Source: Authors' calculations.

Figure 5.10 Liquidity Constraints and Enforcement, by Wealth

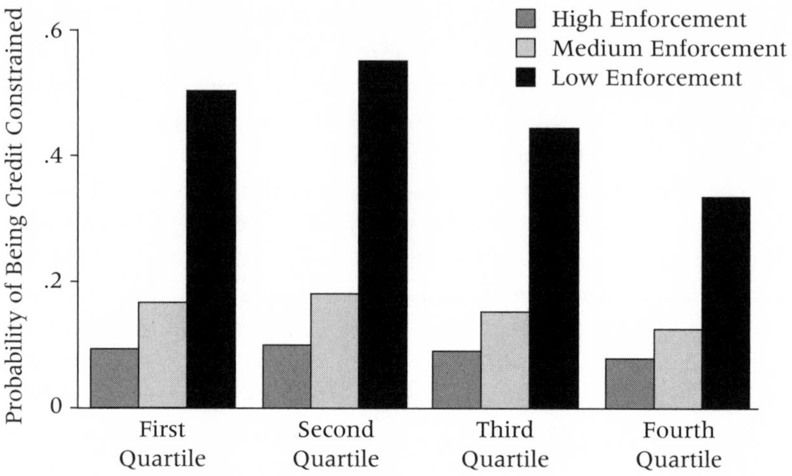

Source: Authors' calculations.

worst judicial district to 8.5 percent in the best and the gap shrinks massively for the higher quartile of the wealth distribution.

Overall, it appears that legal costs are strongly correlated with the probability of being credit constrained, and that poor households are the most affected by an ill-functioning legal system.

Debt Volumes, Legal Enforcement, and Poverty

To test the effect of the legal variable on the amount of debt, we estimate a tobit model, since the data are censored to the left. We include the same independent variables as in the probit analysis. Moreover, we allow for collateral and wealth to separately affect the amount of debt and we let the effect of income and wealth to be nonlinear.[19]

Table 5.7 shows the results of our analysis.[20] In line with the previous evidence, debt volume is positively correlated with the age of the household head in a nonlinear way: the coefficient of age is positive and that of age squared is negative. Moreover, households able to pledge more collateral have a larger amount of debt. Family size and marital status are positively related to debt while being unem-

Table 5.7   Debt Volumes, Enforcement, and Income Distribution

	Real Assets	Estates	Residence	Estates– Residence
Age of the household's head	0.4818 (0.1567)**	0.4775 (0.1566)**	0.4673 (0.1561)**	0.4809 (0.1567)**
Age squared of the household's head	−1.0386 (0.1592)**	−1.0353 (0.1590)**	−1.0327 (0.1586)**	−1.0339 (0.1592)**
Collateral	0.0034 (0.0011)**	0.0050 (0.0013)**	0.0285 (0.0035)**	0.0017 (0.0015)
Years of schooling	0.3428 (0.0759)**	0.3369 (0.0759)**	0.3137 (0.0757)**	0.3506 (0.0759)**
Family size	1.8176 (0.2897)**	1.8245 (0.2895)**	1.7773 (0.2887)**	1.8388 (0.2898)**
Retiree	−4.3143 (1.0028)**	−4.3982 (1.0015)**	−4.4084 (0.9986)**	−4.4236 (1.0030)**
Unemployed	−7.6302 (1.8703)**	−7.7110 (1.8692)**	−7.7076 (1.8635)**	−7.6921 (1.8715)**
Marital status	3.1128 (0.8656)**	3.1208 (0.8652)**	3.1162 (0.8626)**	3.1204 (0.8662)**
Per capita gross domestic product	1.6551 (0.4567)**	1.6602 (0.4563)**	1.6037 (0.4540)**	1.6790 (0.4571)**
Justice × first quartile dummy	−28.2112 (14.0117)*	−27.7331 (14.0037)*	−27.5064 (13.9503)*	−28.0751 (14.0230)*
Justice × second quartile dummy	−12.6464 (13.1193)	−12.3939 (13.1125)	−11.9235 (13.0698)	−12.7931 (13.1291)
Justice × third quartile dummy	−3.8843 (13.1198)	−3.6954 (13.1139)	−2.9617 (13.0707)	−4.0016 (13.1292)
Justice × fourth quartile dummy	17.1265 (13.7076)	17.3311 (13.7004)	18.1333 (13.6621)	17.1164 (13.7157)
Constant	−61.1930 (11.5539)**	−61.4559 (11.5461)**	−63.2319 (11.4949)**	−60.8526 (11.5644)**
Observations	23,556	23,556	23,556	23,556

Source: Authors' calculations.
Note: The dependent variable is the household debt. Standard errors are reported in parentheses. Columns differ for the measure of collateral adopted. This is, in turn, real asset, estates, residence home, and estates minus residence home. All the specifications include a full set of judicial district, year dummies, income, and wealth quartile dummies.
*significant at 5 percent level; **significant at 1 percent level

ployed is negatively related. This is consistent with expectations. Family size proxies for needs and debt is likely to increase with needs. Married couples are more likely to hold mortgages, which explains why the overall debt is higher for them. On the other hand, this is lower for unemployed people. Typically, they cannot borrow to buy a house because they have no income, unless someone guarantees the loan for them.

The coefficient of the variable retiree is negative and significant. Pensioners hold lower volumes of debt, other things equal, which is consistent with most basic theories of intertemporal choices. More educated individuals hold more debt, as pointed by the positive coefficient of the variable years of schooling. This might be capturing the fact that better-educated individuals have a steeper income profile, which is typically associated with higher desired consumption and higher demand for credit early in life. The effect of regional per capita gross domestic product is positive, which shows that debt is higher in richer regions, consistent with what we have seen in Section 3.

Finally, we find that the coefficient of the interaction between the legal variable justice and the first quartile dummy is negative and significant. Recalling that we are measuring the cost of a badly functioning judicial system, a negative coefficient means that if the backlog of pending trials increases, the amount of debt decreases. We interpret this finding as evidence that banks in judicial districts with weak legal enforcement tend to increase the cost of credit, which in turn reduces the availability of funds. We also find that the effect of the cost of enforcement decreases in income distribution and changes sign for high-income households: the coefficient of the last dummy is positive though not significant. In summary, these findings suggest that an ill-functioning legal system redistributes credit toward borrowers with high income.

This evidence is robust to different measures of collateral. The pattern of the results is very similar in the other three columns of table 5.7, where different variables are used to proxy the collateral. Moreover, very similar results (though less precise) are obtained if we consider wealth quartiles, as shown in table 5.8. Again, the cost of the enforcement reduces debt volumes for poor but not for wealthy households.

Table 5.9 quantifies the effect of the legal enforcement on the household's debt. Each entry of this table is the semi-elasticity of

Table 5.8 Debt Volumes, Enforcement, and Wealth Distribution

	Real Assets	Estates	Residence	Estates– Residence
Age of the household's head	0.4877 (0.1567)**	0.4834 (0.1566)**	0.4734 (0.1561)**	0.4868 (0.1568)**
Age squared of the household's head	−1.0428 (0.1593)**	−1.0395 (0.1591)**	−1.0371 (0.1586)**	−1.0381 (0.1593)**
Collateral	0.0033 (0.0011)**	0.0050 (0.0013)**	0.0286 (0.0035)**	0.0017 (0.0015)
Years of schooling	0.3513 (0.0758)**	0.3453 (0.0758)**	0.3221 (0.0757)**	0.3591 (0.0759)**
Family size	1.8259 (0.2896)**	1.8327 (0.2894)**	1.7857 (0.2886)**	1.8470 (0.2897)**
Retiree	−4.2704 (1.0027)**	−4.3543 (1.0013)**	−4.3638 (0.9984)**	−4.3796 (1.0028)**
Unemployed	−7.8511 (1.8693)**	−7.9308 (1.8681)**	−7.9306 (1.8623)**	−7.9112 (1.8705)**
Marital status	2.9968 (0.8647)**	3.0053 (0.8643)**	2.9995 (0.8616)**	3.0050 (0.8653)**
Per capita gross domestic product	1.7066 (0.4565)**	1.7113 (0.4561)**	1.6547 (0.4537)**	1.7301 (0.4569)**
Justice × first quartile dummy	−18.3199 (15.6461)	−17.8901 (15.6367)	−16.9588 (15.5710)	−18.5008 (15.6588)
Justice × second quartile dummy	−5.8674 (13.1665)	−5.5804 (13.1591)	−5.6582 (13.1122)	−5.8830 (13.1764)
Justice × third quartile dummy	−15.3968 (12.3149)	−15.2261 (12.3083)	−15.5327 (12.2652)	−15.4394 (12.3245)
Justice × fourth quartile dummy	4.3696 (13.1841)	4.7558 (13.1793)	6.9714 (13.1502)	4.4107 (13.1921)
Constant	−59.5600 (11.5625)**	−59.8624 (11.5551)**	−61.9660 (11.5039)**	−59.2278 (11.5734)**
Observations	23,556	23,556	23,556	23,556

Source: Authors' calculations.
Note: The dependent variable is the household debt. Standard errors are reported in parentheses. Columns differ for the measure of collateral adopted. This is, in turn, real asset, estates, residence home, and estates minus residence home. All the specifications include a full set of judicial district, year dummies, income, and wealth quartile dummies.
*significant at 5 percent level; **significant at 1 percent level.

Table 5.9   Debt Volumes and Enforcement, Elasticities

	Income Quartiles	Wealth Quartiles
First quartile	−1.6143	−18.3199
	(0.8018)*	(15.6461)
Second quartile	−0.6979	−5.8674
	(0.7240)	(13.1665)
Third quartile	−0.2097	−15.3968
	(0.7083)	(12.3148)
Fourth quartile	0.8970	4.3696
	(0.7179)	(13.1840)

Source: Authors' calculations.
Note: Each entry is the semi-elasticity of the household debt with respect to the legal variable. The first column shows the semi-elasticity corresponding to each quartile of the income distribution, while the second column refers to the wealth distribution. Standard errors are reported in parentheses. In each column the collateral is proxied by the amount of real assets held by the household.
*significant at 5 percent level; **significant at 1 percent level

households' debt with respect to the quality of judicial enforcement. Because the results are very similar for the different proxies of collateral used, we report only those obtained using the whole real wealth as collateral. The first column shows the semi-elasticity corresponding to the four quartiles of the income distribution, and the second to the wealth distribution.

From the first column it arises that, if the cost of enforcement increases by 1 percent,[21] the debt volume decreases by €1,600 for those households belonging to the first income quartile. The effect in the last quartile of the income distribution is less precise: a 1 percent increase of the cost of enforcement increases the debt by around €890. This effect is stronger but much less precisely estimated, if we consider the wealth distribution. A 1 percent increase in the backlog of pending trials causes the debt to reduce by around €18,000 for households in the first quartile, and to increase by more than €4,000 for households in the last quartile of the wealth distribution. Together, these results suggest that judicial costs do affect the average amount of the household's debt and that this effect varies across income and wealth quartiles.

Conclusions and Policy Implications

This work provides robust evidence that poor households are the most affected by an ill-functioning legal system in Italy. The probability that a household in the first quartile of the income distribution is credit constrained ranges from 55 percent in the worst judicial district to 9 percent in the best judicial district. This jump is strongly reduced if we consider households belonging to the last quartile of the wealth distribution: the same probability ranges from 24 percent in the worst judicial district to 6 percent in the best judicial district.

Moreover, we find that a decline in the legal enforcement reduces the amount of debt of low-income households but has no effect on rich households. This effect is found to be significant economically as well as statistically.

Our findings parallel those of Jappelli, Pagano, and Bianco (forthcoming) about the effects of a poor legal enforcement on the corporate credit market in Italy. They also share some similarities with the evidence provided by Gropp, Scholz, and White (1997) for the household credit market in the United States. They document that the size of asset bankruptcy exemptions has a statistically and economically significant, positive effect on the household probability of being turned down for credit. They also find that an increment in asset bankruptcy exemptions reduces the volume of credit for households in the lower half of the asset distribution, and increases the availability of credit to households in the upper half of the asset distribution.

Because an increment in asset bankruptcy exemptions parallels a decline in the performance of courts in reducing creditors' legal protection, the two pieces of evidence go in the same direction. They seem to suggest that a weak legal protection of creditors' rights distorts credit allocation, introducing pronounced inefficiencies.

This evidence also suggests that a reform of the judicial system in Italy would be likely to have both allocative and redistributive effects. An improvement in the ability of judicial districts to reduce the backlog of trials pending would most benefit less-well-off households.

We estimate that a reduction in the annual backlog of trials pending by around 1,500 units (corresponding to the 1 percent of the annual average) would increase the availability of credit of the low-income households by €1,600 but have no effect on wealthy households.

We wish to thank Ailsa Röell, Howard Rosenthal, and David Skeel for very useful comments and suggestions. Financial support from the

Swiss National Science Foundation through the National Centre of Competence in Research "Financial Valuation and Risk Management" (NCCR FINRISK) is gratefully acknowledged.

Notes

1. Unlike in the United States, in Italy most of the loans are secured and people do not use credit cards as a source of finance. In Italy, credit cards work as debt cards. They are similar to personal checks with the difference that the money spent is deducted from the checking or saving account at a fixed date (for instance, the fifteenth of each month).

2. Without self-reported measures, identifying credit-constrained households would require separating the demand from the supply of credit by isolating some overidentifying restrictions. If a plausible restriction is not available, one could split the sample according to a criterion, wealth, for instance. However, this amounts to splitting the sample endogenously, if wealth depends on whether a given household is credit constrained.

3. Roughly, each district corresponds to a region. In some regions (Lombardia, Campania, Puglia, Calabria, Sicilia, and Sardegna) there is more than one judicial district, while Valle d'Aosta is in the Piemonte judicial district. Table 5.4 shows the matching of judicial districts with regions and provinces.

4. This corresponds to an increment of 1,500 trials pending.

5. According to Putnam's argument, the independent city-states of the communal republicanism developed in northern regions encouraged the formation of horizontal networks through a popular involvement in public decisions making and many different forms of horizontal local organizations like: neighborhoods associations, religious confraternities, mutual assistance organizations as well as political parties. This contrasts with the more authoritarian political regimes of the southern Italian regions.

6. They document that an increase in trust raises judicial efficiency, bureaucratic quality, tax compliance (considered as a proxy of government effectiveness), and participation in civic activities and in professional associations.

7. One topic that has been widely discussed is the extent to which the absolute priority rule of secured creditors should be preserved, or, rather, deviations from that rule should be allowed. The debate on this issue is especially intense in the United States in connection with the possible reform of bankruptcy procedures. Part of this research focuses more specifically on the role of collateral in credit contracts and its optimal degree of legal protection.

8. See Andrea Brandolini and Luigi Cannari (1994) for a detailed description of the survey.

9. This is the sum of real and financial wealth.

10. If, for instance, households are indebted to buy both a house and a car, they are counted in both categories of debt.

11. The F-statistic of the null hypothesis that the percentage of loan-applicants is equal in the first, the second, and the third quartile of the wealth distribution is 2.26.

12. The decrease is almost linear: the F-statistic of the null hypothesis that the percentage of credit-constrained households is equal in the first, the second, and the third quartile of the wealth distribution is 1.80.

13. The data used to construct our indicators of legal enforcement include all civil trials except labor and work-related cases.

14. While the length of trials is an important cost of enforcement, there are other costs, such as the fraction of assets actually recovered by the lender in case of borrower's default. These costs are likely to be correlated with our measure of enforcement. However, having measurement errors in the cost of enforcement implies that the real effects of the enforcement are underestimated.

15. "Conti Economici Regionali," ISTAT.

16. The picture is similar if we standardize debt with wealth.

17. The quartiles are defined within Italy. This is justified by the structure of the banking sector. According to Italian regulations, there are no legal restrictions on cross-regional lending or cross-regional branching for financial institutions. Moreover, the regulatory framework is the same across Italian regions.

18. To check that this effect is not driven by the omitted uninteracted income and wealth quartile dummies, we have tested for linearity by estimating a probit where household disposable income and wealth have been replaced by a full set of income and wealth quartile dummies and the cost of enforcement variable is uninteracted. In this specification the relation between credit constraints and income (and wealth) is allowed to be nonlinear and the effect of enforcement is constrained to be the same across the income and the wealth distribution. We find that the hypothesis of linearity cannot be rejected: the F-statistic for linear income effect is 2.16 and for linear wealth effect 3.31.

19. This corresponds to replace disposable income with income quartile dummies and to add to the specification the wealth quartile dummies.

20. The coefficients of the income and wealth quartile dummies are not reported in table 5.7. They suggest that the amount of debt increases along the income and wealth distribution.

21. This corresponds to a 1,500-unit increase of backlog of trials pending, whose sample average is 104,937.

References

Bebchuk, Lucian, and Jesse M. Fried. 1996. "The Uneasy Case for the Priority of Secured Claims in Bankruptcy." *Yale Law Journal* 105: 857–934.

Bebchuk, Lucian, and Randal C. Picker. 1993. "Bankruptcy Rules, Managerial Entrenchment, and Firm-Specific Human Capital." *Chicago Law and Economics* working paper 16. Chicago: University of Chicago Law School, John M. Olin Program in Law and Economics Working Papers.

Berkovitch, Elazar, Ronen Israel, and Jaime F. Zender. 1997. "Optimal Bankruptcy Law and Firm-Specific Investments." *European Economic Review* 41(3): 487–97.

Brandolini, Andrea, and Luigi Cannari. 1994. "Methodological Appendix: The Bank of Italy's Survey of Household Income and Wealth." In *Saving and the Accumulation of Wealth: Essays on Italian Households and Government Behavior*, edited by Luigi Guiso, Albert Ando, and Ignazio Visco. Cambridge, Mass.: Cambridge University Press.

Cristini, Marcela, Ramiro Moya, and Andrew Powell. 2001. "The Importance of an Effective Legal System for Credit Markets: the Case of Argentina." In *Defusing Default: Incentives and Institutions,* edited by Marco Pagano. Washington, D.C.: Inter-American Development Bank.

Duca, John V., and Stuart S. Rosenthal. 1993. "Borrowing Constraints and Household Debt, and Racial Discrimination." *Journal of Financial Intermediation* 3(1): 77–103.

Fabbri, Daniela. 2001. "Legal Institutions, Corporate Governance and Aggregate Activity: Theory and Evidence." *CSEF* working paper 72. Salerno: University of Salerno, Center for Studies in Economics and Finance.

Fabbri, Daniela, and Mario Padula. 2004. "Does Poor Legal Enforcement Make Households Credit-Constrained?" *Journal of Banking and Finance* 28(10): 2369–97.

Gropp, Reint, John Karl Scholz, and Michelle White. 1997. "Personal Bankruptcy and Credit Supply and Demand." *Quarterly Journal of Economics* 112(1): 217–52.

Guiso, Luigi, Paola Sapienza, and Luigi Zingales. 2004. "The Role of Social Capital in Financial Development." *American Economic Review* 94(3): 526–56.

Hall, Robert E., and Frederick Mishkin. 1982. "The Sensitivity of Consumption to Transitory Income: Estimate from Panel Data." *Econometrica* 50(2): 461–81.

Hayashi, Fumio. 1985. "The Effect of Liquidity Constraints on Consumption: A Cross-Section Analysis." *Quarterly Journal of Economics* 100(1): 183–206.

Hynes, Richard. 1997. "Property Exemptions and Loan Repayments." Wharton Financial Institutions Center. Working paper. Philadelphia: Wharton Financial Institutions Center, University of Pennsylvania.

ISTAT. 1999. "Annuario delle Statistiche Giudiziarie Civili." Rome: ISTAT.

Jaffee, Austin. 1985. "Mortgage Foreclosure Law and Regional Disparities in Mortgage Financing Costs." Pennsylvania State University working paper 85. Philadelphia: Pennsylvania State University, Department of Economics.

Jappelli, Tullio. 1990. "Who is Credit Constrained in the U.S. Economy?" *Quarterly Journal of Economics* 105(1): 219–34.

Jappelli, Tullio, and Marco Pagano. 1989. "Consumption and Capital Market Imperfections: An International Comparison." *American Economic Review* 79(5): 1088–1105.

Jappelli, Tullio, Marco Pagano, and Magda Bianco. Forthcoming. "Courts and Banks: Effects of Judicial Enforcement on Credit Markets." *Journal of Money Credit and Banking*.

Knack, Stephen, and Paul Keefer. 1997. "Does Social Capital Have an Economic Pay-Off? A Cross Country Investigation." *Quarterly Journal of Economics* 112(4): 1251–88.

Knack, Stephen, and Paul J. Zak. 2001. "Trust and Growth." *Economic Journal* 111(470): 295–321.

La Porta, Raphael, Florencio Lopez de Silanes, Andrei Shleifer, and Robert W. Vishny. 1997a. "Legal Determinants of External Finance." *Journal of Finance* 52(2): 1127–61.

———. 1997b. "Trust in Large Organization." *American Economic Review Papers and Proceedings* 87(2): 333–38.

Meador, Mark. 1982. "The Effects of Mortgage Laws on Home Mortgage Rates." *Journal of Economics and Business* 34(2): 143–48.

Posner, Richard A. 1992. *The Economic Analysis of Law*. Boston: Little, Brown.

Putnam, Robert. 1993. *Making Democracy Work: Civic Traditions in Modern Italy*. Princeton, N.J.: Princeton University Press.

Zeldes, Stephen P. 1989. "Consumption and Liquidity Constraints: An Empirical Investigation." *Journal of Political Economy* 97(2): 305–46.

Part III

Small Business Loans: Borrowing Together or Borrowing Alone?

Chapter 6

Financing Disadvantaged Firms

Timothy Bates

Scholarly studies have failed to demonstrate that small-business ownership in the United States today is an effective strategy for bootstrapping one's way out of poverty. Thin empirical data coexist with numerous stereotypes about self-employment, particularly regarding the experiences of poor Americans who create small businesses (Bates 1997a). Hard data on small business dynamics are rare: this study focuses on the hard data.

Often advocated but rarely understood, small-business assistance programs often seek to move disadvantaged people out of poverty and into economic self-sufficiency. Typifying widespread sentiment about the need to reduce the dependence of low-income Americans on government assistance, former New York Mayor Giuliani offered this advice to the poor, as Jason De Parle explained in the *New York Times Magazine* ("What Welfare-to-Work Really Means," December 20, 1998, pp. 50, 89–90). "If you can't get a job, start a small business, start a little candy store. Start a little newspaper stand. Start a lemonade stand."

The lemonade stand idea is a poor suggestion. Mainstream literature on entrepreneurship stresses that education, skills, and work experience are prerequisites for aspiring entrepreneurs, be they poor or affluent. Beyond human capital prerequisites, small firm formation often requires financial investment to acquire the tools of the trade. Most new businesses must invest in inventory, equipment, and the like if they are to achieve viability. Working capital is usually needed to finance day-to-day operations. Absent appropriate human and financial capital investments, hard work and initiative alone are often not enough to create lasting firms. People choosing self-employment who lack skills and financial resources generate high business failure and self-employment exit rates (Servon and Bates 1998).

Microenterprise assistance programs commonly recognize that disadvantaged potential entrepreneurs need training as well as lending assistance. Former President Bill Clinton's call to end welfare as we know it was an impetus to the growing microenterprise movement of the 1990s. Small loans and short training courses on business fundamentals were seen as bootstraps for entrepreneurially inclined welfare recipients.

Conducting a substantive dialog about microenterprise finance is complicated by the fact that basic terms—"disadvantaged," for example—lack generally accepted meanings. "Microenterprise" itself is defined in widely differing and inconsistent ways. In this study, microenterprises are referred to as disadvantaged small businesses. "Disadvantaged," in this context, proves to be extraordinarily hard to pin down.

After exploring the origins of microenterprise lending, we examine three concepts of "disadvantage" to illuminate the issue of loan access and business viability among the poor. Applicable concepts are human-capital disadvantage (high school dropouts), income disadvantage (people with very low household incomes), and labor-market disadvantage (people unable to find suitable jobs as employees). Our attempt to operationalize the income-disadvantage concept proved quite difficult.

A final concept—African American firm ownership—was explored to fill out and link some of the fragmentary findings produced in the course of investigating human capital, income, and labor market measures of disadvantage. The role that credit plays in assisting disadvantaged firms is examined, as are several measures of firm viability, including survival rates and financial returns. Despite data gaps and tricky definitional issues, a coherent picture of disadvantaged business financing does emerge from the available evidence.

Origins of Microenterprise Lending Programs

Microenterprise lending often seeks to promote local economic development in geographic areas typified by high rates of underemployment. It is the social welfare motive of alleviating poverty, however, that most profoundly drives microenterprise programs. Part of the appeal of micro-lending, in fact, lies in its simultaneous pursuit of social welfare and local economic development objectives.

Peer Lending

Origins of microenterprise lending are often attached to initiation of the Grameen Bank in Bangladesh. The product of economics professor Mohammed Yunus, the bank began lending in 1979 to help the landless poor start businesses. A "peer" lending model was developed: a group of potential and actual business owners would form a group, receive training, and then decide among themselves who would get the first loan. Other members would achieve eligibility for loans only as long as all group members maintained current payments (Servon 1999).

The Grameen Bank's successful peer lending programs appealed to U.S. policymakers, in part, because they combined social welfare objectives with local economic development. Yet it is not really accurate to equate the origins of large-scale micro-lending programs in the United States with peer-lending models imported from the Third World.

Economic Opportunity Lending

A component of President Lyndon Johnson's War on Poverty, the Economic Opportunity Loan (EOL) program was authorized under Title IV of the Economic Opportunity Act. Targeted solely to those living in poverty, EOL loans were long-term loans extended to business owners by the U.S. Small Business Administration (SBA). The SBA anticipated that most of the EOL loans would finance minority businesses. Amendments to Title IV in 1966 broadened the program to include incomes above the poverty line. To be eligible, one had to be "disadvantaged." This included business owners who "had been denied the opportunity to compete in business on equal terms" (U.S. Small Business Administration 1970, 4). EOL loans were still targeted to low-income borrowers, those whose "family income from all sources (other than welfare) is not sufficient for the basic needs of the family" (U.S. Small Business Administration 1970, 6). Abandoning a strict poverty criterion was seen as a move toward a more flexible definition of disadvantage.

Fiscal year 1972 was the EOL program's highpoint: 5,791 loans were extended to minority business borrowers and average loan size was $12,899 (Bates and Bradford 1979). Plagued by high loan default rates, EOL loans fell steadily in number after 1972, and the program was officially abolished in 1984.

A study of EOL lending in New York, Chicago, and Boston produced representative samples of black-owned firms that received these SBA loans between 1967 and 1970. By 1973, 70.2 percent of the EOL loans that financed firm start-up were in delinquent or default status. Among borrowers financing existing black-owned firms, corresponding delinquency-default figures were 65.0 percent. An econometric analysis delineating current and repaid EOL loans from the delinquent-defaulted ones revealed that higher borrower income at the point of loan application predicted repayment, while lower income was associated with loan default (Bates and Bradford 1979; Bates 1975).

The EOL loan program was in a paradoxical state: the strongest loan recipients often succeeded in business but these borrowers came from mid-to-high-income groups. The truly disadvantaged loan recipients, while clearly eligible, failed in droves. Their failure rates "necessarily have an adverse effect on the credibility of Federal minority enterprise effort" (U.S. Comptroller General 1973, 2). When the EOL program served its targeted clientele, few viable businesses emerged. The program's limited success came about when lending activities missed the target. This problem of missing the targeted clientele was one that would often haunt micro-lending programs of the 1980s and 1990s (Servon 1999; Raheim et al. 1996).

Lisa Servon notes that the EOL program "is the closest U.S. precedent for current microenterprise programs, although there are critical differences" (1999, 21). EOL simply provided loans, while many of the disadvantaged recipients lacked the knowledge and expertise needed to run viable small businesses. The 1990s generation of U.S. microenterprise programs, in contrast, stressed training, which often dominated lending activity.

The Elusive Disadvantaged Business

The Aspen Institute's 1996 Directory of U.S. Microenterprise Programs described 328 active programs operating in nearly every state in the United States; they had assisted, in 1995, more than 36,000 small businesses. Nearly all of these programs defined as disadvantaged those people who had difficulty accessing credit or training. Targeted beneficiaries were low-income people primarily; secondary targets included firms operating in poor neighborhoods, as well as minorities and women (Severens and Kays 1997).

The Small Enterprise and Family Development Program was a microenterprise assistance project in Iowa that was funded by the U.S. Department of Health and Human Services Office of Community Services (OCS). Its mandate was clear: the applicable enabling legislation defined the target population as persons with incomes below the poverty line. Yet examination of the assisted participants revealed that the majority of them were ineligible and "should have been excluded because their incomes were in excess of 125 percent of the poverty line" (Raheim et al. 1996, 93). This microenterprise program had an unambiguously defined target clientele but it was missing its target. This phenomenon was widespread.

San Francisco–based Women's Initiative for Self-Employment (WISE) was one of the first microenterprise programs in the United States, providing both training and lending assistance to disadvantaged women. A 1995 evaluation of clients served by WISE indicated that 75 percent of them had received some college education and only 3 percent had not graduated from high school; 27 percent were college graduates. Among programs operating throughout the United States, similar education profiles typified the assisted clients. Indeed, available evidence suggested that few of the programs primarily served the truly disadvantaged (Servon 1997).

Contrary to their original expectations, staff at WISE and other microenterprise programs often found that they were serving two client pools, the larger of which was more advantaged and ready to borrow, and the smaller less and not. Choosing to serve one of those markets often meant choosing between providing lending and training assistance. Programs serving both markets often segmented their services so that advantaged clients got most of the loans, while the less advantaged got most of the training. "Pressure to control loan losses and to keep the high cost of training down reinforces the tendency to lend to better educated, more affluent clients" (Bates and Servon 1996, 28).

Defining Disadvantage: Three Approaches

In the context of self-employment and small-firm ownership, the concept—*disadvantaged*—suggests low-income persons lacking the expertise and work experience commonly associated with launching a viable business. Microenterprise loan programs, in practice, define the disadvantaged as people having difficulty accessing credit or training. Microenterprise program participants themselves provide an implicit definition of disadvantage when they identify why they want to be self-employed: most stress unemployment and the need for more money (Severens and Kays 1997). Yet employment problems and financial constraints impact many Americans, including college graduates possessing substantial work experience.

This study investigates three measures of small business disadvantage. The first criterion is low income or low economic status among potential and actual small firm owners. This is a difficult measure to operationalize because low income among the self-employed is often a transitory state rooted in changing circumstances. Welfare recipients pursuing self-employment are investigated to provide a proxy for low household-income status.

Criterion two for measuring disadvantage concerns unemployment as a motivation for starting a business. By definition, business owners identifying their inability to find suitable work elsewhere in the job market as their primary reason for starting a firm are labeled "disadvantaged." The inability-to-find-work definition of disadvantage is expedient for two reasons. First, the trait powerfully draws clients to microenterprise assistance programs (Bates and Servon 2000). Second, the U.S. Census Bureau's Characteristics of Business Owners (CBO) database provides a nationwide representative sample of small business owners who list this inability-to-find-work criterion as their primary reason for starting a business.

Analysis of these two measures of disadvantage produced business owner groups of those who tended to be highly educated. The spirit of microenterprise assistance was not to focus primarily on the college-educated individual experiencing hard times, but rather the person lacking the education, skills, and other resources normally associated with the ability to earn a comfortable living. The third measure of disadvantage therefore sought to force the investigation toward those lacking substantial human capital. What about the high school dropout who lacks financial resources? In the very large, nationwide, representative samples of firms available in the Census Bureau's CBO database, I selected a subsample of CBO firms owned by resource-poor owners. Criterion three: I defined as disadvantaged those firms whose owners had not graduated from high school. All of the high-school-dropout owners were further constrained to have launched their businesses with financial capital of $5,000 or less.

Low Income or Low Economic Status

I have stressed that education, skills, and relevant work experience are prerequisites for aspiring entrepreneurs, and studies of microenterprise generally agree with this assessment (see, for example, Servon 1999; Taub 1998). The problem potentially facing microenterprise programs is that few of the potential owners of small firms who in fact have these human-capital prerequisites have low household incomes as well. I have sketched, below, an illustrative example drawn from the quantitative studies conducted by Salome Raheim.

One's income is often highly correlated to one's education, work experience, and specific skills. Welfare recipients possibly offer a pool of low-income potential entrepreneurs who lack such human-capital resources. Raheim analyzed the outcome of the Self-Employment Investment Demonstration (SEID) program, a multistate microenterprise experimental program for AFDC recipients that was implemented in 1986. She concluded that "microenterprise development has proven to be a viable approach to creating economic opportunity for many low-income and unemployed Americans" (1996, 72). Among the businesses created during the SEID program by welfare recipients that were still operating in 1993, Raheim reported that mean firm income for that year was $21,231.

A review of the full report on the SEID project (Raheim and Alter 1995) revealed that Raheim's statement, "the mean income was $21,231" (1996, 78) referred not to microenterprise profits but to their gross sales revenues for 1993. Among the welfare recipient entrepreneurs in the SEID project, deducting mean 1993 business expenses of $18,220 from mean gross revenues of $21,231 produced a modest net profit of $3,011 for the average microenterprise (Raheim and Alter 1995). These low profit and sales figures were derived by studying a survivor group of firms remaining at the end of a time-series analysis. The 21 percent of the firms started by SEID participants that had closed down by 1993 were excluded.

If not profitability, what might underpin Raheim's conclusion about microenterprise being proven as a "viable approach to creating economic opportunity"? Raheim's SEID evaluation studied a self-selected and screened group of 120 entrepreneurial welfare recipients, of whom only 2.6 percent lacked a high school degree. Twenty percent were self-employed before they entered the SEID program, and 74.5 percent were college educated; 40 percent of this subset had graduated from college. In light of their average age (thirty-eight) and demographic profile, these welfare recipients were better educated and more entrepreneurial than the overall adult U.S. population (Bates 1996).

Raheim, in fact, did not measure program success of SEID by using firm performance measures. Rather, she inferred success by the fact that many of the welfare recipients who started businesses exited the welfare roles over the next several years.

Herein lies a major problem with using low income or welfare recipient status as a measure of disadvantage in the small business context. Those pursuing firm ownership, as Raheim has shown in the SEID evaluation, are a highly self-selected subset of the poor. Their human-capital characteristics are not at all typical of the wider universe of poor adults or welfare recipients. At any time in the United States there are a nontrivial number of college-educated people who are either poor or on welfare or both. The transitory choices and misfortunes that produce such poverty include bouts of unemployment, dissolution of a marriage, serious accidents and illness, and lifestyle decisions to depart from secure employment (Servon and Bates 1998).

For the 120 business owners Raheim studied, it is possible that the circumstances that put them in poverty would have been overcome for most, regardless of their SEID participation, because their college educations had equipped them to compete successfully in the job market. Raheim's analysis does not even permit us to reject the possibility that participation in SEID slowed their exit from the welfare rolls. An alternative hypothesis is that their participation in SEID was responsible for their ability to exit welfare. Which explanation is correct?

A control group of 120 welfare recipients with the same demographic and educational credentials as the SEID business owners should have been set up at the beginning of the project. Lacking controls, we can conclude nothing about impacts of training and micro-loans on individual well-being, welfare dependency, or firm viability.

Inability to Find Suitable Work

Popular understanding of the concept, "disadvantaged population" stresses poverty level incomes and lack of resources. Raheim's evidence describing welfare recipient business owners who participated in the SEID program suggests that a lack of human resources typifies few of those participating in microenterprise programs.

Job loss and unemployment frequently spur people to seek assistance from microenterprise programs. The disadvantage criterion we explore identifies those driven to small business by lack of suitable alternatives. People checking "inability to find suitable work elsewhere in the job market" as their primary reason for starting a business are compared in this section to people starting firms for all other reasons. Using CBO data from Census Bureau, businesses started nationwide between 1986 and 1992 were analyzed if they were active in 1992 (as evidenced by grossing at least $5,000 in revenues, having an owner who actively worked in the firm; see Bates and Servon 2000).

Census Bureau CBO data indicate that 4,926,003 small firms fitting these criteria were operating in 1992. Asked why they entered small business, most owners chose two of the numerous alternatives listed on the Census Bureau questionnaire: "to be my own boss," or to "have a primary source of income." Slightly over 2 percent of the respondents (representing on estimated young 100,080 firms) stated that business ownership was primarily motivated by their desire "to have work not available elsewhere in the job market" (Bates and Servon 2000, 27).

The traits of business owners not finding suitable work as employees are summarized in table 6.1 and compared to the broader owner group who are not disadvantaged in the sense of accessing suitable work.

Among the disadvantaged owners described in table 6.1, nearly 33 percent were college graduates. Indeed, owners in this subgroup were nearly five times more likely to be college graduates than high

Table 6.1   Small Businesses and Their Owners (1986 to 1992)

	Disadvantaged Owners: Firm Owner Could Not Find Suitable Work as Employee	All Others
1. Owner traits		
Percentage college graduates	32.6	36.9
Percentage with under four years of high school	7.1	8.0
Percentage experienced in field of self-employment prior to firm formation	78.8*	55.9
Annual owner labor hours (mean)	1,937*	1,782
2. Firm traits		
Total financial capital (mean)	$26,694*	$39,563
Percentage of owners entering the business in 1992	29.0*	20.0
Percentage of owners entering the business in 1991	26.0*	15.3
Percentage of firms still in operation, 1996	66.1*	76.4
n (weighted)	100,080	4,825,922

Source: Characteristics of Business Owners database.

*Difference in mean values is statistically significant at the .05 level.

school dropouts. Amazingly, table 6.1's summary statistics suggest that only 7,106 of the high school dropouts nationwide appeared in the disadvantaged business owner subgroup. Most business owners disadvantaged in the sense of not finding suitable work as an employee were well educated. This finding is consistent with evidence from the SEID evaluation. Recall that less than 3 percent of the business-owning welfare recipients studied by Raheim and Alter (1995) were high school dropouts.

Among those disadvantaged in the labor market, who among them have the necessary skills to establish a small business? Table 6.1's summary statistics offer important clues. Note that 78.8 percent of the disadvantaged business owners had specific work experience in their field of self-employment, and this work experience was acquired before they became business owners. Thus, their pre-existing skills commonly served as their entry ticket into business.

Comparing the traits of table 6.1's disadvantaged owners (and their firms) to others highlights characteristics that may help to clarify what it means to be disadvantaged in a small business context. First, the disadvantaged owners worked, on average, 155 more hours over the course of the year running their firms, relative to the other owners. Working longer hours in their firms was certainly consistent with the fact that the disadvantaged owners could not find suitable work as employees. Second, the average start-up capitalization of the firms launched by disadvantaged owners lagged far behind that of others. The average disadvantaged start-up, capitalized at $26,694, was competing in a small business world where the other-group start-up had 48.2 percent more capital to work with ($12,869 more capital, precisely, for the average start-up in the all-other group). This, too, makes sense. Labor market problems—such as a bout of unemployment—just prior to small business formation dissipate one's savings and lessen one's borrowing ability. The result is a greater likelihood of small business undercapitalization, relative to the other start-ups.

This difficulty in financing start-up operations may partly explain the attraction of micro-loan programs to disadvantaged owners trying to set up firms (Bates and Servon 2000). In particular, the college graduates may have limited access to bank financing precisely because of labor market problems such as unemployment. Hence, lacking alternatives, they turn to microenterprise lenders.

Two firm characteristics sharply delineated the disadvantaged from the others (table 6.1). The first were an extraordinarily young group, with 55 percent of them in operation for two or fewer years. Of the second, 35.3 percent had been in operation for two or fewer years. Very young firm age coexisted with a much higher rate of business closure among the disadvantaged; 33.9 percent of these firms had closed down, discontinuing operations by late 1996. Among the all-other firm group, only 23.6 percent had discontinued operations by 1996. Thus, the disadvantaged were a relatively volatile group.

Why were the disadvantaged closing their firms at the higher rate shown in table 6.1? Past studies consistently link high firm closure rates with undercapitalization and very young firms (Bates 1990). Bates and Servon (2000) applied logistic regression analysis to investigate the closure rates of the table 6.1 disadvantaged and other-firm groups. The dependent variable in this analysis was whether the business operating in 1992 was operating in late 1996.

Logistic regression results identified broadly consistent survival patterns between the disadvantaged and other small business groups, with one important exception. Among the disadvantaged owners, having work experience in the field of self-employment was associated with small business closure. The opposite pattern typified the other owner group (Bates and Servon 2000).

The dynamics of small firm survival depend heavily on a variety of factors beyond those of the entrepreneur's human capital and financial investments. The younger firms, for example, are more volatile and failure prone than older firms, which have built up customer goodwill and an established clientele. Furthermore, a key determinant of whether a small firm survives is the time its owner devotes to the small business: part-time operations are more likely to shut down than full-time (Bates 1990). In all these respects, the firms run by disadvantaged owners behaved much like those run by other owners. Logistic regression analysis revealed only one outstanding difference in the traits that predicted firm survival: owners with work experience in their field of self-employment were less likely to create lasting firms, other factors constant, if they were members of the disadvantaged group. Among the other owners, this experience heightened firm survival prospects (Bates and Servon 2000).

The disadvantaged owners, clearly, often prefer to work as employees if suitable employment is available. Meanwhile, many of them keep their work skills current by pursuing self-employment in the field of their work experience. Self-employment appears to serve, quite often, as a holding pattern for these disadvantaged owners: many are ready, willing, and able to move back to employee status when opportunity comes knocking (Bates and Servon 2000). The small businesses they have created therefore have a greater tendency to cease operations.

Apart from their relative youth and undercapitalization, the firms owned by the disadvantaged were more prone to close down because their owners were pushed into self-employment by lack of suitable work as employees. Being highly experienced and well educated, many obviously had opportunities to return to employee status, and the consequences of their desire to exit self-employment included enhanced firm volatility. This fact complicates the mission of the microenterprise programs that use small business creation and longevity as measures of their success.

Analysis of Firms Started by High-School-Dropout Owners

Among small businesses nationwide operating in 1992, as represented by the Census Bureau's CBO database, 9.0 percent of the nonminority firm owners did not have a high school degree. Corresponding figures for minority owners were 20.1 percent. Because the CBO database heavily oversamples minority business enterprises (MBEs), it is expedient to focus on the subset of MBEs whose owners had not graduated from high school. In this group, Hispanic-owned firms were most common; firms owned by blacks were also numerous; Asian-owned firms were rare.

To focus most directly on resource-poor, disadvantaged firms, this section analyses MBEs begun with $5,000 or less in financial capital headed by owners without high school degrees. Table 6.2 describes minority-owned businesses nationwide whose owners were not high school graduates; all of these started firms between 1979 and 1987 with investments of up to $5,000 in financial capital. More than half had immigrant owners. Nearly half (46.9 percent) of the firms described in table 6.2 were started with no owner investment of financial capital whatsoever. Gross sales in 1987 were typically low, with 61.6 percent of the firms generating total revenues of less than $20,000. Yet these firms were often vitally important contributors to household income; 46.7 percent of the owners reported that earnings from their small businesses were the major source of household income.

Table 6.2 data were derived from the U.S. Bureau of the Census CBO database and are representative of the minority owners (high school dropouts, minimal financial investment) grossing $5,000 or more in annual sales in 1987.

Low household income was commonplace among this subpopulation of self-employed, but certainly was not universal: 48.8 percent of them reported household incomes from all sources of under $15,000 (table 6.2). Self-employment was not a high-yielding activity for most of the high-school-dropout entrepreneurs: 61.6 percent of the firms generated before-tax profits of under $10,000 in 1987. Yet a significant subset did well, with 9.7 percent of the firms netting

Table 6.2   Minority-Owned Businesses, 1979 to 1987

1. Business traits	
1987 gross sales (mean)	$33,054
Percentage with gross 1987 sales under $20,000	61.6
Number of employees (mean)	0.3
Percentage with no paid employees	92.9
1987 net profits (mean)	$11,196
Percentage with net profits in 1987 under $10,000	61.6
Total financial capital (mean)	$1,354
Percentage started with zero financial capital	46.9
Percentage still in operation, 1991	70.8
2. Owner traits	
Annual owner labor input hours (mean)	1,664.7
Percentage reliant on business for 50 percent or more of household income	46.7
Percentage with total household income under $15,000	48.8
Percentage wed, living with spouse	79.3
Percentage black	30.0
Percentage Hispanic	57.4
Percentage Asian immigrants, other	12.6
Percentage male	77.9
3. Industry groups	
Percentage services	35.5
Percentage construction	22.8
Percentage retail	16.9
Percentage other	24.8

Source: Characteristics of Business Owners database.

$25,000 and up. What sort of individual, lacking a high school diploma and financial resources, does well in small business ownership? Looking solely at the firms netting $10,000 or more before taxes in 1987, a clear-cut profile emerged. The successful person pursuing self-employment in this niche was most commonly a male who owned a construction firm (Bates 1997a).

Start-up capital among the firms described in table 6.2 was $1,354, on average, and this figure included the zero amounts of 46.9 percent of the owners. The most common source of capital reported was the household net worth of the owner. Yet firms in the subset that used capital at start-up often relied in part on borrowed funds. The most widely used sources of debt capital were small loans from family and friends. This borrowing pattern contrasts sharply with the reliance on loans from financial institutions that typified the disadvantaged can't-find-suitable-work subset, as well as the broader universe. Owners lacking high school degrees did sometimes report borrowings from financial institutions, but these were commonly forms of consumer credit rather than business loans.

Persons in construction nationwide have the highest self-employment rate (over 22 percent) observed in any major industry group in United States (Devine and Mlaker 1992). The majority of those employed in construction worked in a specific skilled craft, such as carpentry or plumbing, and it was the skilled craftsperson who was most apt to be self-employed. Among those described in table 6.2, immigrant Hispanics in construction were quite common; Asian immigrants and women were rare. This pattern was partially rooted in discriminatory barriers limiting access to training in skilled crafts (Waldinger and Bailey 1991). Women were hardest hit: 1.3 percent of the women-owned firms were in construction, versus 26.4 percent of the male-owned firms.

Every study of "disadvantaged" small business suffers from selection bias because selected parameters have been used to pluck a disadvantaged subset out of a broader small-business universe. By focusing solely on minority-owned businesses grossing revenues of at least $5,000 annually, I have attempted to net out the casual self-employed. The remaining subset—all having owners without high school degrees, all started with less than $5,000 in capital—had a distinct profile: 79.3 percent of the business owners were married and living with their spouse, and 77.9 percent of the owners were males. Overall, 38.4 percent of these disadvantaged firms generated net profits of $10,000 or more in 1987, and 70.8 percent of them were still in business in late 1991 (table 6.2).

More often than not, the business owners were attached to households that had multiple income sources—the presence of other sources acted as a kind of safety net (Servon 1999). For more than 46 percent of the households in which table 6.2 firms were embedded, business earnings were the major source of household income. Business earnings appeared to boost many of these households over the poverty line. Even in cases where they were less than $10,000, these earnings, in combination with other household income sources, often lifted the family out of poverty. It is noteworthy, nonetheless, that most of these businesses, by themselves, did not generate enough earnings to do so.

Table 6.2's overview of disadvantaged businesses owned by minorities revealed gaps between the frequent traits of firm owners—male, married—and the groups often targeted by microenterprise programs—female, often not living with spouse (Raheim and Alter 1995). One goal of microenterprise programs has been to enable groups underrepresented in small business to learn about and pursue self-employment. Clearly, then, some of this mismatch was grounded in program design.

In his study of the Good Faith Fund, a microenterprise loan program operating in Arkansas, Richard Taub observed no instances of poor, single mothers moving from welfare to successful small business operation.

> The success stories come from families who have a safety net of some kind. . . . What the Good Faith Fund model shows, and what I believe a careful analysis of other U.S. adoptions of the Grameen-like program would show, is that they work best not with those who are long term on welfare, but those who have a history of holding jobs and have well-defined skills. When Good Faith Fund borrowers succeed, it is because they are members of low to moderate income families where somebody already has a job and the Good Faith Fund microbusiness loan provides additional or supplemental income. (Taub 1998, 67–68)

The CBO data summarized here are consistent with Taub's assessment.

Black-Owned Small Businesses

In 1992, the Roper organization polled 472 black business owners nationwide to gauge how they viewed their own firms, as well as black businesses generally. Reporter Eugene Carlson covered this survey for the *Wall Street Journal* ("Battling Bias," April 3, 1992, p. R16). Asked why there were so few black-owned firms, 84 percent responded that "black-owned businesses are impeded by lack of access to financing."

A well-established scholarly literature shows that minority-owned businesses have less access to loans from financial institutions than similar firms owned by whites (Cavalluzo et al. 2002; Blanchflower, Levine, and Zimmerman 2003; Bates 1997b). Most of the evidence to date concerns the capital constraints facing black-owned businesses. Average start-up capitalization for young black firms nationwide that were operating in 1992 was $14,108, and median capitalization was under $10,000, according to Census Bureau CBO data; the corresponding figure for the average nonminority firm was $40,065 (Bates 2003).

The Federal Reserve System conducted a survey of 4,637 small businesses in 1993, collecting extensive information about firms that had sought loans over the three previous years (just over 2,000 of the surveyed firms had sought loans). These data, which reflect an oversampling of minorities, are known as the National Survey of Small Business Finances (NSSBF). The major issue stressed by studies using NSSBF data is summarized by Ken Cavalluzzo et al. (1999, 189): "businesses owned by African Americans were two-and-one-half times as likely to be denied credit on their most recent loan request than were businesses owned by white males."

The fact that black-owned firms have less access to financing than whites is well established and not controversial (Pierce 1947; Bates 1997a). The interesting question is whether black-owned firms possessing identical firm and owner traits (other than race) have less access to bank credit than white-owned firms. Recent studies based on the NSSBF data reinforce past findings; the result is a group of studies, all of which demonstrate that the answer is yes: blacks have less access to financial institution loans than otherwise identical white-owned firms (Cavalluzzo et al. 2002; Blanchflower, Levine, and Zimmerman 2003).

Common findings across studies that use the 1993 NSSBF data—(Blanchflower, Levine, and Zimmerman 2003; Cavalluzzo et al. 1999)—are twofold. First, financial institutions are extraordinarily important sources of credit for small businesses, accounting for more than 90 percent of the debt financing flowing to small firms, whether minority or majority owned. Second, black-owned firms have significantly less access to that debt financing than white-owned.

My intent is not to explore the MBE lending discrimination literature exhaustively but rather to draw on selected evidence that contributes to our understanding of how disadvantaged firms, in general, finance their operations. Studies of black-business finance have the dual advantages of being numerous, and providing analyses of nonminority firm comparison groups.

Drawing on the large, representative sample of small firms de-

Table 6.3   Financing Small Business Formation, 1979 to 1987

	Percentage Using Borrowed Funds	Percentage Using Equity Capital Only (No Debt)	Percentage Using No Financial Capital
Nonminority-owned firms	37.2	39.1	23.7
African American–owned firms	28.8	42.3	28.9

Source: U.S. Bureau of the Census, Characteristics of Business Owners database.

scribed in the CBO database, table 6.3 data compare black and non-minority firms regarding types of start-up financing used to launch their firms. Differing financing patterns are apparent in the table 6.3 statistics, but similarities are perhaps more prominent. Well over half of the start-ups—whether white- or black-owned— use no debt financing to begin operations. Indeed, quite a few start out with no financial capital. Among the firms with nonminority white owners, 23.7 percent began operations with zero financial capital; corresponding figures for blacks were 28.9 percent. These zero-capital operations are largely tiny, zero-employee firms, and are concentrated in service industries.

Another 39.1 percent of the nonminority start-ups that began operations with financial capital used no borrowed funds: the firms were launched using equity capital only, and most of this came from the owner's household net worth. Only 37.2 percent of the nonminority start-ups described in table 6.3 used borrowed money to begin operations, but these firms stand out as the larger-scale businesses. Most of the young employer firms were launched using a combination of borrowed funds and owner equity capital to finance start-up. Among the young nonminority firms, the greater size of start-ups beginning with borrowed funds is apparent when mean annual sales revenues for 1987 of borrowers versus nonborrowers were compared: the average borrowing firm had annual sales of $268,373 versus $112,459 for the nonborrower (Bates 1997a). The same pattern typified young black-owned firms.

The nationwide sample of black-owned business start-ups described in table 6.3 indicates that blacks are more likely to start out with no financial capital, less likely to borrow, and more often reliant solely on equity capital, relative to the white-owned firms.

Businesses using borrowed funds, whether black- or white-owned, were the larger scale firms, in terms of annual sales revenues. This relationship—borrowers have greater overall capitalization and larger size than nonborrowers—accounts for the fact that over half of the aggregate start-up capitalization in the overall black and white firm populations is debt capital. Debt as a percentage of aggregate financial capital for all firms described in table 6.3 is 55.6 percent for whites and 50.7 percent for black businesses (Bates 1997b). Where does debt capital come from? CBO data address this issue.

Table 6.4 lists the frequency with which start-up firms tapped the three major sources of debt that finance business formation. Both the white- and black-business borrower groups received start-up financing more often from financial institutions than from the second most important debt source (family). Indeed, the order of importance of sources of debt—financial institutions were most important, family was second, and friends ranked third—was the same for white and black borrowers.

Considering average loan size by borrowing source (table 6.4), in conjunction with borrowing frequency by source, the importance of financial institutions comes into clearer focus. Much larger loans ex-

Table 6.4   Sources of Borrowed Financial Capital Used by Start-Ups, 1979 to 1987

	Financial Institutions	Family	Friends
A. Frequency of borrowings by loan source (percentage)			
Nonminority-owned firms	65.9	26.8	6.4
African American–owned firms	59.1	21.2	11.3
B. Average loan size (dollars)			
Nonminority-owned firms	56,784	35,446	30,907
African American–owned firms	31,958	18,306	16,444
C. Leverage (debt, equity ratio) by source of loan			
Nonminority-owned firms	3.25	2.32	2.03
African American–owned firms	2.61	2.22	2.15

Source: U.S. Bureau of the Census, Characteristics of Business Owners database.
Note: Some firms borrowed from more than one source.

tended by financial institutions add up to a dominance of start-up financing by this loan source.

A valid analysis of financial institution lending to small firms cannot focus narrowly upon availability and terms of business loans because a broader range of financing alternatives—particularly consumer credit—is being tapped by small business start-ups. If one applies for a business loan and is turned down, consumer credit alternatives are numerous. Perhaps reflecting their restricted access to mainstream business loans, black-owned businesses have been particularly active in using consumer credit to finance start-up operations (Bates 1997b). CBO data identify two important forms of consumer credit—home equity loans and personal credit cards—that finance business creation. Among white business start-ups described in tables 6.3 and 6.4 that used borrowed funds, 18.4 percent relied on home equity loans or personal credit cards for business financing. In contrast, 29.6 percent of start-up black-business borrowers used these types of consumer credit.

The table 6.5 OLS regression analysis focuses solely on firms that received loans from financial institutions at the point when business operations began. The dependent variable is the dollar amount of the debt financing the start-up firm used. Explanatory variables are company and owner traits that may be related to the loan amount. Findings suggest that larger loans flow to the owners investing more equity to launch their firms. Greater owner human capital endowments are also associated with larger loan amounts (Bates 1990). Other explanatory variables include owner gender, controls for loan type (consumer credit is flagged), and the most common industry groups in which firms were formed. For complete definitions of these variables, see the Appendix.

In the table 6.5 regression equations (one for black and one for white borrowers), loan dollar amount—the dependent variable—was heavily influenced by the amount of equity capital that the owner invested in the start-up: black borrowers received an extra $0.92 in debt per equity dollar, other factors constant, which was $0.25 below the $1.17 loan increment associated with each equity dollar invested by whites. Blacks were penalized, on balance, by the type of borrowing undertaken: reliance on personal credit card borrowing reduced loan size—$20,776 for blacks and $33,063 for whites—and white borrowers were less likely (6.4 percent) to use

Table 6.5   Explaining Loan Amounts for Start-Up Businesses Borrowing
from Institutional Sources, 1979 to 1987

A. Regression Equations	Regression Coefficient (Standard Error)	
	African American Borrowers	White Borrowers
Constant	20,784.12*	8,730.95
	(8,834.22)	(8,134.32)
Education: high school	−10,998.61	8,061.83
	(6,937.85)	(6,328.80)
Education: one to three years of college	−6,637.85	24,194.79*
	(7,611.44)	(6,847.10)
Education: college graduate	−8,226.75	32,467.54*
	(8,712.17)	(7,432.22)
Education: graduate school	3,864.49	27,905.79*
	(8,361.17)	(7,743.58)
Management experience	11,150.10*	15,208.07*
	(5,501.18)	(4,264.36)
Male	−5,660.92	−2,262.91
	(5,501.18)	(4,819.81)
Wed	5,035.30	2,443.16
	(6,147.70)	(5,321.03)
Equity capital	0.92*	1.17*
	(0.04)	(0.03)
Credit card	−20,775.59*	−33,063.04*
	(6,711.04)	(8,323.64)
Home equity loan	−8,279.45	−21,584.48*
	(6,681.59)	(5,836.43)
Retail firm	4,164.34	−13,030.67*
	(6,206.59)	(4,659.91)
Skill-intensive service firm	6,338.44	−9,816.29
	(6,417.83)	(5,219.33)
Ongoing firm	−5,578.14	20,730.67*
	(6,154.34)	(4,345.04)
R-squared	.185	.247
F	28.1	116.2
N	2,116	6,030

(*Table continues on p. 170.*)

Table 6.5   Continued

B. Mean Values, Explanatory Variables	African American Borrowers	White Borrowers
Education: high school	.286	.317
Education: one to three years of college	.200	.221
Education: college graduate	.128	.170
Education: graduate school	.206	.171
Management experience	.260	.363
Male	.710	.807
Wed	.825	.854
Equity capital	$12,224	$17,488
Credit card	.157	.064
Home equity loan	.139	.124
Retail firm	.206	.251
Skill-intensive service firm	.250	.242
Ongoing firm	.181	.283

Source: Characteristics of Business Owners database.
*Statistically significant at the .05 level.

personal credit cards to finance business formation than blacks (15.7 percent).

The differing constant terms in table 6.5 regressions equations may complicate the interpretation of racial borrowing differences, which are derived from regression coefficient values. A complementary test of black-white differences entails pooling the two firm samples analyzed in table 6.5: a regression model explaining loan size for the pooled sample of black and white borrowers indicates that the racial characteristic—being black—is associated with receiving a loan significantly smaller than that received by a white business borrower otherwise identical regarding the measured traits.

Some of the borrowing firms analyzed in table 6.5 received more than one loan. Nearly 10 percent of bank loan recipients also borrowed from family sources; combining loans from banks and other sources was rare (Bates 1997b).

The greatest difference in loan size determination involved human capital variables: college-educated nonminorities and those with managerial experience received larger loans than other non-minority borrowers, other things equal. In contrast, among blacks, none of the education variables had significant impacts upon loan amount in table 6.5's regression exercise: managerial experience translated into a larger loan but a college degree did not. The primary loan size determinant for black business borrowers was clearly owner equity investment. Note that gender was not a significant determinant (table 6.5).

Family (intergenerational) wealth holdings and the personal net worth of the owner fund the business formation equity investments that serve as the basis for a successful business loan application (Bates 1997b). Among the firms analyzed in table 6.5, borrower debt-equity ratios overall were 3.25 for white firms and 2.61 for black. Closing that gap would benefit black borrowers. A major financing gap, however, lies in the underlying small-business equity investments that owners were leveraging when they received bank loans: that is, mean equity for the white borrowers was $17,488, and for black, $12,224 (table 6.5). Loan size gaps were rooted in black-white firm equity capital differences and in differential black-white loan treatment by banks.

Patterns Among Small Firms Using Debt Capital

The NSSBF data that Blanchflower, Levine, and Zimmerman analyzed in 2003 suggested an overwhelming dominance of loans from financial institutions in the realm of small business borrowing. My CBO-based research, in contrast, indicated that important debt sources for small firms included family and friends, although financial institutions were dominant. Furthermore, a study examining small firms operating in two Chicago neighborhoods—Little Village (which is predominantly Hispanic) and Chatham (predominantly black)—found that "Credit from financial institutions is little used in the start-up phase" (Huck et al. 1999, 485). Personal savings, as well as loans from informal sources such as family and friends, provided most of the start-up capital used by this sample of Chicago firms. Hispanic- and black-owned small businesses dominated the sample on which this study was based (see also chapter 6).

Thus, across three empirical studies, debt capital was provided overwhelmingly by financial institutions at one extreme and predominantly by informal sources at the other. Reconciling these findings points toward a credit continuum. At one end lie the business loans extended by financial institutions; toward the other are the personal credit card borrowings and the loans from family and friends.

Firms in the NSSBF database represent an older, more established, larger scale subset of the nation's small business community: median age among the 4,637 NSSBF firms was 14.3 years; 4.1 percent of these firms had been in operation for less than three years (Cavalluzzo et al. 1999; Blanchflower, Levine, and Zimmerman 2003). Among such established firms, financing was derived predominantly from financial institutions. Data collected from the two Chicago minority communities—Little Village and Chatham—reflected start-up capitalization for firm samples that were largely black- and Hispanic-owned. Over half of these firms were in retailing: among black and Hispanic firms nationwide, relative shares of firms operating in retailing were less than one-third of the Chicago sample proportions. Among blacks, for example, 49.2 percent of those in the Chicago sample ran retail operations; corresponding nationwide figures drawn from CBO data were 13.7 percent. Minority-owned firms in retailing (and black-owned firms specifically) were below average regarding net profitability relative to minority firms (nationwide) in all other fields (Bates 1997a).

The Chicago study was not representative of minority firms nationwide in terms of industry distribution. Nor did it capture minority firms that did not operate in minority communities. My analysis of black-owned firms doing business in twenty-eight large metro areas found that those operating outside of minority communities were better capitalized and more likely to borrow from financial institutions, relative to those in the minority communities (Bates 1993). Relative to the nationwide black-business community, in other words, those examined in the Chicago study represented a disadvantaged subset.

As one examines business subsets that are increasingly disadvantaged, the composition of borrowing sources changes predictably. Family and friends become more common loan sources; business loans extended by financial institutions become less common. If loans from financial institutions are tapped at all, they are likely to be personal loans such as credit card balances. Traits that appear to sort firms along this credit continuum include start-up status versus established firms, nonminority versus minority-owned firms, minority firms operating in minority neighborhoods versus those doing business outside them, resource-poor owners (such as high school dropouts) versus resource-rich owners (college graduates). Broadly, the more advantaged firms tap mainstream borrowing sources; disadvantaged firms rely more on family and friends.

Credit and Small Business Viability

Business start-ups are emphasized because they are particularly vulnerable to problems of limited credit access and undercapitalization. Greater capitalization can serve as a buffer to protect them from the liabilities of newness. New firms, Arnold Cooper et al. (1994) observe, are struggling to establish administrative procedures, define their institutional identity, and gain credibility with customers and suppliers. This "process of experimentation is characterized by iterations of trial and error" (Cooper et al. 1994, 372). Greater financial capital and access to capital at start-up and in the early years of operation help firms survive this process of experimentation and learning; undercapitalization, in contrast, limits the new firm's ability to withstand unfavorable shocks and to undertake corrective actions. More initial capitalization buys time while the entrepreneur learns how to run the business. Without an adequate buffer, poorly capitalized firms may be forced to close down during difficult periods.

Using the U.S. Census Bureau's CBO database, table 6.6 describes young firms in operation in 1987: they were tracked to late 1991 and sorted into groups of firms still operating in 1991, and firms that had discontinued operations by 1991.

Surviving nonminority-owned firms stood out as active borrowers: mean start-up debt was $20,414 for those still in business, versus $8,866 for the firms that had shut down. Survivors, as well, were more likely to borrow than closed firms, and their average leverage was higher. Active borrowing at start-up disproportionately typified the larger scale, more viable small businesses. This same pattern of larger capitalization and higher leverage among black-owned firms delineated surviving firms from those that had gone out of business (see table 6.6).

Table 6.6   Start-Up Capitalization Among White- and Black-Owned Small Businesses, 1979 to 1987: Active Versus Discontinued Firms

	Nonminority		African American	
	Active in 1991	Closed Down	Active in 1991	Closed Down
1987 gross sales (mean)	$185,458	$50,602	$76,971	$29,819
Total financial capital (mean)[a]	$36,301	$17,437	$16,454	$8,013
Debt capital (mean)[a]	$20,414	$8,866	$8,563	$3,459
Equity capital (mean)[a]	$15,886	$8,571	$7,891	$4,554
Percentage started with zero capital	20.2%	35.7%	26.1%	36.6%
Leverage at start-up (debt divided by equity)	1.29	1.03	1.09	0.76

Source: Characteristics of Business Owners database.
[a]Invested in the firm at the point of start-up.

Concluding Thoughts

Evidence, then, points toward financial constraints thwarting the viability of many disadvantaged firms. The start-up, the minority owner, the firm operating in the urban minority community, these and other traits are linked to reduced access to business loans from financial institutions. Family and friends are alternate loan sources, but available evidence (table 6.4) indicates that a dollar of owner equity generates fewer loan dollars (less leverage) from these informal sources than from financial institutions. One result of these constraints is the pattern of higher closure rates that typifies poorly capitalized firms.

None of the evidence discussed suggests that greater loan access, by itself, can be a small business panacea. Owner human capital and financial capital are complements, not substitutes (Bates 1997a). For owners with the requisite human capital—skills, expertise, and experience—for viable small-business operation, many nonetheless fall into the various "disadvantaged" categories. These are the owners most likely to benefit from expanded access to business credit.

A seemingly paradoxical finding is the high incidence of education and skills among members of disadvantaged groups who pursue self-employment. Raheim's analysis of welfare-recipient entrepreneurs revealed that most had attended college. Analysis of those pushed toward self-employment by lack of suitable jobs indicated that nearly 80 percent had specific work experience in their field of self-employment. High school dropouts successfully pursuing self-employment were often working in skilled construction trades. Given the requirements of successful business ownership, these patterns make sense.

From a policy perspective, this evidence points toward traits of disadvantaged persons who are unlikely candidates for success in self-employment. The unskilled adult lacking educational credentials is not a good candidate. Those with histories of loose labor force attachment and few skills—particularly those attached to households lacking alternative income sources—are poor candidates. Poor persons with relevant skills, as well as a safety net, may benefit from starting small businesses. Those who are weak in terms of human capital, without financial resources, having no safety net—the truly disadvantaged—are not likely to achieve self-sufficiency via business formation. Those without the resources associated with viable business operation will most often fail if they pursue this route to upward mobility. A program realistically seeking to move the truly disadvantaged into business ownership would focus first on developing the human capital prerequisites that are the bedrock of small firm viability.

Appendix: Variable Definitions

In this study, summary statistics, along with regression models, are used to analyze firm behavior. Variables appearing in the various regression analyses and tables are formally defined below.

1. Owner characteristics

    a. Education: equal to one under the following conditions (and defined as zero otherwise):

Education: high school: high school graduates only

Education: one to three years college: some college education

Education: college graduate: college graduate

Education: graduate school: have attended graduate and professional schools

b. Experience in field of self-employment: equal to one for those working in the field in which their small business operates prior to owning the business; zero otherwise.

c. Management experience: equal to one for those having at least a year of management experience prior to owning the business; zero otherwise.

d. Gender: male is a dichotomous variable, set equal to one for males and zero for females.

e. Marital status: wed is a dichotomous variable, set equal to one if the individual is married and living with their spouse, zero otherwise.

2. Firm characteristics

a. 1987 (1992) gross sales: dollar amount of gross sales revenues generated by the firm during the 1987 (1992) calendar year.

b. Total financial capital: dollar amount of debt plus equity capital used to start or become the owner of the business.

c. Capital: log of the sum of debt and equity capital used to start or become the owner of the business.

d. Leverage: ratio of debt to equity capital invested in the firm at the point of entry.

e. Number of employees: average number of paid workers reported to the federal government on 1987 quarterly payroll forms.

f. Retail firm: retail = 1; else zero.

g. Skill-intensive service firm: professional services, finance, insurance, real estate, or business services, skill-intensive firm = 1; else zero.

h. Ongoing firm: if the owner entered a business that was already in operation, ongoing = 1; owner was original founder of the business, then ongoing = 0.

3. Loan characteristics

a. Credit card: owner used personal credit card purchases to finance formation and carried an unpaid balance, credit card = 1; else zero.

b. Home equity loan: owner used proceeds of a home equity loan to finance business formation, then home equity loan = 1; else zero.

References

Bates, Timothy. 1975. "Government as Financial Intermediary for Minority Entrepreneurs: An Evaluation." *Journal of Business* 48(4): 541–57.

——. 1990. "Entrepreneur Human Capital Inputs and Small Business Longevity." *Review of Economics and Statistics* 72(4): 551–59.

——. 1993. *Banking on Black Enterprise*. Washington, D.C.: Joint Center for Political and Economic Studies.

——. 1996. "The Financial Capital Needs of Black-Owned Businesses: Reply to Raheim." *Journal of Developmental Entrepreneurship* 1(1): 27–9.

——. 1997a. *Race, Self-Employment, and Upward Mobility*. Baltimore: Johns Hopkins University Press.

——. 1997b. "Unequal Access: Financial Institution Lending to Black- and White-Owned Small Businesses." *Journal of Urban Affairs* 19(4): 487–95.

——. 2003. "Use of Bank Credit to Finance Small Businesses." In *Financing Urban Economic Development in the 21st Century*, edited by Sammis White, Richard Bingham, and Edward Hill. New York: M.E. Sharpe.

Bates, Timothy, and William Bradford. 1979. *Financing Black Economic Development*. New York: Academic Press.

Bates, Timothy, and Lisa Servon. 1996. "Why Loans Won't Save the Poor." *Inc.* (April): 27–28.

——. 2000. "Viewing Self-Employment as a Response to Lack of Suitable Opportunities for Wage Work." *National Journal of Sociology* 12(2): 23–55.

Blanchflower, David, Philip Levine, and David Zimmerman. 2003. "Discrimination in the Small Business Credit Market." *Review of Economics and Statistics* 85(4): 930–43.

Cavalluzzo, Ken, Linda Cavalluzzo, and John Wolken. 1999. "Competition, Small Business Financing, and Discrimination: Evidence from a New Survey." In *Business Access to Capital and Credit*, edited by Jackson Blanton, A. Williams, and S. Rhine. Washington: Federal Reserve System.

———. 2002. "Competition, Small Business Financing, and Discrimination: Evidence from a New Survey." *Journal of Business* 75(4): 641–79.

Cooper, Arnold, Javier Gimeno-Gascon, and Carolyn Woo. 1994. "Initial Human Capital and Financial Capital as Predictors of New Venture Performance." *Journal of Business Venturing* 9(3): 371–95.

Devine, Theresa, and Joyce Mlaker. 1992. "Inter-Industry Variation in the Determinants of Self-Employment." Unpublished paper. State College, Penn.: Pennsylvania State University.

Huck, Paul, Sherrie Rhine, Robert Townsend, and Philip Bond. 1999. "A Comparison of Small Business Finance in Two Chicago Neighborhoods." In *Business Access to Credit and Capital*, edited by Jackson Blanton, A. Williams, and S. Rhine. Washington: Federal Reserve Board.

Pierce, Joseph. 1947. *Negro Business and Business Education*. New York: Harper and Brothers.

Raheim, Salome. 1996. "Micro-enterprise as an Approach for Promoting Economic Development in Social Work: Lessons from the Self-Employment Investment Demonstration." *International Social Work* 39(1): 69–82.

Raheim, Salome, and Catherine Alter. 1995. *Self-Employment Investment Demonstration: Final Evaluation Report*. Washington, D.C.: Corporation for Enterprise Development.

Raheim, Salome, Catherine Alter, and Donald Yarbrough. 1996. "Evaluating Microenterprise Programs: Issues and Lessons Learned." *Journal of Developmental Entrepreneurship* 1(2): 87–103.

Servon, Lisa. 1997. "Microenterprise Programs in U.S. Inner Cities: Economic Development or Social Welfare?" *Economic Development Quarterly* 11(2): 166–80.

———. 1999. *Bootstrap Capital*. Washington, D.C.: Brookings Institution.

Servon, Lisa, and Timothy Bates. 1998. "Microenterprise as an Exit Route from Poverty." *Journal of Urban Affairs* 20(4): 419–41.

Severens, Alexander, and Amy Kays. 1997. *1996 Directory of U.S. Microenterprise Programs*. Washington, D.C.: Aspen Institute.

Taub, Richard. 1998. "Making the Adoption Across Cultures and Societies: A Report on an Attempt to Clone the Grameen Bank in Southern Arkansas." *Journal of Developmental Entrepreneurship* 3(1): 53–69.

U.S. Comptroller General. 1973. *Limited Success of Federally Financed Minority Businesses in Three Cities*. Washington: U.S. Government Printing Office.

U.S. Small Business Administration. 1970. "Evaluation of Minority Enterprise Program, Attachment I: A Brief History of SBA Minority Entrepreneurship Programs." Unpublished paper.

Waldinger, Roger, and Thomas Bailey. 1991. "The Continuing Significance of Race: Racial Conflict and Racial Discrimination in Construction." *Politics and Society* 19(3): 291–321.

Chapter 7

Networks and Finance in Ethnic Neighborhoods

Robert M. Townsend

The Community Reinvestment Act (CRA), the Equal Credit Opportunity Act, and the Fair Housing Act all assign a key role to the formal banking sector, based on the view that it is vital for poor and ethnic minorities to have access to banks and other mainstream financial institutions. The usual regulatory view rarely considers alternatives to this sector, contributing to the impression that rejected bank loan applicants and nonapplicants are left to fend for themselves, perhaps vulnerable to loan sharks and pawn merchants of dubious repute. Without fact-finding missions, this view would go unchallenged. Thus one goal of the research reported here is to measure the importance of the informal sector.

Theory might suggest in fact that the informal sector would be both prevalent and a perfect substitute for the formal. There would be no evident role for formal intermediaries per se. In a world of perfect information and enforcement, individuals could as easily write contracts directly with each other. Without measurement, this view might also go unchallenged. Specifically, there are a few basic questions that need to be answered. Do those without formal access suffer more in consumption from adverse shocks? Are those without formal access restricted in the funds they can use to start businesses?

But answers to these questions beg other questions. If there is an adverse impact to exclusion or to positive yet limited use of the formal sector, then what is it in theory and in practice that limits trade and gives rise to intermediation? Theories of intermediation begin with the idea that information is available only at a cost: intermediaries arise because they minimize the amount of information production. Thus not all adverse events or contingencies are covered, not all individuals need be included, and for that matter not everyone should be an intermediary. Key papers that aid our thinking in this field include Douglas Diamond (1984) and Stefan Krasa and Anne Villamil (1992). However, these studies force a formal structure on the intermediary. Indeed, Philip Bond (1999) shows in such an environment that informal connections among borrowers may economize on transactions costs. But we know little about how such networks operate in practice. There is therefore little to guide the construction of models. We set out in these fact-finding missions to measure salient features of intermediation and networks.

It is by no means obvious from theory that networks should arise in all circumstances or that they should necessarily take the same form. The underlying ingredients of the theory matter. Some of the models emphasize a priori selection, that is, individual joint liability for loans helps to screen out bad apples, as in Maitreesh Ghatak (1999), or individuals choose to link to others from whom they can learn, as in Hal R. Varian (1990). Other models emphasize better internal risk contingencies due to better information on project returns or underlying effort (Holmstrom and Milgrom 1990; Itoh 1993; Prescott and Townsend 2002a), better internal enforcement of implicit or explicit agreements (Besley, Coate, and Loury 1993, 1994), or some combination of these. Christian Ahlin and Robert Townsend (2002) attempt to distinguish among these models. In a general equilibrium market structure we might see some households and business acting on their own, others joining with similar individuals (assortative matching, Becker 1973), while yet others join coalitions with deliberate and striking internal diversity (Prescott and Townsend 2002b). But what do we see in reality? Which networks are thick, lively, and homogenous and which are heterogeneous if not fragmented?

Our goal is to try to answer some of the factual questions. More generally, the purpose is to share what we have learned from a series of intensive fact-finding missions into some of the ethnic neighborhoods of two U.S. cities, and learned in particular from the research, which has used those data. We report on and synthesize here on papers by Daniel Aaronson, et al. (2000), Rebecca Raijman and Marta Tienda (2000), Huck et al. (1999), Maude Toussaint-Comeau and Rhine (2000), Bond and Townsend (1996), Anna Paulson (2003), and Toussaint-Comeau et al. (2003). Our goal is not to report new facts but to draw attention to these papers, and how they fit together. (Readers who wish to see more of the details are urged to consult the original work.)

The primary finding is that there is widespread use of informal credit by both households and incipient businesses. Households use family and friends, or nonfamily partnerships to mitigate the consumption impact of sickness, unemployment, and increased expenses. Likewise, businesses use the informal sector to finance business starts. This may not come as a surprise to economists studying developing countries, but it may seem unusual to those thinking of the United States as an advanced country with a formal financial sector.

A second important finding is that many households are nonetheless not fully insulated against income fluctuations and other shocks, and businesses appear credit constrained in the sense that higher start-up investments lead to more than proportionally higher profits. Formal sector bank access does seem to help households and businesses overcome these consumption and investment effects.

The third finding is that the qualitative nature of networks seems to vary by ethnicity, geography and other factors. The networks among Hispanics are lively and informal, with relatively small transaction values. Yet higher income, greater English proficiency, house ownership, and use of services outside the neighborhood are associated with increased access to the formal sector and a diminished use of networks. In contrast, the networks among the Hmong do not seem to diminish with years of residence in the United States. The network connections among Koreans are formal, less among family, and associated with relatively large amounts of money changing hands. In contrast, the African American communities studied here seem to lack much of an ethnic-based network.

Ethnic Neighborhoods

The initial focus of the surveys was on small ethnic businesses, but collaborators Richard Taub, Marta Tienda, and Robert Townsend decided early on that a companion household survey would also be needed. First, some nonlisted businesses show up in the households themselves. Second, there are barriers to entry into business, failures of existing businesses, and other possible links from households to businesses. So for all neighborhoods there is both a business survey and a household survey, and in most neighborhoods some so-called crossover surveys, to businesses that were also administered the household survey and households that were administered the business survey if a business was uncovered. The questionnaires are largely common across the neighborhoods but translated into or administered in the various languages of the ethnic groups.

The first neighborhood study was Little Village, Chicago, a Hispanic community surveyed in 1994 with Tienda and Taub, under the Center for the Study of Urban Inequality, at the University of Chicago. This community contained Korean and other ethnic businesses in addition to the predominant Mexican businesses. The second neighborhood was Chatham, Chicago, a predominately African American middle-income community surveyed in 1997 and 1998 with the collaboration of the Federal Reserve Bank of Chicago and the University of Chicago. Finally, third and most recently, the Hmong were surveyed in the Minneapolis–St. Paul metropolitan area in 2000 with the collaboration of the Federal Reserve Banks of Minneapolis and Chicago, as was a largely white control group with some blacks and members of other ethnic groups.

Little Village, a neighborhood on the south side of Chicago, is the largest Mexican community in the Midwest. It experienced considerable social and economic change between 1970 and 1990. In 1970, Hispanics constituted only 30 percent of the Little Village population, which numbered 62,895. During the next twenty years they became the predominant ethnic group, comprising 82 percent of all residents by 1990. The process of residential succession generated a crucial market condition for the development of a business sector—that is, a critical mass of ethnic consumers to support ethnic businesses. More generally, Mexican migration to the United States is a significant factor in current U.S. demographic change.

Chatham was chosen as the site of the second study for its distinct and well-recognized ethnic neighborhood. Located also on the south side of Chicago, Chatham became predominantly black during the 1950s (Chicago Fact Book Consortium 1995). According to the 1990 U.S. Census, it had a population of 36,779. All households in the survey are black with a median family income of $35,000, classifying Chatham as a middle-income community. It is not the low-income, crime-ridden community some typically associate with African American urban neighborhoods. Still, key informants tell us the neighborhood may have lost some of its earlier ethnic vitality. The waves of southern black migration to Chicago are well documented.

Hmong immigrants come from a tribal culture indigenous to areas of Laos, Vietnam, Thailand, Burma, and China. Between 1975 and 1991, more than 500,000 people fled Laos and became international political refugees. Most of the Hmong spent several years in refugee camps in Thailand; in our survey data, more than 20 percent of the 1,170 individuals of Hmong families in the United States were born in Thailand. Approximately one-quarter of the nation's Hmong population (41,800) lives in Minnesota. St. Paul is home to more than half of all Hmong living in Minnesota, with an approximate count of 24,389. Minneapolis has the next largest population, with 9,595. The Minneapolis–St. Paul area contains the largest Hmong community in the world outside of Thailand. The largest concentrations of households and businesses are located in the Payne-Phalen neighborhood and along the Penn Avenue North corridor in St. Paul and the Thomas-Dale neighborhood of Minneapolis. These neighborhoods contain well-established commercial strips of aging commercial, industrial, and mixed-use buildings surrounded by older housing stock. It is important to bear in mind that in studying the Hmong one is studying political refugees.

Sampling Issues

The surveys reported here must be understood as case studies. The neighborhoods are not chosen as representative of neighborhoods in general nor are they randomly selected. Likewise, we are not taking a random sample of ethnic groups. Finally, so little is known about networks a priori that it would in any event be difficult to select on that basis. Hopefully these drawbacks are balanced against the insights one gains from implementing an intensive, geographically concentrated instrument. Still, the numbers must be interpreted with some caution.

Within neighborhoods, however, rigorous sampling standards were maintained. The business survey in Little Village was based on a stratified random sample of establishments that were in operation during the spring of 1994. Walking the streets and canvassing the neighborhood, an intensive process, yielded approximately 1000 business establishments. These were then stratified according to primary type of industry, product, or service. Relatively uncommon businesses, such as bridal shops, bakeries, and iron work products and factories were sampled at a rate of 100 percent. Relatively abundant enterprises, like restaurants, bars, auto repair shops, and hair salons, were sampled at a rate of 35 percent. All remaining establishments were sampled at 50 percent. But in the findings presented here, we have not adjusted for the sampling ratios because such adjustments appear to have little impact and, in many cases, the cell sizes are so small as to make such adjustments conceptually problematic.

We drew a sample of 340 establishments, of which 36 were closed by the date of the interview; 10 were franchises or not-for-profit operations, 5 were secondary businesses of respondents in the sample, and 3 were owned by Cantonese-speaking Chinese, which we excluded as it was not cost efficient to translate the survey instrument for these cases. Our target sample was 200; therefore we targeted 286 enterprises and successfully interviewed 204, a response rate of 71 percent.

In addition, Little Village houses a Korean-operated discount mall that accommodates 120 small booths rented by Koreans, Arabs, Asian Indians, Mexicans, and other Hispanic immigrants. We drew a stratified random sample of these booths and interviewed 35 percent of Korean and Hispanic businesses, and all booths rented by other groups. Of the 64 operators contacted for interview from the mall sample, 63 percent were successfully interviewed. This is a highly successful response rate given that we insisted on interviewing owners and not managers or other employees.

For the household segment of the survey, blocks from within the Little Village neighborhood were first drawn at random. A sample of households was then constructed by drawing randomly from a complete enumeration of dwellings within these blocks. Bilingual interviewers successfully conducted the survey in 73 percent of the households in this sample (allowing for vacancies), yielding a total of 327 completed interviews.

As the household and business survey instrument was developed for a multi-ethnic survey, it could be implemented in Chatham with only minor modifications. Relatively common businesses in Chatham (including eating places and hair salons) were drawn at a rate of 22.5 percent and all other businesses at 45 percent. Note that in both surveys medical and legal professionals were excluded from the sample, on the grounds that the educational requirements for these fields result in entrance and financing decisions that have little in common with those of other small businesses. Interviews required about one and a half hours. The response rate for Chatham was 57 percent, lower than in Little Village. Enumerators reported some difficulties in gaining cooperation, and prior links to community leaders were less successful in overcoming difficulties. Chatham as a neighborhood may lack the cohesion of Little Village, though cohesion is difficult to gauge.

The household universe for Chatham was constructed by using a multistage full probability sample model based on the census block groups. The fieldwork resulted in the completion of 191 interviews. The overall response rate was 64 percent.

With less prior information and less-defined neighborhood boundaries, the survey in Minneapolis–St. Paul took a somewhat different form. For the businesses, a list of Hmong-owned businesses was compiled based on information from the Hmong Business Directory, members of the Hmong Chamber of Commerce, and lists provided by the Neighborhood Development Center and St. Paul Planning and Economic Development. The list was screened to verify that the businesses were Hmong-owned and operating. It was also screened to eliminate duplicate businesses. The resulting list consisted of 170 Hmong businesses, most of which were located along two primary commercial strips in St. Paul. Of this total, 121 completed the survey, 36 refused, and 13 were unable to complete the survey within the study period, yielding a final response rate of 71 percent. As it turns out, Hmong businesses are larger than those of the Chicago neighborhoods, leaving open the question of whether the sampling frame in Minneapolis–St. Paul missed existing small businesses. A staff member conducted a spot walking tour and discovered no small business that would have been missed.

The Hmong business locations were used to establish geographic boundaries for a control business sample. A random sample of 6,336 businesses was matched by zip code to the Hmong businesses. Hmong-owned businesses, nonprofits, and government agencies were eliminated from this list. The remaining list was randomized and the first 342 businesses were contacted. Of these, 122 were no longer in business or were found to be nonprofits. Of the 220 remaining, 131 completed surveys, 41 refused, and 48 could not complete the surveys within the study period. The final response rate for this control group was 60 percent. Of this group 74 percent are white, 10 percent black, and 6 percent Asian.

To reach the sample size goal 200 Hmong households, a randomly selected group of 1,083 households was obtained from a sample of blocks with high concentrations of the Hmong population (based on school district and census data). Blocks with public housing developments were excluded. This exclusion seems likely to have biased the education and income numbers upwards, but the numbers for Hmong business owners are larger still. The large measured gap between Hmong households and businesses can only be an underestimate. Of the 1,083 household universe, 313 households were identified as Hmong and contacted. From this group, 202 Hmong households completed the survey. Sixty-six households refused and forty-five surveys could not be completed within the study period, yielding a final response rate of 65 percent. A control group of non-Hmong households was also surveyed. The control households were randomly selected from non-Hmong households living in the same neighborhoods as the Hmong sample. Of the 322 control households contacted, 202 completed the survey. Sixty-eight households refused and 52 surveys could not be completed within the study period, yielding a final response rate of 63 percent.

In summary, the sampling methods used were similar in the case of Little Village and Chatham and distinct from the Hmong and control sample in Minneapolis–St. Paul. The response rates for households are similar for Chatham and the Hmong, and higher for Little Village. The response rates for businesses for the Hmong and control lie between those Chatham surveys (on the low end) and Little Village (on the high end).

Household Characteristics and Risk-Response Networks

Respondents to the household survey in Little Village were overwhelmingly (92.3 percent) Hispanic. Of the remainder, 4.0 percent were white, 1.5 percent African American, and 1.8 percent Arab. A large majority (78.2 percent) were born in Mexico and most of the remainder (19.3 percent) in the United States. For those born in Mexico, the average length of time in the United States was 15.3 years. Of the Hispanics, 18 percent described themselves as very proficient in spoken English, 25 percent as moderately proficient, and 57 percent as not proficient. For written English, the numbers are 14.0 percent, 20.8 percent, and 65.2 percent, respectively. Reported household income is low. The median of $18,720 is lower than the 1990 figure of $22,260 for the same neighborhood (Woodstock Institute 1992).

The principal occupational responses (for men and women, respectively): wage employment (78.2 percent, 39.3 percent), self-employed (8.4 percent, 1.6 percent), unemployed (5.6 percent, 4.9 percent), keeping house (0 percent, 44.3 percent), and retired (6.3 percent, 5.5 percent). The proportion of male respondents who described themselves as self-employed is high compared with the 1990 census figures for Chicago Hispanics—3.1 percent for men (and 1.7 percent for women).

Indeed, of the primary respondents to the household survey in Little Village, 43.6 percent were male and 56.4 percent female; ages ranged from 17 to 90, with a mean of 37.7; the majority (63.0 percent) were married, 8.9 percent were in married-like relationships, 4.0 percent were widowed, 16.0 percent divorced, 6.7 percent separated, and the remaining 12.5 percent single.

Financial difficulties are prevalent. In the sample, 210 households (64.2 percent) reported having experienced a problem that caused financial difficulties in the last five years. The principal problems include death or illness of a relative (38.8 percent), unemployment or periods of low income (49.8 percent), and increases in living expense and/or dependents (38.2 percent). In practice, when faced with actual financial difficulties, there is also widespread use of "new" sources of finance, with 124 respondents (58.5 percent of those responding). But bank loans and the formal sector more generally (finance companies, credit unions) were used by only 11.8 percent, low compared to other options. The formal sector provides a "low" back-stop technology. The informal sector looms larger, with 40 to 50 percent using gifts and borrowing from friends and relatives. Another 31 percent report they delayed or failed to pay debts, though unfortunately the question did not distinguish the source.

There is extensive use of existing savings and assets (35.8 percent). Finally, 41 percent and 45 percent report having to work harder or reduce consumption, an adverse impact.

Another key point: the adverse consumption impact is more severe for those who lack formal sector access. Those borrowing from a bank or lender are less likely to reduce household consumption (but more likely to work harder). Further, informal, network use seems inversely correlated with use of the formal sector, as if the two were substitutes. A perhaps related observation is that networks are less necessary or less effective for longer-term Hispanic residents. That is, assistance from family and friends declines with proficiency in English, quartile of income, house market activity, and links in the city outside the neighborhood, while use of the formal sector increases. In retrospect, with the outcome of the survey in hand, it would seem that this decline in apparent networks should be the object of further study, examining the relationship to age, history, and skill acquisition.

Chatham households are all African American. Median family income is $35,000, and relative to Little Village, there are other sharp contrasts. Strikingly, 63.4 percent of the responding heads are female with only 37 percent of the sample married. Among the unmarried, 11 percent were widowed, 21 percent divorced, and 30 percent never married. Education is relatively high, with 47.9 percent having a high-school degree or the equivalent, 9.6 percent with no degree, and the rest with advanced degrees. Wage or salary employment was about half of the sample only, and professional and managerial occupations are common. The overall average age of forty-nine was also older than the corresponding Hispanic community. Thus a relatively high 22 percent were retired and a relatively high 10 percent were not in the labor force.

Of these Chatham households, only 29 percent had experienced a serious setback, less than Little Village. Still, the distribution among causes is familiar: 41 percent due to illness, 52 percent to unemployment, and 25 percent with increased expenses. Among the responses, the consumption and labor impact seem lower than in Little Village: 23 percent reduced consumption and 14 percent increased labor. More or less the same percent, 35, used existing assets. The number for formal finance at 14 percent is higher than in Little Village while the number for informal finance at 28 percent is slightly lower. Thus black households, though reliant on the informal sector, appear to depend more on formal bank finance. Put another way, short falls in formal finance would impact these households more than in little Village.

The Minneapolis–St. Paul survey of Hmong consists as well of an equal numbered control group (67 percent white and 20 percent black). Hmong households are more likely to have a male head, have more dependents, and have less education than in the other neighborhoods. Only 8.7 percent have a college degree. On the other hand, college degrees increase dramatically with the length of U.S. residence, reaching 28 percent for those living in the United States over fifteen years. Hmong households have a median income of $30,000, lower than Chatham households and the control group ($39,000). Fifty-seven percent are wage or salary earners, mostly in manufacturing, like their Little Village counterparts, although 11 percent are unemployed and 6 percent disabled. Even more notable, 8 percent of the Hmong are on some kind of community or government assistance.

Among the Hmong household respondents, 62 percent had experienced a financial setback, comparable to Little Village and higher than in Chatham. (This does fall with tenure in the United States.) Likewise, of those with setbacks, 38 percent had periods of increased expenditure, 34 percent faced unusually low income, and 29 percent faced substantial unemployment. Notable in the Hmong sample, 13 percent had substantial increases in dependents, and this too falls sharply with tenure. The responses of reducing consumption and working harder are, in contrast, lower than in Little Village, comparable to those of Chatham, and much lower than the control group, begging the issue of how this is accomplished. Hmong households are more likely relative to Mexican Little Village households to borrow from banks, 13 percent, which is comparable to Chatham but lower than the control group, and equally likely to use cash and savings, 35 percent, which is lower than the control group. The use of gifts and borrowing from friends and relatives seems comparable to Little Village and not much different from the control group. Notably, this resort to the informal sector does not decline with tenure. If there are networks, they are persistent, unlike those of the Mexicans of Chicago. Again, this should be studied further. On the other hand, government assistance (emergency cash from the county) under adverse shocks stands out at 39 percent but does decline with tenure. It is hard to know how much of this has to do with the political status of the immigrants. Recall, again, that 8 percent are on more permanent government assistance. Thus formal, informal, and government assistance all seem to play a role in mitigating shocks.

To hazard a summary then, there is a financial sector response to adverse shocks in all these communities. Within this the informal sector is playing a non-trivial role. But the orders of magnitude and types of responses associated with networks seem to differ across the neighborhoods. There is a lively network of assistance among Hispanics in Little Village that declines with tenure in the United States. There is a lively network among Hmong households in Minneapolis–St. Paul that does not decline with tenure. Hmong households use informal assistance, banks, and government assistance to successfully mitigate shocks. Chatham residents seemingly also achieve a low adverse consumption response, but seem relatively more reliant on the formal sector. It must be remembered, however, that the household sample does not allow much stratification by other salient demographic characteristics, which may be helping to determine risk and response.

Small Businesses Finance

One source of variation on the business side is the type of business being run. In a pooled, Chatham–Little Village sample, only 5.3 percent of the businesses are in the manufacturing and wholesale category. For all ethnic groups combined, the bulk of the firms fall into some form of retail or service sector. But black owners are relatively concentrated in the service sector. Manufacturing firms are more common for white owners than for other groups, and Asians have a marked concentration in other retail. Hispanic firms are relatively balanced across industry types, with no single category containing more than 25 percent of the total (although total retail accounts for 68.9 percent of Hispanic businesses). The Hmong business sample differs in having fewer in retail and most in services. The Minneapolis–St. Paul survey did allow professional trades, and 20 percent of the Hmong had them. This is strikingly high relative to the counterpart control group.

For the most part, businessmen are more educated and speak English better than their neighborhood household counterparts. This may be an occupation, selection effect typically studied in the empirical literature. Still, the demographic characteristics of businesses move as one moves across neighborhoods similar to the way household characteristics do. As foreshadowed, an exception to this are the Hmong running business in the Minneapolis–St. Paul sample, in differing radically from their household counterparts.

In the pooled Little Village and Chatham sample, the average age of the business for all groups is about nine years, and firms owned by blacks (thirteen years) and whites (sixteen years) tend to be older than the firms in the remaining groups. Hmong businesses are notably younger (four years), also relative to the counterpart control group. Most firms in the pooled sample employ relatively few workers; the average is 4.5 employees for businesses in all groups. White-owned firms and, to a lesser extent, black-owned firms tend to employ more workers on average (9.2 and 5.1) than firms in the other groups, but even those numbers pale in comparison to the average 10.4 workers in the Hmong business sample and 19.8 in the associated white business control group. Again, this would suggest that the Minneapolis–St. Paul sample of businesses may be biased toward larger, more formal business, something to bear in mind in the discussion that follows.

The average age of the firm owner for all groups in the pooled Chicago sample is about forty-seven years, with black and white owners again tending to be a bit older than owners in the remaining groups. The Hmong at thirty-six are again younger (and younger relative to the corresponding control group). About one-third of all owners in the pooled sample are women. These are Hispanic and especially blacks. In contrast, 92 percent of Hmong owners are male. The majority of business owners are married, 72 percent overall; black proprietors are somewhat less likely to be married and Hmong proprietors more likely, at 91 percent.

Most business owners in the pooled sample are at least high school graduates, and about one-third have a college degree. However, educational attainment varies across racial-ethnic groups. The proportion of Hispanics in the pooled sample that do not have a high school diploma (42.5 percent) is more than twice as high as the proportion for blacks (18.1 percent), the group with the next highest figure. Likewise, Hispanic owners are the least likely to have a college degree (only 18.1 percent have a degree), followed by black owners (34.9 percent). Hmong business owners are the most educated, with 45 percent having at least a college degree.

Hispanic owners (71.2 percent) are moderately or extremely proficient in English, less than the Koreans (89.7 percent), in turn lower than Hmong (98 percent). Finally, an appreciable proportion of the entrepreneurs owned a business previously, ranging from 25.7 percent for blacks, 32 percent for Hmong, and up to 51.0 percent for the Koreans.

An important result from research into the pooled Chatham and Little Village sample is that Hispanic and especially black-owned firms have lower levels of total start-up financing than firms owned by individuals in the other racial-ethnic groups. This all the more striking when one recalls that Chatham is a higher income neighborhood than Little Village. The means of start-up funding are much higher than the medians, indicating that a few businesses with large amounts of start-up funding are pulling the mean away from the median. We avoid this problem by recognizing that start-up funding follows an approximately log normal distribution. Comparing the means of logged start-up funds converted to dollars, we see that the average start-up funding for our sample was fairly modest at $14,737. Further, and much to the point, the amount of start-up funds varies widely by ethnic group. Hispanics ($13,164) and African Americans ($10,812) start their businesses with lower amounts of funds on average than the remaining groups, and Hispanics are higher than blacks. In contrast, the median start-up funding in the Federal Reserve Bank of Minneapolis–Federal Reserve Bank of Chicago study was approximately three times larger at $35,000 for the Hmong, and a larger $55,000 for a white control group. So there seems to be an ethnic effect, but levels seem exceptionally high relative to the Chicago data.

The level of start-up funding for firms in the pooled Little Village–Chatham sample that started their business from scratch is only $10,743, compared with $27,340 for firms that were bought or acquired. This gap holds for each of the ethnic groups. Black owners again start their businesses with about 25 percent less funding than Hispanic owners. In the FRB Minneapolis-Chicago study, the numbers are approximately doubled but come with a slight ethnic gap: from scratch at $21,540 for the Hmong and $22,814 for the control group (bought or acquired at $108,529 and $119,752, respectively).

Again factors beyond ethnicity may affect the level of start-up funding. For example, a grocery store with a requirement for an extensive stock of inventory on the shelves will likely require more start-up funding than a firm that provides a service largely based on the human capital embodied in the owner and key employees. Here we can report on efforts to control for some differences in demographics, human capital, and industry type, to see what ethnic differences emerge.

To account for systematic differences in the required levels of start-up costs across industries, we used a number of industry indicator variables, ranging from manufacturing and wholesaling to business and personal services, in a regression analysis. The ease with which business assets acquired at start-up may be used for collateral may also vary by industry type. Human capital differences might also account for differences in start-up funding. We would expect that more qualified entrepreneurs, all else being equal, would be able to attract more funding. The personal wealth available to entrepreneurs to start a business would also depend, in part, on their human capital. The variables we used to account for this human capital include education, English proficiency, previous experience owning a business, and age at start-up. We included a variable that measures how long ago the owner started the business to account for the possibility that there has been a shift over time in the level of start-up costs. Indicator variables for ethnicity and gender capture differences not due to the industry and human capital variables.

To illustrate the economic effect of regression coefficients in the pooled Chatham–Little Village sample, we calculated estimated levels of start-up funding for each ethnic group using the following baseline characteristics: eating-drinking place, high school education, proficient in English, no previous experience as an owner, thirty-seven years old, male, and business started twelve years ago. The estimated start-up cost for a Hispanic owner with these baseline characteristics is $20,414. For owners in the other groups, the estimated costs are: $11,104 for blacks, $54, 564 for whites, $26,921 for Asians, and $30,479 for others. Thus, a black owner with the baseline characteristics starts a business with an estimated 46 percent smaller pool of funds than a comparable Hispanic. The differential has actually increased. Likewise, a white owner with the baseline characteristics starts with 167 percent more funding than a comparable Hispanic. On the other hand, in the Minneapolis–St. Paul study controlling for industry and demographic characteristics seems to eliminate the difference in start-up costs of the Hmong relative to the white control group. Again, as in the household sample, the Hmong appear to be escaping adverse impacts.

Start-up capital appears to be positively correlated with profit levels, controlling for other characteristics. These findings are supported by regressing profit levels on start-up costs and racial dummy variables, though limited at present to the Little Village sample. An interesting feature is that although nonresident Hispanics report start-up costs similar to those of resident Hispanics, their profits are actually higher than those of Koreans, despite the latter having much higher start-up inputs. Hence, when profitability is considered, Koreans appear to fall back and nonresident Hispanics to move ahead. Recall that the latter group seems less reliant on informal networks, and so again we might say there is a positive correlation in the Hispanic sample between networks and adverse effects. However, dropping the ethnic dummy variables has almost no effect on the results, scarcely surprising given the huge confidence intervals associated with them. Using a profits measure that excludes the owner's salary reduces the estimate of the coefficient on start-up costs by about 0.1, but otherwise has little effect. The main finding of the regression is that each extra dollar invested in the business increases annual profits by $0.70, strong evidence that higher start-up costs are better.

The survey allows the calculation of the proportion of funding from each source for every owner in the sample. Personal savings, on average, are the most important source of funding, 64 percent of the total for all enterprises in the pooled Chicago sample and 60 percent among the Hmong. There are marked ethnic differences in the proportional use of personal savings, with Hispanic, black, Korean, and Hmong owners tending to depend more on personal savings than white and control group owners. Highlighting the importance of personal savings, 55 percent of black owners, 51 percent of Hispanic, and 45 percent of Korean in the sample started their businesses using only personal savings. By comparison, only 19 percent of white owners did. Self-finance via savings could be taken as a priori evidence of constraints, in which case the ordering is consistent with other patterns (that is, more constrained, talented households save more before entering business). Black owners are most constrained, Hispanics second most, then Koreans and Hmong, and finally the white and control group owners.

Formal financing from banks and other formal lenders, at 10.5 percent, is less important for all firms, on average, than personal finance. The ordering appears similar. For Hispanics, for example, only 11 percent (7.2 percent of start-up funding) report using any formal finance. In contrast, a relatively high proportion of white owners (35 percent) use formal financing. The Hmong are the exception, with 25 percent (50 percent of start-up funding) getting formal finance. There may be selection effects at work. Recall also that whites are more likely to enter manufacturing and larger businesses.

Informal financing is more typically the second most important source of funding, at 18.9 percent for all firms in the two Chicago neighborhoods, and this gives us a look at possible network effects. For example, Koreans obtain more funds from relatives outside the immediate family and from friends and business associates than Hispanics do, that is, less from immediate family. It seems likely that Koreans have more personal savings and more connections to other Koreans with greater funds to lend. As evidence, we offer the finding that Koreans talk to a "wider" network of people before starting a business than other groups do. For Koreans, networks are not synonymous with family. There is something more going on. One factor may be greater availability of funds in the Korean community.

Turning the focus to black versus Hispanic differences, black owners begin their businesses with a somewhat higher proportion of start-up funding from personal resources (69.6 percent) than Hispanics (66.0 percent). Black-owned businesses also begin with a lower proportion of start-up funding from informal sources (14.9 percent) than Hispanic-owned (19.0 percent). Black owners start their businesses with a lower proportion of funding from other sources (3.5 percent) than Hispanic owners do (7.4 percent). However, the average proportion of formal funding for black-owned businesses (12.1 percent) is higher than that of Hispanic-owned (7.2 percent). It thus seems that blacks rely more on personal savings and the formal sector relative to Hispanics, and blacks rely less on ethnic networks. This is a salient finding.

Ethnic differences in the level of start-up funding could be the result of differences in personal wealth, or due to some groups facing greater funding constraints than others. But it seems doubtful that Hispanics of Little Village have more personal wealth than blacks in Chatham for a given level of human capital. Recall that blacks do have higher income on average (though they may have higher debt). In any event, some doubt is cast on the hypothesis that wealth differences explain our central finding that black owners begin their businesses with less start-up funding than Hispanic owners for a given level of human capital. It seems at least as likely that the shortfall might be attributed to lack of an ethnic network. The Hmong, though relatively well financed from banks, do seem to be helped by a network effect. Hmong rely more on informal sources than the control sample does.

Of course attitudes toward risk may also vary across the neighborhoods. Mexicans relative to African Americans and Koreans appear more willing to risk windfall gains in current or new businesses. There is no evidence in our surveys here of discrimination in lending.

Ethnicity, Geographic Proximity, and Trade Credit

The neighborhood surveys contain information for up to three suppliers for each business owner. Trade credit is available to many of the businesses in the Little Village and Chatham surveys, as 49.7 percent of the firms report at least a credit offer. Hispanics (32.9 percent) and black firms (30.8 percent) are about equally likely to work with a supplier of the same ethnicity. The questionnaire further elicits information on the supplier's geographic location. We found that a Hispanic-owned business working with Hispanic suppliers is significantly more likely to receive an offer of trade credit than other Hispanic-owned firms. The data show no statistically significant corresponding relationship for black-owned firms working with black suppliers. Indeed, black-owned firms dealing with a neighborhood supplier rather than one outside the MSA suffer a reduced probability of being offered trade credit by between 15 to 27 percent, statistically significant and robust against a battery of industry and socioeconomic controls. The opposite relationship is observed for Hispanic-owned businesses, as dealing with a supplier closer to home increases the likelihood of trade credit offers, between 26 and 35 percent more likely relative to having the supplier located outside the MSA, and there an additional positive effect for a supplier in the neighborhood itself. These results suggest that Hispanics benefit from some kind of ethnic and geographically concentrated business network, as was evident on the household side, while African Americans either suffer from fragmented communities or perhaps have network-like associations outside their own ethnic group. Given the shortfall in black finance it might seem the former is a plausible story.

One wonders of course if these neighborhood specialty results are representative of U.S. cities more generally. Again, the neighborhood studies suffer from various kinds of bias. Data from the National Survey of Small Business Finances shed some light on this issue. The presence of other Hispanic businesses in an MSA with more Hispanic-owned businesses is associated with an increased frequency of cash discount offers and usage and a reduction in the likelihood of being rejected for trade credit. For example, the difference for use of cash discounts would disappear if we compare a Hispanic-owned firm in a city with no other Hispanics versus an MSA with 10 percent Hispanic business base. For black-owned firms, as in the case of the neighborhood studies, only one trade credit measure suggests a benefit from concentration with other black-owned businesses, and for two other measures there is an apparent adverse effect.

References

Aaronson, Daniel, Raphael Bostic, Paul Huck, and Robert M. Townsend. 2000. "Supplier relationships and small business use of trade credit." Working Paper Series WP-00-28, Federal Reserve Bank of Chicago.

Ahlin, Christian, and Robert M. Townsend. 2002. "Determinants of the Prevalence of Cooperative Borrowing." Unpublished paper. Chicago: University of Chicago.

Becker, Gary. 1973. "A Theory of Marriage, Part I." *Journal of Political Economy* 81(4): 813–46.

Besley, Timothy, Stephen Coate, and Glenn Loury. 1993. "The Economics of Rotating Savings and Credit Associations." *American Economic Review* 83(4): 792–810.

——. 1994. "Rotating Savings and Credit Associations, Credit Markets and Efficiency." *Review of Economic Studies* 61(4): 701–19.

Bond, Philip. 1999. "Joint Liability and the Structure of Financial Intermediaries." Unpublished paper.

Bond, Philip, and Robert M. Townsend. 1996. "Formal and Informal Financing in a Chicago Ethnic Neighborhood." *Economic Perspectives (Q 3).* Chicago: Federal Reserve Bank of Chicago.

Chicago Fact Book Consortium. 1995. *Local Community Fact Book— Chicago Metropolitan Area 1990.* Chicago: Academy Chicago Publishers.

Diamond, Douglas. 1984. "Financial Intermediation and Delegated Monitoring." *Review of Economic Studies* 51(3): 393–414.

Ghatak, Maitreesh. 1999. "Group Lending, Local Information and Peer Selection." *Journal of Development Economics* 60(1): 27–50.

Holmstrom, Bengt, and Paul Milgrom. 1990. "Regulating Trade Among Agents." *Journal of Institutional and Theoretical Economics* 146(1): 85–105.

Huck, Paul, Sherrie L.W. Rhine, Philip Bond, and Robert M. Townsend. 1999. "Small Business Finance in Two Chicago Minority Neighborhoods." *Economic Perspectives (Q 2)* 23(2): 46.

Itoh, Hideshi. 1993. "Coalitions, Incentives, and Risk-Sharing." *Journal of Economic Theory* 60(2): 410–27.

Krasa, Stefan, and Anne P. Villamil. 1992. "A Theory of Optimal Bank Size." *Oxford Economic Papers* 44(4): 725–49.

Paulson, Anna. 2003. "The Financial Assimilation of Immigrants: Evidence from the Hmong Community in Minneapolis–St. Paul." Unpublished manuscript.

Prescott, Edward S., and Robert M. Townsend. 2002a. "Collective Organizations Versus Relative Performance Contracts: Inequality, Risk Sharing, and Moral Hazard," *Journal of Economic Theory* 103: 282–310.

——. 2002b. "Firms as Clubs in Walrasian Markets." Manuscript. Chicago: University of Chicago.

Raijman, Rebecca, and Marta Tienda. 2000. "Immigrants' Pathways to Business Ownership: A Comparative Ethnic Perspective." *IMR: International Migration Review* 34(3): 682–706.

Toussaint-Comeau, Maude. 2000. "Immigrant Small Business Formation, Financing and Networks: An Analysis of Hmong Businesses in Minneapolis–St. Paul." Unpublished paper.

Toussaint-Comeau, Maude, and Sherrie L.W. Rhine. 2000. "Access to Financial Credit and Services among Black Households." *Consumer Issues Research Series.* Chicago: Federal Reserve Bank of Chicago.

Toussaint-Comeau, Maude, Art Rolnick, Robin Newberger, Jason Schmidt, and Ron Feldman. 2003. "Credit Availability in the Minneapolis–St. Paul Hmong Community." Paper presented to the Federal Reserve System Research Conference, Sustainable Community Development: What Works, What Doesn't, and Why. Washington, D.C. (April).

Varian, Hal R. 1990. "Monitoring Agents with Other Agents," *Journal of Institutional and Theoretical Economics* 146: 153–75.

Woodstock Institute. 1992. *The 1992 Community Lending Fact Book.* Chicago: Woodstock Institute.

Chapter 8

Microcredit Repayment Insurance: Better for the Poor, Better for the Institution

Loïc Sadoulet

The "microcredit revolution" of the past twenty years has led to a shift of the image that many had of the poor. While previously they were seen as unproductive individuals who could only be helped through welfare programs and subsidies, microcredit programs have demonstrated that the poor can become economically viable actors in the economy. Repayment rates for well-managed programs are typically above 95 percent (Morduch 2000), and "commercially minded" programs tend to achieve operational self-sufficiency after two to three years, even when servicing a very poor clientele (for example, SafeSave in Dhaka slums, Génesis Empresarial in Guatemalan highlands). Consequently, microcredit initiatives have expanded at an exponential rate: twenty years after the birth of the Grameen Bank, the World Bank estimates that there are over seven thousand programs in more than sixty countries, serving more than fourteen million borrowers with US$7 billion in outstanding loans.[1]

However, as successful as microcredit programs have been in less developed countries (LDCs), the results to date in *developed* countries are far from being uniformly positive. Many institutions have failed, most are struggling to control costs, and only a few have managed to generate profits. For example, Calmeadow—an NGO focused on providing affordable financial services to low income self-employed individuals in Vancouver, Toronto, and Nova Scotia—abandoned its lending activity in 2000 because of lack of commercial viability. Similarly, the Good Faith Fund, a Grameen replica set up in rural

Arkansas by then Governor Bill Clinton, was forced to eliminate their lending program after repayment rates fell to a dismal 48 percent after two years of operation (Taub 1998). Even ACCION—an organization with a long and successful experience in setting up microcredit programs in Latin America (including the famous BancoSol in Bolivia)—is not managing to cover costs in their programs in the United States.

Why have programs struggled in developed countries? Based on an extensive review of experiences in developed countries, Emanuele Massetti and Loïc Sadoulet (2003) identify four factors that affect the success of programs: product design and methodology, efficient processing and delivery infrastructure, a sufficient range of product and services to generate sufficient revenues, and institutional credibility. In most failed attempts, the institutions have fallen short on at least one of those dimensions. Poorly designed financial contracts lead to little uptake, or to short-term opportunistic behavior from participants. Reaching poor clients entails extremely high fixed costs, due to the extensive network of branches that needs to be set up to service clients ("local banking"), and to the evaluation and processing costs of loans of very small amounts. Furthermore, financial institutions that do not fall under national banking regulations—as is the case for most NGOs that start microcredit programs—are forbidden to provide savings or insurance products, thus limiting the revenue-generating opportunities for institutions. Last, the perception of microcredit programs as public assistance or charitable endeavors undermines borrowers' incentives to repay: why repay if one can get away with not repaying, or if the institution is going to disappear anyway? Institutional credibility is thus a crucial factor to induce repayment.

The question then is to determine what type of institution could satisfy those four crucial factors. In Massetti and Sadoulet (2003), we suggest that commercial banks, with an appropriate microfinance methodology, could reach the microenterprise sector profitably. The costs of processing and delivering financial services are lowered by their existing extensive network of branches and ATMs and their financially trained staff. Furthermore, commercial banks can offer a range of loan, savings, and—in countries that permit it—insurance products. And, last, commercial banks would not suffer from a "welfare program" image (as long as the microfinance products are clearly represented as a commercial venture and not as philanthropy), which would help the issue of institutional credibility.

Here we return to the first factor—the issue of product design. For commercial banks to be successful in microfinance, they need to provide financial products that serve the demands of the target market. And for this, we can learn from the experience of programs in developing countries. The high rates of exclusion and client dropout in microfinance institutions (MFIs) have been linked to the reluctance of individuals to incur debt to avoid exposing their assets to foreclosure risk (Meyer 2002; Wright 2001). Indeed, in most microfinance programs, borrowers are obligated to borrow continually if they are to remain in the program, whether they need it or not. Furthermore, the vulnerability of personal account balances to seizures from banks to compensate for delinquent loan accounts has also contributed to nonparticipation in the formal banking sector (Réseau de Financement Alternatif 2002). We thus propose an important complementary product to micro-loans that would reduce the vulnerability of borrowers' assets to credit risk while increasing repayment rates to lending institutions: repayment insurance. The contract is very simple: borrowers build a credit record according to their past repayment behavior. Those with good credit records can use their good past behavior to insure themselves in case they cannot repay. The cost is a higher premium and a downgrading of their credit record, but it remains better than losing access to future loans. Individuals with bad credit records do not qualify for insurance. Our point here is to demonstrate that there is high demand for repayment insurance, that the provision of repayment insurance requires no additional information from lending institutions, and to provide simple guidelines to price and manage insurance contracts to minimize the problems of adverse selection and moral hazard. Our goal is to develop the contractual conditions that allow these contracts to be sustainable for the institution and for the borrowers.

What is Microfinance?

Financial markets are typically characterized by important informational asymmetries between lenders and borrowers. Lenders have difficulties assessing the true riskiness of loans they extend and must thus rely on average-pricing approaches and collateral requirements to limit adverse selection and moral hazard behavior. The pledge of assets that can be seized in case of default discourages excessive risk taking and induces borrowers to repay their loans to the best of their ability. However, a consequence of this practice is that the poor— because of their lack of collateral assets—have traditionally been excluded from formal sector loans.

Microfinance capitalizes on this limited access to credit to create repayment incentives despite poor entrepreneurs' lack of collateral. The fundamental principle is to offer borrowers a sequence of un-collateralized inexpensive loans (as compared to borrowers' alternative sources of credit, typically local money lenders) to which they maintain access as long as they repay; any default, however, is punished by the loss of future access to these loans. The incentive for borrowers to repay comes not from the fear of losing collateral in case of default, but from their desire to maintain access to these future (bigger) loans. The lack of collateral favors outreach;[2] the access to future loans creates incentives to repay for those who value future loans.[3]

Microfinance loans have been extended in two types of contracts: individual loans, in which borrowers are individually responsible for their debt; and group loans, in which loans are given to a group and each member of the group is liable for the entirety of the group loan: if *any* part of a group loan is not repaid, *all* members of that group are considered in default and are punished by the lending institution. Group lending has, by far, been the most frequent approach.

Joint liability has often been presented as the crux behind the success of microcredit programs. By making borrowers' access to future loans depend on their partners' repayment behaviors through joint liability, financial institutions—the story goes—harness local information and enforcement mechanisms to reduce adverse selection and moral hazard behavior. Joint liability would induce borrowers to screen out bad risks in their groups (Stiglitz 1990; Wydick 1995), pressure each other to repay (Armendáriz 1999), or threaten to punish moral-hazard behavior with social sanctions (Besley and Coate 1995) for fear of losing access to future loans.

However, these theories cannot explain why some programs prosper with individual lending contracts (as is the case of Caja de los Andes in Bolivia), while others fail miserably in close-knit societies such as villages in the Ivory Coast or Venezuela (Accion International 1999). Joint liability is not what creates repayment incentives.[4]

This is not to say that joint liability may not have other important roles, such as reducing loan processing and collection costs (Meyer 2002), facilitating the detection of groups of bad borrowers (Wydick 1995), or preventing a "market for lemons" problem in which all safe borrowers would drop out of the market due to the presence of risky borrowers, by concentrating the cost of risky borrowers on the groups with risky members rather than on the borrower population as a whole (Ghatak 1999).

Another important role of joint liability—and the one that practitioners have long focused on—is the "mutual help" aspect of group lending. Jointly liable borrowers may come together and repay each other's loans in case of trouble. As reported on the Grameen Trust's website, "the Group Model's basic philosophy lies in the fact that shortcomings and weaknesses at the individual level are overcome by the collective responsibility and security afforded by the formation of a group of such individuals" (n.p.).[5]

But why join a credit group to get this help? Sadoulet (1999) argues that joint liability allows borrowers to set up credible informal insurance agreements in environments in which individuals have limited access to outside sanctions. One major risk in insurance arrangements is for the insurer to renege on the insurance promise. By denying access to future loans to *all* group members of a defaulting group, joint liability helps make insurance promises credible within credit groups: if a partner does not fulfill an insurance promise ex post, the partner too will lose access to future loans. The financial institution, despite being uninformed about behavior within the credit groups, thus provides a sanctioning mechanism to punish borrowers who do not conform to the insurance arrangement.[6]

However, joint liability, by imposing the responsibility of repayment on the credit group, imposes part of the credit risk to the credit group. Transferring part of this credit risk back to the financial institutions could have important welfare and efficiency benefits. Furthermore, repayment insurance is a potentially important complementary financial product to MFIs' lending activities. Insurance allows MFIs to retain their more experienced clients and improve outreach. This is particularly important given the important dropout rates that MFIs are facing after the few first loan cycles.[7]

Repayment insurance is thus good for the borrowers and good for the institution. Our objective is to demonstrate how MFIs can use the observable data they have on borrowers (repayment outcomes) to design an insurance contract that is actuarially fair, and limits adverse selection and moral hazard to any predetermined acceptable level. Note that the contract we propose is not set up as an "optimal contract"—a nonlinear contract based on the whole credit history cannot do worse than the contract we propose (see, for example, Townsend 1982). However, it is a simple and implementable contract, which improves the financial services currently offered.[8]

Repayment Risk Is a Big Issue for Borrowers

Our interest in exploring insurance mechanisms for the poor stems from three observations. First, the poor are subject—and vulnerable—to substantial risk. Low-income households, due to their higher consumption requirements as a share of their incomes and to their limited capacity to buffer the effects of shocks because of low asset holdings, find themselves at risk of falling below binding subsistence-level consumption constraints whenever there are changes in income or consumption needs (Rosenzweig and Binswanger 1993). Second, to make up for income shortfalls, the poor engage in risk-mitigation strategies which often induce a reduction in future income-generation capacity. Households diminish exposure to risk by choosing less variable activities at the expense of more profitable ones (Reardon et al. 1994), or by remedying the lack of income through (often disadvantageous) changes in asset position and resources (Alderman and Paxson 1994; Dercon 2000).[9] This leads the poor to suffer severe and often long-term consequences of even temporary downturns. Third, while informal risk-sharing mechanisms exist,[10] they are insufficient as households—particularly poor households—remain subjected to considerable uninsured risk (Jalan and Ravallion 1999; Paxson 1993; Townsend 1994). Microcredit, by imposing another immutable claim on resources, actually heightens this vulnerability.

How important is it for borrowers to mitigate this risk? Evidence from a microfinance program in Guatemala suggest that the insurance needs are frequent and for significant amounts of money. In a 1995 survey, we interviewed the 782 members of 210 credit groups that were clients of Génesis Empresarial, a Guatemalan nongovernmental organization providing short-term loans for working capital (table 8.1 provides descriptive statistics). Borrowers were small informal market sellers, very typical of the vendors found in markets in low and middle-income countries, characterized by low sales ($400 to $500 in good weeks) and variable sales (sales in a bad weeks were around 40 percent lower than good weeks on average). They kept low stocks of merchandise and had a high rate of capital turnover (as demonstrated by nearly half the sample buying merchandise more frequently than two to three times a week). Their activity was confined to only one business, and this was the only source of income for 40 percent of the households. Prior to Génesis, their access to credit was limited: only 4 percent of the sample had access to formal banks. The main credit sources were money lenders and wholesale credit, although these tended to charge very high interest rates (15 to 25 percent over the loan). Family and friends were also possible sources of credit, but for small and short-term amounts.

Borrowers were offered a *choice* of two types of loans from Génesis: individual or group. Both carried the same monthly interest rate (2.5 percent, as is the case for consumer loans from the formal banking sector in 1995).[11] They were for the same term and purpose: two-month loans for working capital, with regular payment schedules (weekly, fortnightly, or monthly). The amounts were the same: initial loans were relatively small ($60) but grew rapidly upon successful repayment, typically by 10 to 30 percent from one loan to the next. On average, loans represented around two weeks worth of inventory. In fact, the individual and group contracts were identical in every aspect except for the extra joint liability. And yet, two-thirds of borrowers *chose* group loans.[12] A question thus naturally arose: why would borrowers ever choose group loans? Part of the answer, we want to suggest, stems from insurance that emerges in these credit groups.

As described, Génesis created repayment incentives by making access to future loans conditional on repayment behavior. Génesis uses a "three strikes and you're out rule": one late payment resulted in no increase in loan size; two late payments reduced the loan size;

Table 8.1 Descriptive Statistics

Variables	Mean	Standard Deviation[a]	Minimum[a]	Maximum[a]	Median[a]	5 percent[a]	95 percent[a]	Number Observed
Personal business characteristics								
Average weekly sales in good weeks (in U.S. dollars)	531	770	14	13333	381	112	1203	782
Bad week sales, as a fraction of good week	0.58	0.17	0.03	1.00	0.58	0.29	0.84	782
Buying merchandise daily	0.19	—	—	—	—	—	—	782
Buying two to three times per week	0.29	—	—	—	—	—	—	782
Buying once a week	0.35	—	—	—	—	—	—	782
Only one business	0.79	—	—	—	—	—	—	772
Sole income provider to household	0.40	—	—	—	—	—	—	782
Loan characteristics								
Loan size (in U.S. dollars)	740	555	56	5000	650	167	1700	782
Loan size as percentage of average daily purchases	17	20	1	93	12	2	47	647

Weekly payments	0.30	—	—	—	—	—	—	782
Fortnightly payments	0.32	—	—	—	—	—	—	782
Monthly payments	0.38	—	—	—	—	—	—	782
Payment size (in U.S. dollars)	124	97	5	718	93	29	276	782
Payment as percentage of average daily purchases	2.98	3.40	0.02	27.69	1.92	0.29	8.73	647
Group characteristics								
Group size	3.7	0.94	3	8	3	3	6	210
Groups of three	0.50[b]							105
Groups of four	0.34[b]							72
Groups of five	0.12[b]							26
Groups of six	0.01[b]							3
Groups of seven	0.00[b]							1
Groups of eight	0.01[b]							3

Source: Author's compilation.

[a]Standard deviation, minimum, maximum, median, and 5 percent and 95 percent points are not reported for dummy variables.

[b]As a percentage of total number of groups.

and three late payments within the past twelve months resulted in permanent exclusion from any further loan. Borrowers wanting to maintain access to future loans had to minimize the probability of finding themselves unable to repay. Because payments start after the first week of the loan, a fair share of borrowers (19 percent) put part of the loan aside in order to make the first one or two payments, to reduce the chance of going into default. Nonetheless, a fair share of them still had difficulties making payments. Table 8.2 reports the number of times borrowers declare having to resort to help to make their loan payments. In over 60 percent of groups, at least one member needed help making a payment in the past twelve months. Typically, these shortfalls in income to make the payment arise because of low sales or bad planning (74 percent), or of shocks such as robbery and family illness (23 percent)—shocks that can be classified as idiosyncratic (although not necessarily exogenous).[13]

It ends up that the credit group plays an important role in addressing these income shocks. When borrowers had difficulties making the payment, in 69 percent of the cases help came from someone within the group. Only in 23 percent did the help come from personal resources: either friends or family outside the group, or from personal savings or borrowing from a moneylender. Furthermore, the help required is for nontrivial amounts given that it covers around 20 percent of the payment due by the person who cannot repay.[14]

To summarize, the evidence from the Guatemalan data suggests that credit groups are an important source of insurance for their members. Yet, it is clear that a financial institution is much more capable to absorb credit risk than are small credit groups. Transferring the credit risk from a lending institution to the (certainly more risk-averse) borrowers has efficiency and welfare costs.

Incorporating Insurance in Loan Contracts

One way of transfering credit risk back to lending institutions is by adding insurance clauses to credit contracts based on dynamic incentives.

Dynamic Incentives in Microfinance Contracts

Repayment incentives in microfinance contracts are created by promising future loans to borrowers who repay their current loan. How-

Table 8.2   Insurance Occurences in 210 Credit Groups

	N	Percentage
Insurance need in past year (someone in group has had trouble making own payment in past year)		
None	79	0.38
Once	34	0.16
Two times	26	0.12
Three to four times	35	0.17
More than four times	36	0.17
Total	210[a]	
Reason insurance was needed		
Low sales	155	0.63
Bad planning	30	0.12
Robbery	7	0.03
Family illness	49	0.20
Other	6	0.02
Total	247[b]	
Who provides insurance?		
A member of the group	128	0.52
The whole group	42	0.17
Someone from outside	49	0.20
Self insurance (savings, money-lender)	8	0.03
Resulted in late payment (insurance failed)	20	0.08
Total	247[b]	

	Amount (in Dollars)	As Fraction of Payment[c]
How much?		
Mean	28	0.24
Median	17	0.17
Five percent	5	0.04
Ninety-five percent	88	0.67
Minimum	2	0.01
Maximum	167	1.25

Source: Author's compilation.

[a] A total of 468 times in past year.

[b] The question was only asked for the past two times $(34 + (26 \times 2) + (35 \times 2) + (36 \times 2) = 228$ events) and more than one answer was possible (19 cases) = 247.

[c] As we have only current payment information, and not the payment information at the time insurance was given, these are only approximations.

ever, these dynamic incentives do not ensure that all borrowers will indeed repay. Repayment strategies are governed by borrowers' ability and willingness to repay. When borrowers' projects fail, they may be unable to repay their loans; they thus have no other choice but to default. Moreover, when their projects succeed, they are faced with a choice of actions: they are able to repay, but might not be willing. Willingness to repay has straightforward consequences: if they choose to repay, they maintain access to future loans; if they choose not to, they will be considered in default and excluded from access to any future loans. Willingness to repay thus depends on the value they place on future loans.

The value of future loans is influenced by the size of future loans (that is, the growth rate of loans), but also by a borrower's perspective of future expected returns and alternatives. Unskilled borrowers, for example, may not be willing to repay after a successful project because future projects would in all likelihood fail, so they may prefer to keep the lucky return rather than undertake the cost of maintaining access to future loans. Similarly, a borrower with high fallback options may choose to take greater risks to maximize gains as the losses are less in case of project failure. These borrowers are not desirable borrowers from the standpoint of the financial institution. While the prospect for the institution of screening them out is low due to the limited information, these types of borrowers tend to drop out early, when loan sizes are small.

Furthermore, there is an issue of credibility of the financial institution. In the same way that the financial institution has to be credible on its threat of foreclosure on posted collateral in traditional banking practices, there are two credibility issues for MFIs. First is the credibility of rules—to generate an incentive to repay, borrowers must perceive that defaulters *will* lose access to future loans; it might take a while for young institutions to gain their reputation of being "tough." Second is the credibility of survival—since the incentive to repay emerges from the promise of future loans, borrowers, in making their project/repayment choice, assess the probability of survival of the lending institution. Turbulence in the local microfinance industry, or doubts regarding the continued existence of the lender may generate avalanches of defaults (which are rational, because they are self-fulfilling). In particular, credibility of rules—particularly in light of past failed targeted credit programs that disappeared because of dismal repayment rates—may be particularly important to signal the objective of permanence of MFIs.

However, credibility of rules means that the institution will have to exclude some "good" borrowers when they do not repay, despite the fact that their projects genuinely failed and were not excessively risky. One such example is a case at Génesis involving a group of three borrowers in their seventh year of problem-free borrowing. The death of the mother of two of the members led to the group being unable to repay their loan. The staff at Génesis was faced with a difficult choice: follow the rule and deny any further loans to the group, or refinance the group and risk diluting the repayment incentives for the rest of its portfolio. Excluding the defaulting group was perceived as a waste by the loan officers; these clients had been very good borrowers and accidents do happen occasionally.

This case, and the prevalence of insurance in credit groups discussed in the previous section, raises the question as to whether—and how—the financial institution could improve on current contracts by introducing an insurance contract tied to the loan. We turn to this next.

Adding Repayment Insurance to the Credit Contract

The basic idea of the proposed insurance contract is that, since the institution has no information on the actual outcome of projects in any particular period, insurance will be awarded conditional on a measure of borrowers' reputation. Individual borrowers, through their repayment behavior, build up a credit record. As long as borrowers are in good standing with the financial institution, their insurance claims will be honored, thus protecting them from default.

The timing of the loan and insurance contracts is as depicted in figure 8.1. At the beginning of each loan sequence, borrowers in good standing receive a loan. They choose whether to subscribe to the insurance contract, and pay the according premium out of the loan they just received. They invest the remainder of the money in their project, which succeeds or fails. They then make their repayment decision: repay their loan, file an insurance claim, or default. If the borrower repays or if the insurance claim is accepted, then the borrower remains in good standing and can receive a loan in the next cycle; if not, the borrower is excluded forever.

The financial institution starts with some prior distribution of

Figure 8.1   Timing of Loan and Insurance Contract

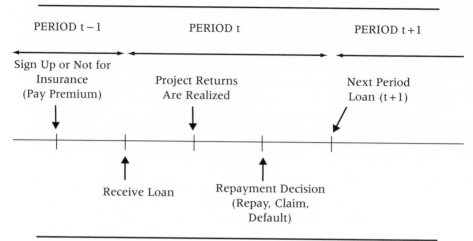

Source: Author's compilation.

borrower risks. Since the institution initially has no information on any particular borrower, all borrowers start at the same reputation, say the mean of the institution's prior on the distribution of types.[15] In order to clarify the discussion below, let us denote this initial reputation by $\mu_i^{[1]}$:

$$\mu_i^{[1]} = E^{[1]}(P_i) = \mu^{[1]}$$

where $E^{[1]}$ denotes the expectation taken by the financial institution at the beginning of the first period (that is, before observing i's repayment outcome after the first loan), and P_i is the probability of success of borrower i's project.[16]

As time passes, the institution updates individual borrower reputations according to observations of repayment. Borrower i's reputation based on her repayment behavior after t loans is thus given by $\mu_i^{[t]}$, which is equal to:

$$\mu_i^{[t]} = E^{[t]}(P_i \mid c_i^{[t]}) \tag{8.1}$$

where $E^{[t]}$ denotes the expectation at the beginning of period t; P_i is the probability of success of borrower i's project; and $c_i^{[t]}$ is the number of claims i has made up to the beginning of loan t.[17] An example is depicted in figure 8.2. Successful repayment of a loan increases i's reputation; an insurance claim decreases her reputation.

Figure 8.2 Evolution of Borrower Reputation

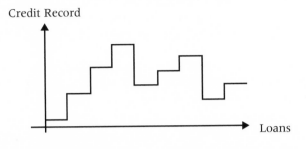

Credit Record

Loans

Source: Author's compilation.

To finance the insurance, the financial institution charges an insurance premium. The premium is payable at the time the loan is disbursed. We constrain the financial institution to charge actuarially fair premiums to each subscriber.[18] The premium $\Psi_I^{[t]}$ for borrower i in time t depends therefore on her reputation $\mu_i^{[t]}$ in time t:

$$\psi_i^{[t]} = (1 - \mu_i^{[t]})L$$

where L is the cost of repaying the loan. From period to period, the premium is updated according to this formula as more information becomes available.

The financial institution has to protect itself from two sources of abuse coming from asymmetric information. The first stems from the undesirable borrowers described in the previous section (excessive risk-takers and strategic defaulters) wanting to sign up for insurance schemes in order to have access to more loans before they get excluded from the credit scheme; the second one from borrowers filing false claims (moral hazard). We examine each in turn.

Excluding Undesirable Borrowers Taking Insurance

Undesirable borrowers are the ones who are excessively risky, either by skill or by choice. In the microcredit contract without insurance, they tend to drop out early since the cost of repaying a loan outweighs the benefit of maintaining access to future loans. However, the new possibility of insurance could allow these borrowers to default more than once before being evicted from the program. Some would thus sign up for the insurance contract to benefit from a second loan on which to default, as long as the insurance premium they have to pay is not too large.

An easy way to avert this adverse selection is for the financial institution to deny insurance coverage to any borrower who does not have a reputation above a certain threshold μ. As long as the threshold is such that it takes sufficient rounds of successful loan repayment to reach it, the institution can weed out some of the borrowers wanting to strategically default on the insurance contract. The longer the waiting period, the fewer the number of borrowers that will undertake the waiting period rather than default immediately. Note that since the contracts are one-period contracts, borrowers have no incentive to sign up to the insurance until they have repaid enough loans to reach the threshold reputation $\mu^{[T]} = \mu$ where $\mu^{[T]}$ denotes the reputation the financial institution ascribes at the beginning of period T to a borrower who repaid all the previous $T - 1$ loans.

The insurance contract must thus provide some incentive mechanism encouraging borrowers to claim insurance only when they need it, and allow the financial institution to deny claims from borrowers it considers opportunistic. The insurance contract will therefore display the following property:

Property 1: Limiting Adverse Selection
To protect itself against adverse selection, the financial institution provides incomplete insurance in the sense that:

- No borrower with reputation below some reputation cutoff $\mu^{[T]}$ is insured;
- There is no insurance in the first round of loans: $\mu^{[T]} > \mu^{[1]}$

The intuition is that, to keep undesirable borrowers from participating, the financial institution must put an entry cost to the insurance contract. This, as demonstrated, can take the form of several preliminary rounds of successful repayment. It can also take the form of a series of discouragingly high premiums, until borrowers establish their reputation as willing repayers.

A waiting period discourages the riskier borrowers, who prefer to strategically default immediately rather than undertake the cost of repaying several loans before qualifying for insurance. However, not all strategic defaulters will be excluded. Sadoulet (2003, proposition

3) demonstrates that to eliminate all strategic defaulters would take an infinite waiting period; yet, while the financial institution cannot eliminate adverse selection completely, it can reduce the cost of adverse selection in the insurance contract so that it is lower than the one in the no-insurance case. The reason is that, in the case of no insurance, a whole segment of borrowers strategically defaulted on their first loan. In the insurance case, either they are discouraged from participation, in which case the cost of the adverse selection coming from these borrowers is the same as in the no-insurance case: they simply default on their first loan. Or they repay $T - 1$ loans before defaulting on two loans in a row, after which they are denied insurance. For T large enough, the present discounted value of losses from strategic default for the institution in the insurance case is smaller than in the no-insurance case, since defaulters repay $T - 1$ loans before defaulting on two.[19]

The waiting period and the premium allow the financial institution to screen some of the bad risks from participating in the insurance contract. The question is whether "good" borrowers would ever choose to participate in the insurance scheme. Ignoring fraudulent claims for an instant, if the financial institution had perfect information on borrower risks, an actuarially fair insurance contract would be priced such that the premium is exactly the expected cost of insurance, namely:

$$\mu_i^{[T]} = (1 - P_i)L$$

where P_i is the probability of success of borrower i's project. The benefit of insurance for borrowers is to ensure access to future loans. Denote by Z_i the discounted expected value of future loans, by ER_i the expected return of the current project, and by V_i the value of the fallback option for borrower i. If borrower i decides not to take insurance in the current period, the expected return is:

$$ER_i + P_i(-L + Z_i) + (1 - P_i)V_i \qquad (8.2)$$

that is, the expected return of the project and, when successful, the cost of repayment plus the expected benefit of access to future loans. If the project fails, borrower i is pushed to the fallback option. However, if borrower i subscribes to the actuarially fair insurance contract, the expected return becomes:

$$-(1 - P_i)L + ER_i + P_i(-L) + Z_i \qquad (8.3)$$

that is, the actuarially fair premium is paid, and then the borrower gets the expected return minus the cost of loan repayment when successful, plus the expected value of future loans with certainty. Clearly, as long as the cost of repaying the loan (L) is less than the extra value future loans have over the fallback option $(Z_i - V_i)$, then borrower i will sign up:

$$\text{equation } (8.2) < \text{equation } (8.3) \Leftrightarrow L < (Z_i - V_i)$$

However, the institution does not have perfect information on types. Nonetheless, as long as the financial institution's assessment of a borrower risk is close enough to the actual risk, the borrower will participate. By virtue of the fact that borrowers must have been successful in *all* periods before signing up for insurance for the first time, the premium that borrowers face before signing up for the first time is decreasing over time and tends to zero; the reputation of successful borrowers increases over time. The premium will eventually become low enough that any borrower who values future loans over the fallback will sign up.

The cost of the waiting period is that some "good risks" that the financial institution would have liked to insure may end up failing before being insured. But that is the cost of the asymmetric information. The benefit of this insurance scheme is that at least some of the "good risks" do end up getting insurance eventually. We now turn to the second source of abuse: fraudulent claims.

Deterring Fraudulent Claims

Because the financial institution has very little information on borrowers in the early rounds of the loans, the gains and losses in reputation for borrowers are greatest in those rounds. Each repayment or insurance claim represents a large proportion of the information that the institution has at its disposal to assess individuals.

However, as the number of loan rounds gets large, this difference in reputation from an extra observation shrinks to the point that it becomes negligible. The effectiveness of the drop in reputation as a deterrent for false insurance claims thus diminishes over time. The insurance contract thus has to rely on additional sanctions to deter false insurance claims.

Property 2: Limiting Moral Hazard
To deter fraudulent claims, the institution must impose costs beyond simple updating of reputation after insurance claims.

Figure 8.3 illustrates the problem. It represents borrowers' reputations as a function of the numbers of loans undertaken. The top curve is a borrower's reputation with no defaults; the second is a borrower's reputation after one default; and so on. Any default drops the borrower down one curve.

By filing a false claim, the borrower gains the fact of not repaying the current loan. The costs of filing a claim are twofold: an increase in the future premia due to a loss of reputation, and an increase in the probability of falling below the reputation cutoff after repeated failures (that is, the borrower drops down by one curve in figure 8.3, bringing her closer to the reputation cutoff below which she is denied insurance). However, after enough loan repetitions, these two changes become infinitesimal since the effect of an added claim on a borrower's reputation is negligible (right-hand side of figure 8.3), that is:

$$\lim_{t \to \infty} \frac{\partial \mu_i^{[t]}}{\partial c} = 0$$

To discourage false claims, the institution must thus impose an extra cost of claiming insurance beyond simple Bayesian loss of reputation.

In Sadoulet (2003), we derive sufficient sanctions to deter moral hazard. It involves increasing the premium and diminishing the probability of being covered by insurance in the future by more than Bayesian updating. Formally, the sanctioning is equivalent to downgrading a borrower's reputation by reducing her acquired "experience" (by which we mean the number of loans she participated in). For example, a borrower at point A in figure 8.3 might find his reputation and experience downgraded to point B after an insurance claim. Reducing a borrower's reputation by more than dictated by the Bayesian updating rule (8.1) pushes the defaulting borrower

Figure 8.3   Evolution of Borrower Reputation $\mu_i^{[t]}$

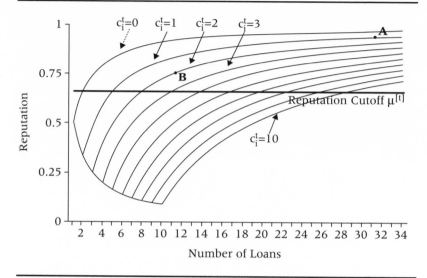

Source: Author's compilation.

closer to the cutoff below which she will be denied insurance; stripping away experience and considering her as a newer borrower than she actually is (that is, using a lower t to calculate updates on her reputation) increases the risk that she will actually reach the cutoff due to repeated failures. Financial institutions can customize these losses in reputation and in experience to achieve exactly the punishment they intend to deter false claims. The resulting borrower reputations in the insurance contract thus follow something resembling the case depicted in figure 8.4. It takes time to reach the minimum reputation to qualify for insurance. Any claim is sanctioned by an update in the reputation, which is larger than what would follow under simple Bayesian updating.

The idea of imposing large negative reputation effects upon insurance claims, forcing individuals to reengage in the slow process of rebuilding a reputation, is an idea that is present in other contracts. Automobile insurance contracts typically function in a similar way. New drivers sign up for insurance at a very high premium, corresponding to the average risk of a broad category of new drivers. If a driver were to have an accident early, most insurance companies

Figure 8.4 Evolution of Reputation in Proposed Contract

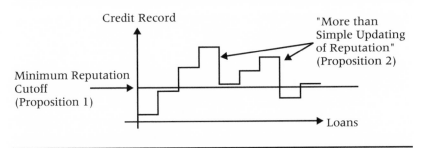

Source: Author's compilation.

would refuse to renew the driver's policy. Over time, responsible driving is met with decreasing premia and increased coverage. However, to discourage moral hazard behavior on the part of experienced drivers, insurance claims are followed by high increases in premia (and deductible) that take several years of faultless records to erase. Similarly, credit-rating ratings for consumers function in similar manner: past behavior becomes the most highly weighted factor in credit-scoring model. A bad credit experience inordinately lowers credit records, which then take a long time to reestablish.[20]

Conclusion

As documented, borrowers are vulnerable to repayment risk. Insurance is thus an important byproduct of group-lending contracts. However, by the virtue of transferring risk to groups of borrowers less able to absorb it than the lending institution, these contracts entail an important loss in efficiency.

We illustrate here a simple credit-with-insurance contract that financial institutions could implement in environments in which insurance mechanisms are incomplete. It is based on the main incentive mechanism in microlending contracts, namely the repetition of loans: borrowers repay to maintain access to future (bigger) loans. The contract we propose uses this repetition to allow borrowers to build reputations. These reputations can then be used by borrowers in good standing to insure themselves when they are unable to repay. The lending institution limits adverse selection by not insuring borrowers below a certain reputation cutoff. False claims and excessive risk taking are discouraged by imposing large reductions in reputation and "experience" (the number of loans used to calculate updates in reputation) after claims.

This contract is simple to implement in that no new information is required. It certainly improves welfare given that building reputation is less costly than building savings. It also transfers credit risk from poor individuals to a better diversified and less risk-adverse institution and allows the institution to cover shocks that are beyond the capacity of joint-liability groups to absorb through mutual help arrangements. The insurance contract is also beneficial for the financial institutions, since it is complementary to their lending activity: insurance allows institutions to keep experienced borrowers who suffer unforeseen shocks, whereas defaulting borrowers would have had to have been excluded from further loans under the existing loan rules.

The question is to understand why institutions do not implement such contracts. In one sense, institutions have begun to do so. Warren Brown and Craig Churchill (2000) document explicit insurance contracts in a number of institutions worldwide that are experimenting with life, health, and property insurance. Furthermore, implicit insurance arrangements exist whereby institutions are more flexible on the terms of repayment with older groups. But these rescheduling of loan payments are typically kept under cover to avoid contagion to the rest of the portfolio.

Nevertheless, explicit repayment insurance contracts have three important hurdles to clear. First, in microfinance, as in any other institution offering both loans and insurance, providing repayment insurance can impact institutional credibility. Incentives to repay are weakened when defaults are not followed by a cost. This is particularly true for microfinance institutions because they are often in areas in which public targeted-credit programs have failed due to lax enforcement of rules. Borrowers did not repay their loans as they perceived them as temporary welfare programs. If the current institutions are seen as "soft" on the rules due to insurance, they may—like their predecessors—be faced with waves of default. Second, many of these institutions are preparing for an eventual transition to becoming formal banks in order to increase their access to funds—in particular, to be allowed to accept deposits. Repayment insurance runs the risk of being viewed by regulators as a "creative accounting" way to make the portfolio appear in good standing, and thus derail the process of formalization. Third, institutions offering insurance must be able to cover potential large-scale shocks. Because microfinance institutions operate in relatively small geographical areas, they are not immune to a large fraction of their loan portfolio suffering bad outcomes (such as floods, fire in a market, and earthquakes). While large covariate shocks are easily observable, the ability of the institution to provide insurance is then in question. MFIs must then be able to reinsure these risks, and these markets are often too small (and opaque) to attract the interest of large reinsurance companies.

This suggests a very important direction for policy regarding accounting practices. For institutions to successfully manage loans and insurance, strict accounting rules are needed to separate true instances of insurance from nonperforming loans. As we have seen in recent banking sector crises, even developed countries are far from adhering to the standards advocated by the Basel Accords. Transparency, however, is crucial for institutions to gain credibility: in the eyes of their clients, of their national regulatory agency, as well as with potential reinsurers.

The author was research fellow at ECARES at the Free University of Brussels while working on this chapter. This chapter was prepared for the conference on "Credit Markets for the Poor" held at Princeton University, May 2–3, 2003. Many thanks to the organizers, Patrick Bolton and Howard Rosenthal, to the discussant, Erik Berglöf, and to the participants for interesting comments and discussions. The usual disclaimer applies.

Notes

1. Data reported on the virtual microfinance library website (available at: www.gdrc.org/icm/data/d-snapshot.html [accessed January 28, 2005]). While the statistics commonly reported vary wildly—the Microcredit Summit Campaign report (2000, n.p.), for example, gives much higher numbers of people served by fewer institutions: "as of December 31, 2001, 2,186 microcredit institutions reported reaching 54,904,102 clients"—it is clear that the microcredit sector is of important size.

2. Although there is a debate as what types of poor microcredit actually reaches. In particular, there is increasing evidence that it does not directly help the poorest of the poor (Navajas, Gonzalez-Vega, and Gonzalez 2001).

3. To reinforce these dynamic repayment incentives, loans tend to be small short-term loans with frequent payments (to minimize the benefits of deviation from repayment) and display a sharp growth upon repayment (to increase the benefits from repayment of the current loan; Varian 1990; Jain and Mansuri 2003).

    However, Stuart Rutherford (2000, 51) correctly points out that the term "microfinance" actually usually refers to "microenterprise finance" (loans to start and run small businesses) rather than "microfinance" per se (financial services for the poor). The incentive to repay hinges on the borrower's desire to maintain access to a "microenterprise loan." A recent focus on the substantial dropout rates in microfinance programs has generated a discussion on the need to better adapt financial products to the clients' needs—not only for their business, but also for their personal and life-cycle needs (Meyer 2002; Wright 2001). We will return to this later.

4. These arguments have mainly been based on the assumption that groups were fixed. Once we allow for groups to be endogenously formed, as is the case in practice, the issues of self-selection out of groups with non-aligned goals and of collusion against the lending institution emerge (Sadoulet 1999).

5. Grameen Trust website is available at www.grameen-info.org/mcredit/cmodel.html (accessed January 28, 2005).

6. Note that borrowers in good standing can change credit groups, form new credit groups, or borrow individually at the beginning of any two-month loan cycle (as long as *all* previous loans for which they were responsible—including their partners' in a group loan—are fully repaid). The extortion possibilities are thus relatively limited.

7. MicroSave-Africa, in a study of 13 MFIs in East Africa, find dropout rates ranging from 13 to 60 percent per year. There are in fact now more MFI dropouts in East Africa that there are active clients (Matin and Helms 2000). In a survey in Bangladesh, Timothy Evans et al. (1999) similarly find that 11 percent of the households that they identify as eligible for a microloan from BRAC, a MFI, were in fact former members that had dropped out of the program.

8. The discussion in this paper is based on the technical results derived in complementary paper—"Reputation as Insurance? Extending the Range of Financial Services for the Poor" (Sadoulet 2003)—which contains the formal argumentation.

9. Examples include pulling children out of school (Jacoby and Skoufias 1997), canceling or postponing investments (Morduch 1999), over-exploitation of natural resources (Platteau 2000), diminishing nutritional intake (Dercon and Krishnan 2000), and running down rela-

tionship-based insurance benefits (Goldstein, de Janvry, and Sadoulet 2001).

10. Partially contingent contracts have been documented in the case of quasi-credit contracts in which the repayment conditions of the contract depend on the relative outcome of the contracting parties— Marcel Fafchamps and Susan Lund (2003) report evidence for the Philippines; Franque Grimard (1997) for Côte d'Ivoire; and Christopher Udry (1990) for Nigeria. This is also the case for remittances (Jensen 1998; Lucas and Stark 1985) and informal insurance arrangements (Coate and Ravallion 1993; Morduch 1999).

11. With 11 percent inflation in 1995, this amounts to a real monthly interest rate of 1.65 percent (IMF 1998). Génesis covered all operational expenses with the interest spread between the cost of funds it borrowed from the commercial sector at 16 percent and its on-lending rates of 35 percent.

12. While there is some differential screening in practice, borrowers can opt for an individual loan easily after just a few rounds of group lending. Note that the transactions required to renew a group loan are exactly the same as those required to switch to an individual loan. People in older groups who remain in group loans therefore reveal their preference for those groups over individual loans (behavioral inertia, à la James J. Choi et al. [2001], is an unlikely explanation for persistence in group loans given the coordination costs for members to collect and time repayment).

13. While it is probable that the risk of robbery and family illness varies little from group member to group member, repayment ability being affected by low sales or bad planning is typically the result of borrowers' choices of liquidity strategy. Borrowers who save earlier for the purpose of making the payment encounter fewer problems in case of bad sales the last days before the payment is due. However, this is at a high opportunity cost considering the high turnover of capital (payments represent two to three days of merchandise purchases, with half of the borrowers buying merchandise at least two to three times a week—see table 8.1). The trade-off for borrowers is thus between risk and return.

14. We refer to this "mutual help" as insurance because we have strong anecdotal evidence that suggests that members of groups pay each other risk premia to compensate for differential risks in the credit groups.

15. Recall, borrowers have no assets or other sources of income. They are thus unable to signal their type by any type of investment or bond posting.

16. The square brackets are used to distinguish the notion of "at the beginning of time t" from exponential powers.

17. Note that, since the returns for individuals are independent and identically distributed over time, the order of claims does not matter. More

generally, this could be written as conditional on the history of repayment $h_i^{(t)}$.

18. In fact, the premium is not quite actuarially fair since the institution will punish borrowers by more than a Bayesian loss of reputation in case of insurance claim, as we will see below. The pricing rule we impose is that the institution cannot charge more than the minimum premium that would make the insurance contract incentive compatible.

19. Note that repayment rates always increase if there is one period of waiting, since the repayment rate was zero from these borrowers when no insurance was offered. However, repayment rate, in this case, is not an appropriate measure of performance.

20. In practice, credit rating agencies' policies seem to reflect a belief that a bad credit experience may contain information about a change in the conditions for the borrower (from presentations by Fair-Isaac and Wells Fargo at the World Bank's conference "New Technologies for SME Finance," December 4–6, 2002). Whether financial institutions impose additional disproportionate risk-adjustment costs to borrowers with low ratings as a sanction to discourage moral hazard behavior is difficult to verify.

References

Accion International. 1999. *Annual Report.* Somerville, Mass.: Accion International. Available at: http://www.accion.org/about_annualreports_newsletters.asp (accessed January 27, 2005).

Alderman, Harold, and Christina Paxson. 1994. "Do the Poor Insure? A Synthesis of the Literature on Risk and Consumption in Developing Countries." In *Development, Trade and the Environment,* edited by Edmar L. Bacha. Vol. 4 of *Economics in a Changing World.* London: Macmillan.

Armendáriz de Aghion, Beatriz. 1999. "On the Design of a Credit Agreement with Peer Monitoring," *Journal of Development Economics* 60(1): 79–104.

Besley, Timothy, and Stephen Coate. 1995. "Group Lending, Repayment Incentives and Social Collateral." *Journal of Development Economics* 46(1): 1–18.

Brown, Warren, and Craig Churchill 2000. "Insurance Provision in Low-Income Communities. Part II: Initial Lessons from Micro-Insurance Experiments for the Poor." *Microenterprise Best Practices.* Bethesda, Md.: Development Alternatives, Inc.

Choi, James J., David Laibson, Brigitte C. Madrian, and Andrew Metrick. 2001. "For Better or For Worse: Default Effects and 401(k) Savings Behavior," NBER Working Papers: 8651. Cambridge, Mass.: National Bureau of Economic Research.

Coate, Stephen, and Martin Ravallion. 1993. "Reciprocity Without Commitment: Characterization and Performance of Informal Insurance Arrangements." *Journal of Development Economics* 40(1): 1–24.

Dercon, Stefan. 2000. "Income Risk, Coping Strategies and Safety Nets." Background paper for *World Development Report 2000/01*. Washington, D.C.: The World Bank.

Dercon, Stefan, and Pramila Krishnan. 2000. "In Sickness and Health: Risk Sharing Within Households in Rural Ethiopia," *Journal of Political Economy* 108(4): 688–727.

Evans, Timothy G., Alayne M. Adams, Rafi Mohammed, and Alison H. Norris. 1999. "Demystifying Nonparticipation in Microcredit: A Population-Based Analysis." *World Development* 27(2): 419–30.

Fafchamps, Marcel, and Susan Lund. 2003. "Risk Sharing Networks in Rural Philippines." *Journal of Development Economics* 71(2): 261–87.

Ghatak, Maitreesh. 1999. "Group Lending, Local Information and Peer Selection." *Journal of Development Economics* 60(1): 27–50.

Goldstein, Markus, Alain de Janvry, and Elisabeth Sadoulet 2001. "You Can't Always Get What You Want: Inclusion and Exclusion in Mutual Insurance Networks in Southern Ghana." Working paper. London: London School of Economics.

Grimard, Franque. 1997. "Household Consumption Smoothing through Ethnic Ties: Evidence from Côte D'Ivoire," *Journal of Development Economics* 53(2): 391–422.

International Monetary Fund (IMF). 1998. *International Finance Statistics Yearbook*. Washington, D.C.: IMF.

Jacoby, Hanan G., and Emmanuel Skoufias. 1997. "Risk, Financial Markets, and Human Capital in a Developing Country," *Review of Economic Studies* 64(3): 311–36.

Jain, Sanjay, and Ghazala Mansuri. 2003. "A Little at a Time: The Use of Regularly Scheduled Repayments in Microfinance Programs." *Journal of Development Economics* 72(1): 253–79.

Jalan, Jyotsna, and Martin Ravallion. 1999. "Are the Poor Less Well-Insured? Evidence on Vulnerability to Income Risk in Rural China." *Journal of Development Economics* 58(1): 61–81.

Jensen, Robert T. 1998. "Public transfers, private transfers and the crowding out hypothesis: evidence from South Africa." Working paper. Princeton, N.J.: Princeton University.

Lucas, Robert E. B., and Oded Stark. 1985. "Motivations to Remit: Evidence from Botswana," *Journal of Political Economy* 93(5): 1–18.

Massetti, Emanuele, and Loïc Sadoulet. 2003. "Extending the Revolution': An Analysis of Success and Failures of Microfinance Programs in Developed Countries." Working paper. Free University of Brussels.

Matin, Imran, and Brigit Helms. 2000. "Those Who Leave and Those Who Don't Join: Insights from East African Microfinance Institutions." *CGAP Focus Note* 16(May): entire issue. Washington, D.C.: CGAP.

Meyer, Richard L. 2002. "The Demand for Flexible Microfinance Products:

Lessons from Bangladesh," *Journal of International Development* 14(3): 351–68.

Microcredit Summit Campaign Report. 2000. "Empowering Women with Microcredit." Available at: www.microcreditsummit.org/campaigns/report00.html (accessed January 27, 2005).

Morduch, Jonathan. 1999. "Between the State and the Market: Can Informal Insurance Patch the Safety Net?" *World Bank Research Observer* 14(2): 187–207.

———. 2000. "The Microfinance Schism." *World Development* 28(4): 617–29.

Navajas, Sergio, Carlos Gonzalez-Vega, and Adrián Gonzalez. 2001. "Do Lending Technologies Exclude the Poor? The Case of Rural El Salvador." Working paper. Columbus: Ohio State University.

Paxson, Christina. 1993. "Consumption and Income Seasonality in Thailand," *Journal of Political Economy* 101(1): 39–72.

Platteau, Jean-Philippe. 2000. *Institutions, Social Norms, and Economic Development.* Amsterdam: Harwood Academic Publishers.

Reardon, Thomas, Amadou Abdoulage Fall, Valerie Kelly, Christopher Delgado, Peter Matlon, Jane Hopkins, and Ousmane Badiane. 1994. "Is Income Diversification Agriculture-led in the West African Semi-Arid Tropics? The Nature, Causes, Effects, Distribution and Production of Off-farm Activities." In *Economic Policy Experience in Africa: What Have We Learned?* Nairobi: African Economic Research Consortium.

Réseau de Financement Alternatif. 2002. *Dépêche de Finance Ethique et Solidaire* 6. Namur, Belgium: Réseau de Financement Alternatif.

Rosenzweig, Mark, and Hans Binswanger. 1993. "Wealth, Weather Risk, and the Consumption and Profitability of Agricultural Investments." *Economic Journal* 103: 56–78.

Rutherford, Stuart. 2000. *The Poor and Their Money.* New Delhi: Oxford University Press.

Sadoulet, Loïc. 1999. "The Role of Mutual Insurance in Group Lending." In *Credit for the Poor: An Analysis of Microfinance Contracts with Applications to Guatemala,* by Loïc Sadoulet. Ph.D. Dissertation, Princeton University.

———. 2003. "Reputation as Insurance? Extending the Range of Financial Services for the Poor." Working paper. Free University of Brussels.

Stiglitz, Joseph. 1990. "Peer Monitoring and Credit Markets." *World Bank Economic Review* 4(3): 351–66.

Taub, Richard P. 1998. "Making the Adaptation Across Cultures and Societies: A Report on an Attempt to Clone the Grameen Bank in Southern Arkansas," *Journal of Developmental Entrepreneurship* 3(1): 1–20.

Townsend, Robert M. 1982. "Optimal Multi-Period Contracts and the Gain from Enduring Relationships Under Private Information." *Journal of Political Economy* 90(6): 1166–86.

———. 1994. "Risk and Insurance in Village India." *Econometrica* 62(3): 539–91.

Udry, Christopher. 1990. "Credit Markets in Northern Nigeria: Credit as Insurance in a Rural Economy," *The World Bank Economic Review* 4(3): 251–69.

Varian, Hal R. 1990. "Monitoring Agents with Other Agents." *Zeitschrift für die gesamte Staatswissenschaft* 146(1): 153–74.

Wright, Graham. 2001. "Dropouts and Graduates: Lessons from Bangladesh." *The MicroBanking Bulletin* 6(6): 14–16.

Wydick, W. Bruce. 1995. "Group Lending as a Credit Delivery Mechanism in Guatemala." Working paper. Berkeley, Calif.: University of California.

Chapter 9

Can Microcredit Reduce Poverty? The Effect of the Loan Contract on Loan Size

Malgosia Madajewicz

A major transformation in credit markets for the poor began in the 1970s. Nonprofit, nongovernment organizations (NGOs) began experimenting with models of lending which would allow them to offer business investment loans to poor people on a large scale. Microcredit, as such lending became known, grew rapidly, spreading to almost all developing countries and to low-income neighborhoods in developed countries.[1] The goal was to help small businesses grow and thus to reduce poverty. Microcredit NGOs have been embraced by international development donors, government aid agencies, and foundations as one of the most effective ways of raising the incomes of the poor.

The attention notwithstanding, we still know little about the impact of microcredit on poverty. It does not seem to lift people out of poverty, as was once hoped. Businesses tend to remain small and their owners poor, though some NGOs seem to achieve more than others. A significant obstacle to a better understanding of microcredit is lack of good data. There are a number of program evaluations, but almost all are simple comparisons of incomes of borrowers and nonborrowers, which ignore the fact that borrowers have different incomes from nonborrowers for reasons other than access to credit.[2] Donors often rate NGOs on the basis of their financial performance, that is, repayment rates and profitability, because data on impacts are not available. Financial performance differs widely, but the reasons and consequences may not bear any relation to impacts on poverty.[3] One general fact is that NGOs in developed countries perform worse financially than those in developing countries, and anecdotal evidence suggests that they also have less of an impact (Otero and Rhyne 1994).

I develop an explanation for the variation in the NGO performance based on the difference between the two main loan contracts the NGOs use, the joint-liability loan contract, also known as the group contract, and the individual-liability contract. In the group contract, borrowers form groups of typically five to seven individuals. Each person gets a loan for her own business, but all group members are responsible for repaying each loan. The payment made for another's debt is the joint liability. The alternative lending methodology is the individual-liability contract, in which each borrower is responsible only for her own loan. The lender typically threatens that if any loan is not repaid, the group or the individual will not get credit in the future, while timely repayment will be rewarded with larger future loans.

The great majority of NGOs use only the group contract. The group lending organizations are the best known and the ones that attract most of the funding.[4] This may explain why the effect on poverty seems to be small. Anecdotal and some econometric evidence suggest that NGOs offering individual loans have a better record of funding businesses that grow than group lenders do.[5] They may thus have more of an impact on poverty, but their effect is less visible, because they are few. I also suggest that the loan contract may explain some differences in financial performance and that the reliance on group loans may be partly responsible for the poor performance of microcredit NGOs in developed countries. However, exclusive reliance on individual loans would disadvantage the poorer among the borrowers.

One possible explanation for the difference between group and individual loans is the incentive effects of joint and individual liability. Consider one of several problems that can affect lending—moral hazard.[6] Borrowers may undertake riskier projects than the lender would like when the lender cannot observe which project a borrower has chosen and when liability is limited. Joseph Stiglitz and Andrew Weiss (1981) describe the problem. Limited liability means that borrowers who do not have enough wealth to repay the loan fully if the project fails pay the lender less if the project fails than if it succeeds, because no other punishment is available for the failure. This makes the riskier project, which is more likely to fail, more attractive to the borrower but less attractive to the lender. Under reasonable assumptions, the larger the loan is for a fixed amount of collateral, the more likely the borrower is to choose the riskier project. Moral hazard therefore leads to credit rationing. A lender will restrict the loan size to ensure that the borrower chooses a safer project.

As Stiglitz (1990) points out, joint liability can reduce this incentive problem and allow the lender to offer a larger loan. The reason is that joint liability induces borrowers to monitor each other. When borrowers are responsible for each other's loans, the choice of a riskier project by one group member increases the probability that the others will have to pay the liability. Group members will therefore want to invest effort in monitoring each other's choice of project, even if this effort is costly, because a monitor who observes that the riskier project has been chosen can punish that choice, for example, by confiscating the returns to the project. The threat of such punishment will prevent the borrower from choosing the riskier project. Because borrowers are policing each other, they may choose a safe project even when offered a loan that would cause an individual borrower, not linked by joint liability, to choose the riskier project. Then, the lender can offer a larger loan to a member of a group.

However, joint liability also has a negative incentive effect, which Stiglitz (1990) does not point out. This effect appears only if borrowers are risk averse. Borrowers in a group face a risk, which is absent from an individual contract. If a borrower's project succeeds, in an individual contract she receives a high payoff. In a group, however, she faces a lottery. She will receive a high payoff if all her partners' projects succeed, but a low payoff if anyone else's project fails, because she then has to help repay that person's debt. Call the event in which the borrower has to help repay someone else's loan the bad state. If the risky project yields a higher return when it succeeds than the safe project does, borrowers can guarantee themselves a larger payoff in the bad state if they choose the risky project, simply because they have more left over after paying the joint liability. If borrowers are sufficiently risk averse, then they care enough about the outcome in the bad state that the concern about the size of the payoff in this state may outweigh the concern about the probability of having to pay the liability. This concern leads them to choose the riskier project. As a result, borrowers in a group may monitor little and choose the riskier project even when offered a loan that would induce an individual borrower, who does not face the risk imposed by joint liability, to choose the safe project. An individual loan will then be larger than a group loan.

The result indicates that monitoring by the borrowers may not help reduce the moral hazard problem even when borrowers cannot offer enough collateral for as large a loan as they would like. It is true even when the lender does not monitor the borrowers in the individual contract. Of course, the lender may also monitor and often does, which further raises the amount of the individual loan relative to the group loan.

Interestingly, the balance between the positive and negative effect of joint liability can be shown to vary with the amount of wealth that borrowers can offer as collateral. The positive effect tends to dominate when wealth is low, and the negative begins to dominate above some level of wealth. The reason is that the amount to be gained in the bad state by choosing the risky project increases as the loan size grows with wealth, and the return to the risky project grows with the loan size. The implication is that poorer borrowers will get larger loans from group lending programs, while the wealthier can borrow more if the loan is individual.[7]

Evidence based on data from loan contracts in Bangladesh indicates that individual loans appear to become larger than group loans at rather low levels of borrower wealth. The data includes loans offered by the Grameen Bank, the flagship of microcredit programs and one of the main proponents of group loans. If larger loans lead to larger investments and profits, then NGOs that offer individual loans may have a better record of funding businesses that grow, because they allow the wealthier borrowers to get more credit. The widespread reliance on group loans may generate a poverty trap. The contractual form prevents the poor from accumulating capital, which they could either invest or use as collateral for more credit to expand the business.[8] The policy implication is that lenders should offer both loan contracts, allowing borrowers to graduate from group loans to individual loans as they grow wealthier. Recently, some group lending NGOs have begun doing just that.

These results may help to explain why microcredit has been less successful in the United States. In general NGOs in the United States experience higher default rates and lower profitability than the best NGOs in developing countries. NGOs in the United States offer only group loans. The evidence from Bangladesh suggests that individual loans there are larger than group loans even for households that are poorer than the poorest households in the United States. The level of wealth above which individual loans are larger would have to be much higher in the United States than in Bangladesh to justify NGO policies. Therefore, default rates in the United States might be high because many people do not value future access to the loans given how small they are. Lower profitability may be partly a result of the high default rates and partly of low demand for the loans, again due to how small they are.[9]

An Example

The example illustrates the effect of wealth on contracts without formalizing the results. A formal treatment is in Madajewicz (2004). An individual-liability contract can result in higher welfare and larger loan size than a joint-liability contract, even when the borrower is credit constrained and the lender does not monitor the individual borrower. Stiglitz (1990) explains a mechanism that results in larger utility and possibly larger loans in the joint-liability contract if monitoring is costless. I explain this mechanism later in this chapter. When monitoring is costly, the mechanism Stiglitz proposes is still active, but it is no longer the only mechanism at work.

Consider two identical risk-averse borrowers and one risk-neutral lender. They operate in a competitive credit market with many lenders and borrowers. While the market for credit is not likely to be perfectly competitive, it is not clear that any other assumption is more realistic. Low-income individuals get credit from a variety of sources, from informal ones such as moneylenders and community networks to formal microcredit NGOs and occasionally commercial banks. The degree of competition varies from place to place and from borrower to borrower. Furthermore, the assumption about market structure does not affect the qualitative nature of the results as long as lenders who offer different contracts face the same market conditions. Assuming competition allows me to derive the results in the simplest setting. Because the market is competitive, the lender will offer a contract that maximizes the welfare of the borrowers subject to the constraint that the lender break even.

The borrowers choose between a safe and a risky project. The safe project yields a return $R_s = 2$ with probability $p_s = 0.9$ and zero otherwise, and the risky project yields $R_r = 3$ with probability $p_r = 0.5$ and zero if it fails. Note that $R_r > R_s$ but $p_r R_r < p_s R_s$. Borrowers need a minimum loan of size 1.7 to carry out a project that yields these returns. Note that in this example a larger loan confers no benefit because project returns do not increase with loan size.

Project returns are observable only to the borrower undertaking the project. The lender does not observe which project a borrower chose unless he monitors and neither does the other borrower. Everyone knows (costlessly) whether a project succeeded or failed and this information is verifiable.[10]

The borrowers' utility is a von Neumann-Morgenstern utility function which is piecewise linear. The slope of the function is 5.3 for payoff levels from 0 up to and including 0.7, 4 for $0.7 <$ payoff $\leq$ 1, 3.6 for $1 <$ payoff ≤ 1.7, and 3.3 for payoff > 1.7. Assume that borrowers have wealth, $w = 0.5$, which they can offer as collateral. This wealth is observable and verifiable to all parties.

Credit rationing may occur when borrowers' expected utility from choosing the risky project is higher than the expected utility from choosing the safe project, while the lender cannot break even if he funds the risky project. Stiglitz and Weiss (1981) show that this structure of returns may arise when there is limited liability. Limited liability here means that borrowers do not have enough wealth to repay the loan fully if the project fails, and no other punishment for failure is available to the lender. In this case, borrowers have to pay more if the project succeeds than if it fails. Therefore, the expected utility from the risky project, which succeeds less often, may exceed the expected utility from the safe project even when the expected return to the risky project does not cover the opportunity cost of the loan.

In the example, suppose that the borrower does not have any wealth. Then, the expected utility of a borrower who undertakes the safe project and obtains the minimum size loan at the opportunity cost of capital is:

$$V_s = p_s \times u_s (R_s - \rho L + w) = 0.9 \times 5.3(2 - 1.7) = 1.43$$

L is the loan size, ρ is the opportunity cost of capital and u_s is the von Neumann–Morgenstern utility function. I assume that $\rho = 1$. The risky project yields the following expected utility:

$$V_r = p_r \times u_r \, (R_r - \rho L + w) = 0.5 \times 3.6(3 - 1.7) = 2.34$$

Therefore, the borrower will prefer the risky project. Since this is true for a loan offered at the opportunity cost of capital, it will certainly be true at any interest rate that will actually be offered, since such an interest rate will be higher as long as the project is risky and the borrower cannot repay fully if the project fails.

The safe project yields a positive social surplus at the minimum required loan size, but the expected return to the risky project is less than the opportunity cost of the loan. Therefore the lender does not want to fund the risky project. Because for a given interest rate the borrower prefers the risky project, he or she may face credit rationing. The lender may not offer the minimum required loan if the borrower chooses the risky project when offered that loan amount.

The lender can use two instruments to induce the borrower to choose the safe project, collateral and monitoring. Collateral is limited by the borrowers' wealth. Borrowers can monitor each other.[11] Monitoring is a two-part process of gathering information and imposing punishment.[12] The monitor observes the actions of the borrower before returns are realized. She or he observes the project which the borrower is choosing as the borrower implements the project. A monitor who observes that the borrower chose the risky project can punish the borrower after returns are realized—by confiscating the returns, for example. The threat of punishment prevents the borrower being monitored from choosing the risky project, therefore punishment does not need to be imposed.[13]

The monitor detects that the borrower is choosing the risky project with some probability, $b < 1$. She learns nothing with probability $(1-b)$. The monitor chooses this probability—for example, by visiting the borrower's business more often, spending more time, and being more inquisitive during the visits. If the monitor does determine that the borrower chose the risky project, she can impose a punishment of size d, also chosen by the monitor.[14] The monitor can vary the expected punishment faced by the borrower by varying the probability of detection, b, or the punishment imposed in case of detection, d. The monitor chooses the *certainty equivalent* (CE) of the expected punishment, c = CE(b x d).

Monitoring costs the monitor W(c) and this cost increases with c. For the purpose of the example, assume that W(c) = c.

The borrowers know how much they are being monitored, so they know what punishment to expect when they choose their projects. The lender cannot observe whether the borrowers are monitoring each other.

The Contracting Process

The lender offers a contract consisting of the loan size, L, and vector of payments, S, which the borrower has to make in each state of the world and which depend on outcomes observable to the lender *without monitoring*. The borrowers decide whether to accept the contract. If they accept, then the borrowers play the following noncooperative game. Knowing the terms of the contract, both borrowers simultaneously choose levels of expected punishment. Borrowers observe each other's choices, but the lender does not. Monitors begin to monitor.[15] Then borrowers simultaneously choose projects. Finally, returns are realized and payments are made. Figure 9.1 shows the time line.

I assume that borrowers abide by the contract. This may be because the contract states that they will not obtain a loan in the future if they do not, though I do not model this explicitly. The incentive problem is the choice of project, because it affects the borrower's ability to repay. This is a realistic representation of the problem faced by lenders who serve the poor. The denial of future credit very successfully induces borrowers to repay. However, borrowers do not always repay fully, because they may not be able to do so.

The Individual-Liability Contract

If the lender offers a contract in which each borrower's payment does not depend on the outcome of the other borrower's project, then the contract is individual liability. In this case, borrowers do not

Figure 9.1   Time Line

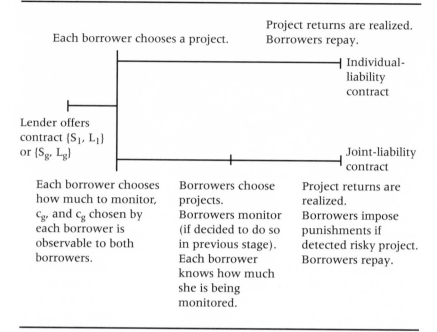

Project returns are realized.
Borrowers repay.

Each borrower chooses a project.

Individual-
liability
contract

Lender offers
contract {S_1, L_1}
or {S_g, L_g}

Joint-liability
contract

Each borrower chooses
how much to monitor,
c_g, and c_g chosen by
each borrower is
observable to both
borrowers.

Borrowers choose
projects.
Borrowers monitor
(if decided to do so
in previous stage).
Each borrower
knows how much
she is being
monitored.

Project returns are
realized.
Borrowers impose
punishments if
detected risky project.
Borrowers repay.

Source: Madajewicz (2004).

monitor and each chooses a project to maximize the expected utility, independently of the other's choice. Each borrower chooses the safe project if

$$V_s(\mathbf{S}_1, L_1) \geq V_r(\mathbf{S}_1, L_1) \tag{9.1}$$

where $V_s(\mathbf{S}_1, L_1)$ is the expected utility of the borrower who implements the safe project and $V_r(\mathbf{S}_1, L_1)$ is the analogous expression when the borrower chooses the risky project. The subscript 1 denotes the individual-liability contract.

The lender offers terms that maximize the borrower's utility subject to the incentive constraint represented in equation 9.1, the constraint that the lender break even on the loan and the limited liability constraint that the borrower never pay more than her available wealth. In the example, the solution to the problem is that the borrower pays all of his or her wealth if the project fails, $S_1^f = w = 0.5$, where superscript f stands for the state in which the project failed.[16] She or he pays an amount that gives the lender an expected profit of zero if the project succeeds,

$$S_1^u = \frac{\rho L_1 - (1 - p_s)w}{p_s} = 1.1L_1 - 0.06$$

where superscript u stands for the state in which the borrower's own project succeeded.

In general, the solution to the problem depends on the degree of risk aversion. However, the contract with maximum possible collateral maximizes utility when the probability of success of the safe project is large enough. The more collateral the borrower pledges, the less incentive she or he has to choose the risky project, therefore the larger is the loan which the lender can offer. However, the maximum possible collateral imposes risk. The bigger the probability of success of the safe project, the less likely is failure to occur, since the borrower chooses the safe project in equilibrium, and therefore the smaller is the imposed risk. If the probability of success is large enough, maximum collateral is best regardless of the degree of risk aversion.

Given the contract terms, the incentive constraint in equation 9.1 determines the loan size the lender will offer. The expanded constraint is:

$$p_s u_s (R_s - S_1^u + w) \geq p_r u_r (R_r - S_1^u + w)$$

Substituting in the values chosen for the example, the incentive constraint is:

$$0.9 \times 5.3(2.56 - 1.1L_1) \geq 0.5 \times 3.6(3.56 - 1.1L_1)$$

The constraint dictates that the maximum loan size the lender can offer is $L_1 = 1.77$. This loan is slightly larger than necessary to allow the borrower to undertake a project.

The Joint-Liability Contract

If the lender offers a contract in which each borrower's payments depend on the outcome of the other borrower's project then the contract is joint-liability. In this case, borrowers play the noncooperative game described earlier. The borrowers implement the strategies, level of monitoring, and choice of project, which constitute the Pareto dominant subgame perfect Nash equilibrium (SPNE) of this game. I assume that the probability distributions of projects chosen by different borrowers are independent of each other.

By backward induction, consider the subgame in which borrowers choose projects after both choose not to monitor. If her partner chooses the risky project, the probability that a borrower who chooses the safe project will have to help repay her partner's loan rises from $p_s(1 - p_s)$ to $p_s(1 - p_r)$. The borrower then obtains the same gain as her partner from choosing the risky project, plus a (larger) decrease from $p_s(1 - p_r)$ to $p_r(1 - p_r)$ in the probability that she will have to pay the liability. Thus, if one chooses the risky project, the other one will as well. In this subgame, this is the only Nash equilibrium (NE). It is also the only NE in each of the subgames after asymmetric monitoring decisions.

An NE in which both borrowers choose the safe project exists only in the subgame after both borrowers choose to monitor. It is an NE, because a borrower who monitors chooses a level of monitoring such that the other borrower prefers to choose the safe project if the monitor chooses the safe project, that is,

$$V_{ss}(\mathbf{S}_g, L_g) \geq V_{rs}(\mathbf{S}_g, L_g) - c_g \qquad (9.2)$$

where $V_{ss}(\mathbf{S}_g, L_g)$ is the expected utility when both the borrower and her partner choose the safe project, and $V_{rs}(\mathbf{S}_g, L_g)$ is the expected utility when the borrower chooses the risky project and her partner chooses the safe project. c_g is the level of monitoring chosen by each borrower.

Consider the game as a whole. The decisions whether to monitor are also symmetric. A SPNE in which both borrowers monitor and both choose the safe project exists if the terms of the contract satisfy the following group incentive constraint[17]:

$$V_{ss}(\mathbf{S_g}, L_g) - W(c_g) \geq V_{rr}(\mathbf{S_g}, L_g) \qquad (9.3)$$

where $V_{rr}(\mathbf{S_g}, L_g)$ is the expected utility when both the borrower and her partner choose the risky project. This SPNE is not always unique, but it is the Pareto dominant one.

The lender offers terms that maximize the borrower's utility subject to the incentive constraints in equations 9.2 and 9.3, the constraint that the lender break even and the limited liability constraint that the borrower never pay more than her available wealth. The terms will be that the borrower pay all of her wealth when her project fails, $S_g^f = w = 0.5$. When her project succeeds but her partner's project fails, she pays the *joint liability*, which consists of her wealth and the return to the safe project, $S_g^{uf} = R_s + w = 2.5$, where superscript uf denotes that the borrower's project succeeded and the partner's failed. The borrower pays an amount determined by the lender's break-even constraint when both projects succeed,

$$S_g^{uu} = \frac{\rho L_g - (1 - p_s^2)w - p_s(1 - p_s)R_s}{p_s^2} = 1.23L_g - 0.34$$

where superscript uu denotes that both projects succeeded.

As in the case of the individual-liability contract, in general the solution depends on the degree of risk aversion. However, when the probability of success of the safe project is large enough, the contract maximizes utility. It takes away all of the borrower's wealth if the borrower's own project fails and if her partner's project fails but her own succeeds, that is, her payoff is zero unless both projects succeed. The borrower pays the maximum possible when her own project fails for the same reason as before. The maximum joint liability is optimal for two reasons. It lowers the payment in the state in which both projects succeed as much as possible, thereby rewarding the choice of the safe project by both borrowers. This minimizes the cost of monitoring and allows the lender to offer the largest possible loan. Also, by imposing the maximum possible punishment on a borrower for the partner's failure, the contract expands the range of loan sizes for which borrowers will monitor.

The contract with a maximum joint liability is very risky for the borrower and is optimal if the probability of success of the safe project is large enough. However, this probability must be larger for the maximum liability to be optimal than it does for maximum collateral to be optimal, holding all else constant.

The constraints (2) and (3) determine the maximum loan size which the lender can offer through a group contract. The expanded constraint (3) is:

$$p^2 u_s^{uu} (R_s - S_g^{uu} + w) - W(c_g) \geq$$
$$p_r^2 u_r^{uu}(R_r - S_g^{uu} + w) + p_r(1 - p_r)u_r^{uf} (R_r - R_s)$$

Constraint (2) determines c_g. Combining the two constraints and substituting in the values assumed for the example yields:

$$0.9^2 \times 3.6(2.84 - 1.23L_g) + 2.3 - 1.73L_g \geq$$
$$0.5^2 \times 3.3(3.84 - 1.23L_g) + 0.5^2 \times 4$$

The maximum group loan which the lender can offer is $L_g = 1.48$. This loan is not large enough for a borrower to undertake a project.

Comparing Contracts: Loan Size

In the example, the loan the lender can offer through the individual contract is just large enough that the borrower can undertake a project. The loan the lender would offer through the group contract is too small to be worth taking. The outcome seems surprising, because the borrowers are credit constrained because of their scant wealth and the asymmetric information about investment decisions. The lender does not monitor in the individual contract, therefore the contract relies only on wealth to provide an incentive for borrowers to choose the safe project. In the joint-liability contract, two instruments are available for this purpose, wealth and monitoring by the other borrower.

The outcome is less surprising once we take into account the trade-offs between the two contracts. Consider the advantages of joint liability first. Borrowers in a group have an incentive to monitor each other and thereby induce each other to choose the safe project. They do so to reduce the probability of having to pay the liability. They may monitor and choose the safe project even when the loan size is such that an individual borrower who is not being monitored would choose the risky project. Therefore, the lender may be able to offer a larger loan to members of a group than he could to borrowers who have unmonitored individual contracts. Furthermore, the extra collateral embodied in the partner's liability reduces the payment, which the borrower has to make when her project succeeds and thereby rewards the choice of the safe project.

However, joint liability is not free from drawbacks. The joint liability imposes a risk on borrowers that the individual contract does not and the monitoring it induces is costly. Consider the risk first. If a project fails, the individual contract and the group contract yield the same payoff, zero, because the borrower surrenders all wealth. If the project succeeds, an individual contract offers a sure payoff, while the group contract offers a lottery. In the group contract, the borrower receives a high payoff only if both (or all) projects succeed. If a partner's project fails, the borrower has to pay the joint liability. All borrowers guarantee themselves a larger income in the low-payoff state of this lottery (the state in which they have to pay the liability) when they choose the risky project simply because it yields a larger return when it succeeds.[18] If borrowers are sufficiently risk averse, so that they care enough about the low payoff, the value of the insurance, which the risky project provides in the state in which the borrower has to pay the liability may dominate the value of reducing the probability of paying the liability. Then the risky project becomes more attractive under the group contract than under the individual one because the risk imposed by joint liability is absent from an individual contract, and the lender can offer a larger loan to an individual borrower than to members of a group.

If monitoring were cost free, the advantages of joint liability would be enough to ensure that the group loan is always larger than an individual loan, as Stiglitz (1990) points out. The reason is that a very small liability, one that represents only a marginal increase over the payment the borrower makes when both projects succeed, would be sufficient to elicit monitoring and raise the loan size above the size of a loan in an individual contract. The risk imposed by such a small liability would not reduce utility or affect incentives, because it would be too small to have a first-order effect.[19] The difference between a group and individual loan and utility may be small, but it would be positive.

When monitoring is costly, such a small liability will generally be insufficient to elicit monitoring, since the benefit of the somewhat larger loan will not outweigh the cost of monitoring. Furthermore, the cost of monitoring reduces the range of loan sizes for which monitoring will be worthwhile for borrowers. Ample evidence indicates that monitoring is indeed costly.[20] In fact, borrowers' main complaint about group loans is that time spent monitoring is very costly to them.

I should note that the result in the example is not an artifact of the group contract in which the joint liability is the maximum that it can be. This large liability maximizes utility in the joint-liability contract when the probability of success of the safe project is high enough.

Comparing Contracts: Utility

In the example, the individual contract yields a higher utility simply because it allows the borrower to undertake a project. The joint-liability contract does not. However, suppose that a borrower can implement a project with the loan amount the joint-liability contract offers. This assumption does not work well in the example, because there is then no benefit to the larger individual loan, given that project returns do not increase with loan size. The larger loan increases the amount that has to be repaid with no change in benefits. Even in this case, the utility generated by the individual contract with a loan of 1.7 is higher than the utility generated by the joint-liability contract with a loan of 1.48. The reason for the lower utility in the group contract is the cost of monitoring and the risk imposed by the liability, reflected here in the smaller probability of the high payoff. This point would be even stronger in the more realistic case in which project returns increase with loan size, provided that the return to the risky project is always larger than the return to the safe project, conditional on success.

The joint-liability contract may not yield higher utility than the individual contract even when it offers a larger loan. The loan has to be sufficiently larger to compensate for the cost of monitoring and the risk imposed by the liability.

Comparing Contracts: Effect of Wealth

Would borrowers ever prefer the joint-liability contract in the example? Suppose that borrowers can implement a project with a loan smaller than 1.7, and a larger loan is valuable because it increases returns without changing the difference between the returns to the safe and the risky projects, conditional on success. Then borrowers who have no wealth would prefer the joint-liability contract. The largest individual loan that a borrower who has no wealth can obtain is $L_1 = 1.05$. However, the joint-liability loan for a borrower who has no wealth would be 1.1. As long as this loan is large enough to implement a project, the joint-liability contract would yield higher utility. Therefore, there is some amount of wealth between 0 and 0.5 such that borrowers who own that amount of wealth are indifferent between the two types of contracts. Poorer borrowers prefer joint-liability loans and wealthier borrowers prefer individual loans.[21]

General Results

Please see Madajewicz (2004) for a detailed exposition of general results. The model is similar to that in the example. However, project returns increase with loan size and I assume that the return to the risky project, conditional on success, increases with loan size faster than does the return to the safe project.[22] I first determine what terms the lender offers conditional on the choice of liability and then I compare welfare under the joint-liability contract to welfare under the individual-liability contract with no monitoring given the terms of each contract. I also consider a contract in which liability is individual and the lender monitors.

The contracts presented in the example maximize utility as long as the probability of success of the safe project is large enough.[23] Considering a large probability of success of the safe project is one way of imposing the condition that the borrower faces credit rationing.[24] If the solution is such that the borrower does not give up all available wealth in case of failure, then the borrower does not demand a larger loan at the equilibrium interest rate. The lender can always increase the loan size and the collateral while holding the interest rate fixed, as long as the borrower has more collateral available. If such an increase lowers utility, one could argue that the borrower is not facing credit rationing.

The general result states that if borrowers at some level of wealth are indifferent between the joint-liability and the individual-liability, unmonitored contract, then under some conditions wealthier borrowers prefer the individual-liability contract. For borrowers who are just barely wealthier than those who are indifferent, a joint-liability loan may be larger than an individual-liability loan. However, the individual contract will yield higher welfare due to the cost of monitoring and the risk imposed by joint liability. At some, possibly higher, level of wealth, individual-liability loans actually become larger than joint-liability loans.

The discussion of the example conveyed the intuition for the result. Joint liability has two incentive effects. One induces borrowers to monitor each other and thereby makes the risky project less attractive, allowing the lender to offer a larger loan. The second effect, caused by the risk imposed by the joint liability, works in the opposite direction. The result states that the positive incentive effect dominates below some level of wealth, while the adverse effect dominates at higher levels of wealth.

The incentive to monitor increases with borrowers' wealth, because the liability increases as borrowers have more wealth to offer as collateral and as increases in loan size offered increase the return to the safe project. The incentive effect of the risk imposed by joint liability also grows with wealth, because wealthier borrowers obtain larger loans and, by assumption, the difference between the return to the risky and the safe project grows with loan size. Therefore, the insurance which choosing the risky project offers in the state in which the borrower has to pay the liability grows with the borrowers' wealth. Under some conditions, the effect of the risk grows faster.

I consider only risk-averse borrowers. The incentive problem does not rely on risk aversion. In fact, risk-averse borrowers have a weaker preference for the risky project than do risk-neutral borrowers. Risk aversion is essential to the trade-off between the individual-liability and the joint-liability contract, because the risk imposed by the joint liability does not affect the utility or the incentives of risk-neutral borrowers. In fact, risk-neutral borrowers always prefer the joint-liability contract.

The result holds under some conditions, a large difference between the returns to safe and risky projects, high degree of risk aversion of borrowers and large opportunity costs of funds. These conditions seem to accurately characterize circumstances faced by lenders who serve the poor. Therefore the result may hold precisely in the case in which it provides a useful explanation for the performance of lenders. The types of projects available to borrowers in Bangladesh, for example, differ widely with respect to the returns on success and the risks involved. Evidence is anecdotal but suggestive. The most common type of small business funded with microcredit is raising chickens. Most borrowers undertake this activity on a regular basis even without a loan, and are thus very familiar with it. Credit allows them to increase the scale. The investment is safe but far from lucrative. By contrast, projects offering higher profits are often more capital intensive and far riskier. One example is a rice mill, used to process large quantities of the crop. The more common method of processing rice is manual threshing. A rice mill is far riskier than raising chickens, but is also capable of generating much larger profits. This project is almost never undertaken with group loans.

If the wealthier among credit-constrained borrowers prefer an individual, unmonitored contract, they will also prefer a lender-monitored contract as long as the lender chooses the level of monitoring optimally. Poorer borrowers may prefer group loans. However, a lender-monitored contract can offer a larger loan than an unmonitored contract can, therefore even those who prefer a joint-liability contract to an unmonitored one may prefer a lender-monitored contract to the group one. In summary, if any borrowers prefer the joint-liability contract, they are the poorer ones. Wealthier borrowers may prefer individual-liability contracts, either monitored by the lender or not.

Evidence

In a world in which all contracts are available, the theory predicts that wealthier borrowers should choose individual loans, lender-monitored or unmonitored, and poorer borrowers should choose group loans. However, in Bangladesh and in most places borrowers do not have a choice of loan contracts.[25] As mentioned, most NGOs offer only one type of contract, most often group loans. Other lenders, such as moneylenders and banks also use one type of contract. The poor may have access to loans from both an NGO and a moneylender, but even in this case, the amount they can borrow from each source is restricted in ways which I will discuss in more detail. Thus the type of contract is most often dictated by lender rules, and not by borrower preferences.

In this case, the theory predicts that those among the poorer borrowers who get group loans will have larger loans than those who obtain individual loans, and individual loans should be larger than group loans for wealthier borrowers.

The Data

The data were collected in a survey of 1,798 households in eighty-seven villages in Bangladesh in 1991 and 1992.[26] The survey was designed to study the impact of three nonprofit microcredit programs on borrowers' welfare. The three programs—the Grameen Bank, the Bangladesh Rural Advancement Committee (BRAC), and the Bangladesh Rural Development Board's (BRDB) RD-12 program—offer only group loans.

The survey contains information about households that have access to a group lending program as well as a control group of households that do not have access either because they are not eligible for a group loan or because they live in a village in which no program operates. All three programs use the same eligibility criterion to target poor households; households should own no more than one-half of an acre of land. Thus, each household in the survey belongs to one of five categories: borrower from a group program, eligible nonborrower in a village with a program, eligible nonborrower in a village without a program, ineligible household in a village either with or without a program.

All households have access to individual loans from several sources. Moneylenders, commercial and government banks offer only individual loans, and some of these lenders monitor.

The data contain information on all loans obtained by a household over the last four years by source of loan, and detailed information about household characteristics. Table 9.1 presents the means and standard deviations of loan sizes and of the amount of land owned by the household, which serves as a proxy for a household's wealth. Land is the only measure of wealth that can be argued to be exogenous, because the markets for land were not very active at the time at which the data was collected. It is the most easily observable component of wealth and is closely correlated with

Table 9.1 Means of Loan Sizes and Amount of Land Owned

Variable	Mean	Standard Deviation
Amount of land owned (acres)	0.84	1.14
Loan size, all loans (taka)	2,166.37	110.11
Size of group loans (taka)	3,414.34	153.98
Size of loans from banks (taka)	4,801.06	504.55
Size of loans from moneylenders (taka)	2,709.21	222.70
Size of loans from family and friends (taka)	3,688.62	369.51

Source: Madajewicz (2004).
Note: Means are adjusted by sampling weights. The exchange rate for the relevant years was thirty-three taka per U.S. dollar.

other components, which is why microcredit lenders use it to target the poor. It is also the form of wealth most commonly accepted as collateral by banks. The range of wealth in the data is from zero to five acres of land.

The Hypothesis

The hypothesis is that group loans are larger for poorer borrowers than individual loans are, while individual loans are larger for wealthier borrowers, because access to loan contracts is restricted by institutional rules. Only the microcredit programs offer group loans, and they offer only those. The loans are not available to everyone. Households should own less than one-half acre of land when they get their first loan. Although this rule is not strictly enforced, it does strongly affect a household's probability of getting a group loan. Furthermore, residents of villages in which no microcredit program is present do not have access to group loans.

The individual-liability loans are available from banks and moneylenders. Banks offer only individual-liability loans. They rarely lend to low-income people. Poor households that do get bank loans generally have personal connections, such as a relation or a friend who knows someone at the bank and who is willing to vouch for the borrower. Thus, poor borrowers who prefer individual loans may not be able to get them simply because they do not have the requisite relationship with a potential lender.[27] All households in my sample would be considered low to low-middle income by a bank.

Moneylenders primarily offer individual loans, though they do also lend when someone other than the borrower takes responsibility for repaying the loan. They also primarily lend to people whom they know personally or through others whom they trust.[28] The difference between banks and moneylenders is that the loans offered by moneylenders are often components of interlinked transactions (Braverman and Stiglitz 1982). Moneylenders often have relationships with their borrowers in other markets, for example the borrower may be the moneylender's tenant, an employee on his land or in his factory or a client in his shop. Thus the terms of loans from moneylenders may not behave in accordance with the presented model because the model does not take into account the interlinked transaction.

In sum, then, households with more than one-half acre of land have more restricted access to group loans than poorer households, and households who live in villages without a microcredit program have no access to group loans. All households in the sample have restricted access to bank and moneylender loans.

Descriptive Results

Table 9.2 reports the mean values of loan size by type of lender and wealth. The amount of land owned by each individual in the poorer portion of the sample is less than or equal to 0.04 acres. The reason for this cut-off is that it is the largest amount of land owned such that the average group loan for households that own less is larger than the average individual loan. If I separate the sample at higher wealth levels, the average individual loan is larger than the average group loan for borrowers in both groups.[29]

Table 9.2 shows that the average group loan is larger for poorer borrowers, and that the average individual loan is larger for wealthier borrowers. The mean estimates are weighted to correct for oversampling in the survey. The differences between all the means are significant at the 1 percent level. The evidence in table 9.2 is not conclusive, but is suggestive.

The descriptive results are not conclusive because they do not ad-

Table 9.2 Mean Loan Size

	Average Loan Size by Type of Contract	
Borrowers' Wealth	Group	Individual
Amount of land is less		
than or equal to 0.04 acres	3,310 taka	2,266 taka
Standard error of mean estimate	232.87	281.81
Number of observations in cell	465	5
Amount of land is greater than		
0.04 acres	3,564 taka	4,925 taka
Standard error of mean estimate	158.60	523.75
Number of observations in cell	1,571	75

Source: Madajewicz (2004).
Note: The exchange rate for the relevant years was thirty-three taka per U.S. dollar.

dress a problem with identifying the effect of the contracts on loan size—that is, selection bias. Households able to get group loans may differ from those getting individual loans or those not getting any loan on the basis of characteristics not observable in the data that might affect the relationship between loan size and wealth regardless of the contract. For example, practitioners generally note that microcredit organizations engage in "cream-skimming," that is, carefully choosing the best risks among the poorer individuals. NGOs may be better at this than banks for poorer individuals but worse than banks for wealthier individuals. The difference in loan sizes would then simply reflect the difference in unobserved (in the data) abilities of those borrowers who get group and individual loans.

Furthermore, group lending programs choose villages in which they locate using information not in the data, but that might affect the relationship between loan sizes and borrower wealth for all lenders in the village. For example, NGOs may choose villages in which the poor can more easily establish a profitable business because communication networks are good. These advantages may be less important for wealthier borrowers.

In Madajewicz (2003), I estimate a regression model that addresses both types of selection bias. The results are very similar to the descriptive results reported here.

The individual loans reported in table 9.2 are from commercial and government banks. The average loan from moneylenders given in villages with group lending organizations is always smaller than the average group loan and the average in villages without them is always larger. This suggests that there is competition between microcredit NGOs and moneylenders, which affects moneylenders' behavior. This is not surprising given that moneylenders serve a similar clientele and charge much higher interest rates than microcredit NGOs.[30] NGOs present less competition for banks because the poor are a very small portion of the banks' clientele and banks charge similar or lower interest rates than NGOs. Furthermore, as mentioned, loans from moneylenders are likely to show a different pattern due to interlinkage of the transaction.

The importance of the finding is twofold. First, it suggests that the negative incentive effect of joint liability identified in the theory may be real and of practical importance. The most plausible candidate for an alternative explanation is that group lending programs have a rule that they do not offer loans larger than a specific amount.[31] However, there is no obvious truncation point in the data. Furthermore, only eight out of ninety-four bank loans are larger than the largest group loan.

The second reason the result is important is that it has a simple policy implication. People who own 0.04 acres are very poor. The level of land ownership is much lower than the eligibility level for group loans. If larger loans result in larger investments and larger profits per dollar invested, then the reliance on the group contract prevalent among microcredit organizations yields smaller profits and less growth of businesses over time than would occur if lenders offered a menu of contracts, the group contract to the poorest borrowers, and the individual to somewhat wealthier borrowers.

The estimated level of wealth above which individual loans dominate suggests that reliance on group loans is particularly misguided among microcredit NGOs operating in developed countries. The caveat to this conclusion is that the level of wealth at which individual loans become larger may be different in developed countries than in Bangladesh. The model suggests that this level will depend on returns to risky and safe projects and the rate at which these increase with loan size, on the degree of risk aversion, and on the opportunity cost of capital. All of these parameters may well differ across countries, and across rich and poor countries in particular.

Conclusion

Joint liability in credit contracts may have a negative incentive effect, which causes a group of borrowers linked by joint liability to choose riskier investments than individual borrowers would choose. Consequently, contrary to intuition, a lender may offer smaller loans to members of a group who are monitoring each other than to an unmonitored, individual borrower even when borrowers are credit constrained because they cannot offer much collateral. This negative incentive effect is likely to dominate the positive incentive effect of joint liability for the wealthier borrowers.

There is evidence that the negative incentive effect of joint liability is empirically important. The evidence is based on data from Bangladesh, which show that individual loans are smaller than group loans for the poorest borrowers, but become larger than group loans for borrowers who are wealthier but still poor. The disincentive effect of joint liability seems to provide the only plausible explanation for this pattern.

The disincentive effect of joint liability has a simple and potentially important policy implication. Microcredit NGOs most commonly use joint-liability loans to provide credit for very small businesses and thus reduce poverty. Somewhat oddly, most of these lenders offer only joint-liability loans. The policy may reduce loan sizes and therefore the poor borrowers' ability to invest. The NGOs may have a bigger impact on poverty if they offer group loans to the poorest borrowers, but allow wealthier borrowers to take out individual loans. The focus on group loans may be a large part of the explanation for the failure of microcredit NGOs operating in developed countries to match the repayment rates and numbers of borrowers that such NGOs achieve in poor countries.

The model here considers only the effect of the loan contract on loan size. The loan contract may well affect other aspects of outcomes. Empirical analysis in Madajewicz (2003) suggests that the loan contract also affects the productivity of the chosen investment. Also, the effects of wealth predicted here may appear in contexts other than lending to the poor—for example, in the choice between a partnership and an individual form of ownership of a firm.

I am grateful to Abhijit Banerjee and Eric Maskin for guidance and detailed comments. I would also like to thank Glenn Ellison, Jonathan Morduch, and Tomas Sjöström for helpful discussions. The usual disclaimer applies.

Notes

1. Examples of programs in the United States include ACCION International's programs in various cities, Working Capital in New England, the Trickle-Up Program in New York, Women's Self-Employment Project in Chicago.

2. For an example of an evaluation which ignores the problem that borrowers are a self-selected group, see David Hulme and Paul Mosley 1996). Three studies that do address the problem are Mark Pitt and Shahidur Khandker (1998), Jonathan Morduch (1998), and Madajewicz (2003).

3. The better-managed nonprofits have repayment rates as high as 95 percent, higher than most commercial banks. A few have reorganized as commercial banks and are fully profitable. See Robert Christen, Elizabeth Rhyne and Robert Vogel (1994), Maria Otero and Rhyne (1994), Morduch (1999a).

4. The World Bank lists *group-based* microcredit as a best practice for reducing poverty (Narayanan 2000).

5. See Otero and Rhyne (1994, chapter 10) and Hugo Pirela Martínez (1990) for anecdotal evidence, and Madajewicz (2003) for econometric evidence.

6. Joint liability can reduce several incentive problems, adverse selection, moral hazard, and the problem of strategic default. See Beatriz Armendáriz de Aghion and Christian Gollier (1996), Timothy Besley and Stephen Coate (1995), Maitreesh Ghatak (1999), Karla Hoff and Joseph Stiglitz (1990), Stiglitz (1990), Hal Varian (1990).

7. An intuitive reason why wealthier borrowers may prefer an individual contract is that wealthier borrowers have a higher opportunity cost of time and additional credit is not sufficiently valuable to them to compensate for the cost of monitoring. The result in the paper holds for borrowers who are not so wealthy that this intuitive effect is important.

8. This point is an extension of Abhijit Banerjee and Andrew Newman's (1994) remark that the use of collateral in response to information problems in credit markets causes a poverty trap since poor people cannot borrow to invest because they are poor.

9. It is also partly due to higher costs.

10. A motivation for this information structure is that a coarser signal, such as whether a business exists or not, may be more easily observable than is a finer one which reveals the exact return and/or the risk-

iness of the project. The borrower can affect the riskiness of her investment in many ways which are difficult to observe and which she prefers to hide from the lender, such as the choice of strategy, choice of inputs, and so forth.

11. In the general version of the model, I also allow the lender to monitor, but not for the purpose of the example.

12. The monitoring model is based loosely on Banerjee, Timothy Besley, and Timothy Guinnane (1994).

13. The threat is credible. If the punishment is the confiscation of returns, it yields a benefit to the monitor and she has an incentive to carry it out.

14. The punishment d has two potential interpretations. I will think of it as confiscating the returns to the risky project. In models of peer-monitored contracts, the typical assumption is that other borrowers impose social sanctions against any borrower who misbehaves. In this case, d is the disutility associated with the exclusion from benefits associated with social networks, for example, getting help from one's neighbors, or simply feeling accepted in the community. This interpretation is also consistent with my model.

15. One can think of monitoring as beginning prior to the choice of project and extending until after projects have been chosen, since a borrower may be able to costlessly change her project from a safe to a risky one if she is not being monitored. For example, she may be able to change the inputs.

16. I state formally and prove this result and all subsequent ones in Madajewicz (2004).

17. The constraint can be interpreted as a no-collusion constraint.

18. The return in this state for a borrower who chooses the risky project is $R_r(L_g) - R_s(L_g)$.

19. More precisely, the reason is that a utility function is linear around a point.

20. See for example Otero and Rhyne (1994) and Irfan Aleem (1990).

21. In the example, it is not obvious that such a switch cannot occur more than once. I show that it cannot in the general results.

22. One then has to restrict the range of loan sizes for which the analysis is relevant.

23. However, the general results are also valid if the group liability is not the maximum that it can be, but rather is some fraction of the wealth available to the borrower when her project succeeds, as long as the liability is large enough.

24. Interestingly, almost every study of microenterprises notes that businesses undertaken by low-income entrepreneurs have very high success rates. The evidence is anecdotal. One indirect indicator of rates of success are repayment rates, which vary between 92 percent and 98 percent in well-managed programs, both individual-liability and

joint-liability ones. See for example Christen, Rhyne, and Vogel.
(1994), Mahbub Hossain (1988), Charles Mann, Merilee S. Grindle,
and Amy Sanders (1989), Otero and Rhyne (1994).

25. This statement may appear to contradict the reasons given for assuming a competitive market in the model. It does not, because competition occurs between lenders who use the same loan contract—
moneylenders and rural banks. However, microcredit lenders and
moneylenders do compete for some range of borrowers.

26. The description of the data is partly drawn from Pitt and Khandker
(1998).

27. Banks allow borrowers who live in villages other than where the bank
branch is located to borrow from the branch, thus the location of a
bank is not the same type of constraint as is the location of a group-
lending program.

28. Similarly to a bank, the location of a moneylender does not restrict
who can borrow as much as the location of a group lending program
does.

29. Madajewicz (2003) finds the cut-off level of land using regression
analysis. The exact number varies depending on the estimator used,
but all are of the same order as reported here and considerably smaller
than the eligibility criterion for group loans.

30. Clive Bell (1993) provides some evidence regarding the effect of new
lending institutions on moneylenders in India.

31. One could also object that the explanation for the pattern in the data
is based on a model in which the agents behave optimally, while I
have stated that the observed contracts are not offered optimally. One
could argue that the agents in reality do not optimize, hence one cannot explain their behavior with a model that assumes that they do.
However, it is difficult to explain how non-optimizing behavior might
result in the observed pattern in which the relationship between loan
size and wealth depends on the loan contract offered.

References

Aleem, Irfan. 1990. "Imperfect Information, Screening and the Costs of Informal Lending: A Study of a Rural Credit Market in Pakistan." *World
Bank Economic Review* 4(3): 329–49.

Armendáriz de Aghion, Beatriz. 1999. "On the Design of a Credit Agreement with Peer Monitoring." *Journal of Development Economics* 60(1):
79–104.

Armendáriz de Aghion, Beatriz, and Christian Gollier. 1996. "Peer Grouping
in an Adverse Selection Model." *University College London Discussion
Paper* 96/24. London: University College.

Banerjee, Abhijit V., Timothy Besley, and Timothy W. Guinnane. 1994. "Thy

Neighbor's Keeper: a Theory of Credit Cooperatives." *Quarterly Journal of Economics* 109(2): 491–515.

Banerjee, Abhijit V., and Andrew F. Newman. 1994. "Poverty, Incentives and Development." *American Economic Review* 84(2): 211–15.

Bell, Clive. 1993. "Interactions Between Institutional and Informal Credit Agencies in Rural India." In *The Economics of Rural Organization,* edited by Karla A. Hoff, Avishay Braverman, and Joseph E. Stiglitz. New York: Oxford University Press.

Besley, Timothy, and Stephen Coate. 1995. "Group Lending, Repayment Incentives and Social Collateral." *Journal of Development Economics* 46(1): 1–18.

Braverman, Avishay, and Monica Huppi. 1991. "Improving Rural Finance in Developing Countries." *Finance and Development* 28(1): 42–4.

Braverman, Avishay, and Joseph E. Stiglitz. 1982. "Sharecropping and the Interlinking of Agrarian Markets." *American Economic Review* 72(4): 695–715.

Christen, Robert C., Elizabeth Rhyne, and Robert C. Vogel. 1994. "Maximizing the Outreach of Microenterprise Finance: The Emerging Lessons of Successful Programs." Consulting Assistance for Economic Reform Paper. Arlington, Va.: IMCC.

Gale, Douglas, and Martin Hellwig. 1985. "Incentive-Compatible Debt Contracts: The One-Period Problem." *Review of Economic Studies* 52(4): 647–63.

Ghatak, Maitreesh. 1999. "Group Lending, Local Information, and Peer Selection." *Journal of Development Economics* 60(1): 27–50.

Hoff, Karla, and Joseph E. Stiglitz. 1990. "Imperfect Information and Rural Credit Markets—Puzzles and Policy Perspectives." *The World Bank Economic Review* 4(3): 235–50.

Hossain, Mahbub. 1988. *Credit for Alleviation of Rural Poverty: The Grameen Bank in Bangladesh.* Washington, D.C.: International Food Policy Research Institute.

Hulme, David, and Paul Mosley, editors. 1996. *Finance Against Poverty.* London: Routledge.

Huppi, Monica and Gershon Feder. 1990. "The Role of Groups and Credit Cooperatives in Rural Lending." *The World Bank Research Observer* 5(2): 187–204.

Itoh, Hideshi. 1993. "Coalitions, Incentives and Risk Sharing." *Journal of Economic Theory* 60(2): 410–27.

Levitsky, Jacob, ed. 1989. *Microenterprises in Developing Countries.* Warwickshire, U.K.: Intermediate Technology Publications.

Madajewicz, Malgosia. 2003. "Does the Credit Contract Matter? The Impact of Lending Programs on Poverty in Bangladesh." Unpublished paper. Columbia University.

——. 2004. "Joint liability versus individual liability in credit contracts." Working Paper. Columbia University.

Mann, Charles K., Merilee S. Grindle, and Amy Sanders (eds.). 1989. *Seeking Solutions.* West Hartford, Conn.: Kumarian Press.

McKernan, Signe-Mary. 2002. "The Impact of Micro-Credit Programs on Self-Employment Profits: Do Non-Credit Program Aspects Matter?" *Review of Economics and Statistics* 84(1): 93–115.

Morduch, Jonathan. 1998. "Does Microfinance Really Help the Poor? New Evidence on Flagship Programs in Bangladesh." Unpublished paper. New York University.

——. 1999a. "The Microfinance Promise." *Journal of Economic Literature* 37(4): 1569–1614.

——. 1999b. "The Grameen Bank: A Financial Reckoning." Unpublished paper. New York University.

Narayanan, Deepa, ed. 2000. *Empowerment and Poverty Reduction. A Sourcebook.* Washington, D.C.: The World Bank.

Otero, Maria, and Elizabeth Rhyne, eds. 1994. *The New World of Microenterprise Finance.* Bloomfield, Conn.: Kumarian Press.

Pirela Martínez, Hugo. 1990. "The Grey Area in Microenterprise Development." *Grassroots Development* 14(2): 33–40.

Pitt, Mark M., and Shahidur R. Khandker. 1998. "The Impact of Group-Based Credit Programs on Poor Households in Bangladesh: Does the Gender of Participants Matter?" *Journal of Political Economy* 106(5): 958–96.

Stiglitz, Joseph E. 1990. "Peer Monitoring and Credit Markets." *The World Bank Economic Review* 4(3): 351–66.

Stiglitz, Joseph E., and Andrew Weiss. 1981. "Credit Rationing in Markets with Imperfect Information." *American Economic Review* 71(3): 393–410.

Varian, Hal 1990. "Monitoring Agents with Other Agents." *Journal of Institutional and Theoretical Economics* 146(1): 153–74.

Part IV

Inequality and Credit Markets

Chapter 10

Inequality and Credit Markets: An Introduction to Political Economy Perspectives

Howard Rosenthal

Inequality matters to social outcomes. We ask here both how inequality influences the operation of *private* credit markets that are subject to political intervention and how market outcomes affect inequality. Topics of central interest to researchers include whether equity can be achieved without substantial efficiency losses, what mix of leniency and enforcement should apply ex ante to debt contracts, and whether governments should, in exceptionally dire times, intervene ex post to alter the terms of existing contracts.

Credit markets can contribute to the reduction of inequality. Credit becomes especially important when reducing inequality by direct redistribution is not politically feasible.[1] Credit markets can reduce inequality in short-term consumption. They can provide for redistribution of capital from rich to poor. Investment by the poor might then reduce inequality. At the same time, all boats must rise, because the rich will lend only if lending is expected to be profitable.

Although all participants in a credit market expect to benefit, inequality in benefits can be affected by political intervention. Intervention in a credit market might not only reduce inequality but also improve average consumption. To focus solely on the effects of the operation of private credit markets, I will largely ignore government intervention that takes the form of direct redistribution. The emphasis, therefore, will be on government regulation.

Studying government action in private credit markets puts this discussion in the growing field of political economy. The literature here is nascent. For example, the highly regarded graduate text of Torsten Persson and Guido Tabellini (2000) covers direct redistribution and government debt but ignores private debt (but see Pagano and Volpin 2001). So I will concentrate on just a few buds and provide a fairly detailed summary of a small set of papers. Even among these, not all had government regulation as a focus. None directly evaluated the implications of the models for inequality; I will emphasize the inequality topic.

An Overview of the Impact of Regulation

Political institutions can either improve or worsen the operation of credit markets. The important points developed here are:

- Government regulation can reduce inequality. Inequality reducing policies include usury laws, regulation of the capital requirements of banks, and forcing firms to be controlled by bondholders rather than equity owners. Many inequality reducing policies may come at a cost in efficiency (Glaeser and Scheinkman 1998; Dewatripont and Maskin 1995; Perotti and von Thadden 2002). On the other hand, some policies that benefit debtors can increase aggregate output (Ayotte 2002; Bolton and Rosenthal 2002).

- Private credit markets, government regulated or not, can cause all boats to rise, but at a cost of increased inequality. Because productive talents can create a "winner take all" situation, consumption may be less equally distributed when credit markets operate than when they collapse (Dewatripont and Maskin 1995; Bolton and Rosenthal 2002). Unless societies can engage in direct redistribution, societies with private credit markets may become highly unequal. The papers I discuss in detail here are all short-run models in which the economy terminates after one or two periods of production. But the potential for private credit markets to increase inequality has been noted in dynamic models (Matsuyama 2000; Aghion and Bolton 1997).[2]

- Inequality should not be evaluated solely on a one-time snapshot of the economy. An unregulated market may initially lower inequality more than a regulated one, but the current reduction in inequality comes at a cost of increased inequality as debts are repaid (Glaeser and Scheinkman 1998).

- When lenders have monopoly power, showing leniency to failed debtors may largely benefit relatively well endowed debtors. (Ayotte 2002; Jappelli, Pagano, and Bianco 2002). Thus stricter enforcement can be in the interest of the poor. On the other hand, lax enforcement may benefit the poor if there are social costs to the liquidation of failed debtors (Biais and Récassens 2002).

- Increases in political equality may not promote increases in economic equality (Bolton and Rosenthal 2002). For example, anticipation that an underclass will always vote for debt cancellation may cause credit markets to collapse, allowing no boats to rise.

Regulatory Policies

The development and implementation of regulatory policies in credit markets is becoming an active area of research in political economy. Before turning to the political economy models, let us review several important policy areas and their implications for inequality.

- Market structure. Political processes decide how creditors can operate. For example, political decisions have circumscribed the entry of banks into local markets (Kroszner and Strahan 1999). How legislation that determines the concentration of creditors affects the poor is a complex matter. While a decentralized system may be more efficient, a centralized system may be more beneficial to the "poor" (Dewatripont and Maskin 1995). Other legislation can affect the organization of debtors. For example, government constraints on household credit markets may help maintain rotating and other cooperative credit arrangements in industrializing economies (Besley 1995).

- Interest rate regulation. Political processes can be used to set maximum or minimum interest rates. A high minimum rate would represent legalized price-fixing, a cartel to the benefit of lenders. A low maximum rate could cause lending to dry up, to the detriment of all. On the other hand, a usury law that set a maximum rate somewhat below the market-clearing rate could provide a desirable form of social insurance (Glaeser and Scheinkman 1998).

- Debt repayment regulation. There is widespread agreement that credit markets benefit from the "rule of law" that allows for the efficient enforcement of debt contracts. Private enforcement is typically regarded as an inefficient substitute for an honest court system (Straub and Sosa 2001; Pinheiro and Cabral 2001).[3] On the other hand, complete enforcement or overly harsh punishment might result in an inefficient loss of productive resources held by the poor.

  The severity of enforcement has been an important issue in the United States from the early days of the republic (Mann 2002) through the current debate over the availability of "fresh start" bankruptcy for credit card debtors and the unlimited household exemptions some states afford to debtors (Nunez and Rosenthal 2004; Posner, Hynes, and Malani 2001).

  The policy debate on enforcement is echoed in theoretical models that study the degree of leniency the courts will grant debtors with regard to the collection of both the debtor's return and collateral (Jappelli, Pagano, and Bianco 2002). When the debtor has information unknown to the creditor, creditors might prefer contracts where debtors' prison type punishment accomplishes only enforcement and does not benefit the creditor (Diamond 1984). Debtors might prefer contracts where punishment is proscribed and monitoring costs are incurred (Townsend 1979).

- Ex post intervention in debt contracts. Some regulations, such as bankruptcy law, pertain to individual debt contracts ex ante. Is there also a case for more contingent regulation that might occur, ex post, to avoid a macroeconomic collapse? In practice, the courts have allowed for ex post intervention in unusual circumstances such as the Great Depression (Kroszner 2003; Alston 1983; 1984; Rucker and Alston 1987). Patrick Bolton and Howard Rosenthal (2002), moreover, point to circumstances where politics provides an opportunity for debt relief that is ex ante, as well as ex post, optimal. Indeed, the United States has a long history of ex post intervention in credit markets (Rothbard 1962; Mann 2002; Warren 1935; Balleisen 1996).

- Loan Guarantees, Direct Subsidies, and Bailouts. One way to make things easier for the poor is to up front reduce the risk or increase the return to lenders. Loan guarantees and subsidies are pervasive in the housing and post-secondary education markets, air transportation and other markets in the United States. A bailout can be thought of as a probabilistic loan guarantee, one that pays off only when the borrower has enough political muscle (Chrysler) to get it through. Economy wide bailouts in unusual circumstance have similar implications for efficiency as government cancellation of private debts. Debt cancellation and bailouts do differ mightily in who bears the costs of government intervention (Bolton and Rosenthal 2002; Biais and Récassens 2002).

- Regulation of Information and Negotiation. Political processes might be used to redress asymmetries in information and bargaining skill. A wide variety of "consumer protection" legislation applies to credit markets. The topic is beyond the purview of this paper.[4]

- Investment Incentives and Stakeholder Protection. Inequality of individuals can be affected by the regulation of credit in investments where individuals are not directly borrowers. The channel is the firm-specific human capital individuals have in their workplaces. Their rents from this capital depend on the success or failure of the individual firms. If firms undertake relatively risky investments, some individuals will do relatively well and others poorly. Enrico Perotti and Ernst-Ludwig von Thadden (2002) have begun to explore these issues in a model where the entire economy is driven by political decisions that determine, first, the level of firm-specific rents that accrue to stakeholders, second, whether "lenders" or "equity holders" control firms, and, third, the degree to which taxation can be used to redistribute across individuals. In their model, inequality can be lowered if firms are controlled by lenders who have a limited, nondiversifiable claim on the firm's return.

Modeling the Politics of Credit Markets

Political economy models of credit markets are inherently models where inequality is present. If all agents were identical, there would be no reason for credit markets to operate. So credit markets flourish as a result of inequality. Initial inequality can occur in three ways. First, there can be inequality in endowed wealth, either in money or physical assets, including those assets that can serve as collateral for loans. Second, there can be inequality in endowed abilities, in productivity. Third, there can be inequality in political rights. For example, voting rights might be restricted to a subset of the agents. I concentrate on the first two, economic forms. But I do ask if some form of political inequality is beneficial to the reduction of economic inequality. I evaluate political intervention in credit markets in terms of its effect on ex post inequality in the form of utility or consumption differences.

The models I look at all have a common basic structure with regard to the sequencing of political and economic decisions by agents. A political process is used to determine constraints on actions in the economy. Sometime it is useful to think of the political process as taking place "behind the veil of ignorance" before capital endowments or abilities are known. The political process can also occur at an interim stage, either after endowments are known or even after markets have operated to produce returns and information. In a final stage, the economy operates subject to the regulatory constraints imposed by the political process. Final payoffs are then realized.[5]

Against the background of the common structure or timing, the models are differentiated along two dimensions. First, one model, that of Perotti and von Thadden (2002), seeks to analyze institutions that govern the economic organization of a society. Credit is embedded in a consideration of corporate governance institutions and, specifically, whether "debt" or "equity" dominates. I treat this model last. The other models look at specific issues in the operation of credit markets. Second, models differ in the information structure that surround contracting. In some cases, debtors and creditors are completely informed. In others, at least the creditors are incompletely informed about the characteristics of debtors.

I start with models where debtors and creditors contract in a setting of complete information. In each model, there is a case for political intervention. I begin with Edward Glaeser and Jose Scheinkman (1998), where the motivation for borrowing is to provide for consumption smoothing. It illustrates the role that risk aversion plays in making a case for regulation. The focus is different in Kenneth Ayotte (2002), Tullio Jappelli, Marco Pagano, and Madga

Bianco (2002), and Bruno Biais and Gilles Récassens (2002). These scholars are concerned with government regulation of defaulting debtors. Ayotte examines the government's role in regulating the terms under which defaulting debtors get refinanced. Jappelli and his coauthors pursue government policy toward seizing the income and collateral of borrowers. Biais and Récassens show how liquidation versus continuation (with no refinancing) is affected by social costs and legal corruption.

When it comes to incomplete information settings, Mathias Dewatripont and Eric Maskin (1995) pursue the refinancing problem when there is asymmetric information between borrowers and lenders. Bolton and Rosenthal (2002) study the situation where both borrowers and lenders are incompletely informed and contracts are necessarily incomplete.

Regulating Credit Contracts Under Complete Information

The first two studies can be seen as exploring interest rate regulation, an important avenue for government policy. When credit markets are fully competitive, a regulated interest rate can provide insurance to the poor as shown by Glaeser and Scheinkman (1998). When lenders have monopoly power in credit markets, regulation can increase aggregate output. Ayotte (2002) shows this in the context of the "fresh start" theme in the bankruptcy literature. In his work, a fresh start is captured by reduced repayment terms for future loans to borrowers currently in default. The reduced terms are equivalent to a reduction in the interest rate on the loan. Jappelli, Pagano, and Bianco (2002), and Biais and Récassens (2002) focus on the regulation of default.

Inequality, Social Insurance, and Usury

Usury laws, laws that regulate maximum interest rates, are pervasive in human history. What might lead to political adoption of such laws? Glaeser and Scheinkman (1998) investigated this question.

Creditors will lose from an usury law. At the regulated interest rate, debtors have unsatisfied demand for loans. If the regulation is removed, lender volumes and profits will rise. On the other hand, debtors can benefit. A usury law effectively reduces competition among borrowers. Although borrowers will be able to borrow less, the loss in available credit will be more than offset by the reduction in price. Beyond the veil of ignorance, when individuals are uncertain whether their destiny is to be rich creditors or poor debtors, a society might well unanimously opt for a usury law. Ex ante, an optimal usury law maximizes expected utility from the credit market. The law provides social insurance by correcting for a pecuniary externality in the competitive market.

THE ECONOMIC ENVIRONMENT   In the Glaeser and Scheinkman model, there are two classes of individuals, rich and poor. There are two periods, and in each both the rich and poor receive endowments. A rich individual receives more than a poor individual in both periods. The rich, however, are relatively less rich in the second period than in the first; they have a smaller share of the second period pie. There is no storage, so endowments must be consumed. The economy is an extremely simple one. There is no uncertainty, no production, no time preference, and no money.

The second period endowments, in the aggregate, are at least as large as the first period's, so there can be exogenous growth in the economy. A loan contract is simply a transfer of consumption from rich to poor in the first period in exchange for a transfer from poor to rich in the second period. Loan contracts are enforced. All loans are repaid. There is strictly decreasing marginal utility of consumption.

For the model to give rise to a market for credit to accomplish consumption smoothing, the poor must have an incentive to borrow and the rich an incentive to lend. This requires, with respect to the starting point represented by the endowments, the following condition on marginal utility, denoted MU:

$$\frac{MU(\text{poor at } t = 1)}{MU(\text{rich at } t = 1)} = \frac{MU(\text{poor at } t = 2)}{MU(\text{rich at } t = 2)}$$

Consider the case where there is no growth. That is, two equal-size pies are distributed, one at $t = 1$ and the other at $t = 2$. Because the poor are poor, they always have higher marginal utility for consumption. They have especially high marginal utility at $t = 1$, so they are willing to give up second period consumption to get more in the first period. Indeed, they are even willing to pay interest. That is, they are willing to give up more second period consumption than they gain in the first period. The loans smooth consumption for the rich as well as the poor.

MARKET CLEARING IN THE ABSENCE OF POLITICAL INTERVENTION   The loan market is characterized by two variables, L, the per capita loan amount, and R, the interest rate. In the absence of political intervention, the market equilibrium reduces to a simple supply and demand analysis. This leads directly to market-clearing values R_M and L_M.[6]

POLITICS BEHIND THE VEIL   Political intervention might be considered to take place "behind the veil of ignorance," when the citizens do not know their types (rich or poor). Behind the veil, all individuals have identical preferences.

FIRST BEST BEHIND THE VEIL   Behind the veil, all citizens should agree to expropriate all wealth in both periods and give all citizens equal shares. This would maximize ex ante utility and, obviously, eliminate future inequality. Since there are no labor supply or similar disincentive effects to expropriation, the Glaeser-Scheinkman model implicitly assumes that expropriation has out-of-the-model costs that are just too high. Identifying the wealthy types, collecting their endowments, and redistributing is presumably very costly relative to the type of redistribution that takes place in a decentralized system where the wealthy are voluntarily matched with the poor in loan contracts.[7] In contrast, it is assumed that government can costlessly enforce and regulate private debt contracts.[8] Throughout this chapter I am going to adopt the approach implicit in the Glaeser-Scheinkman paper. First, governments find direct redistribution so costly that capital and consumption transfers will have to take place through credit contracts. Second, governments will, at no cost, enforce these contracts, subject to information constraints (as in Bolton and Rosenthal 2002). As the Fabbri and Padula (chapter 5, this volume) and several papers in Pagano (2001) make clear, enforcement is in fact very costly. I am, to get at other issues, simply sweeping enforcement costs under the rug.

Intervention in the Credit Market: Usury Laws   A usury law, setting an upper limit to the interest rate, R_U, would be a second-best behind the veil policy that all would agree to. Since individuals have de-creasing marginal utility of consumption, the socially optimal inter-est rate is lower than the market-clearing rate. The socially optimal rate depends on the supply elasticity of loans by the rich. The more elastic the supply, the less the usury law should depart from the market-clearing rate. Since the socially optimal rate is a binding constraint on lending, the loan amount L_U is that which results when the rich maximize utility subject to the constraint that the in-terest rate is R_U. At this interest rate, there is excess demand for loans by the poor, and the rich, if they could, would charge a higher rate to clear the market.

Let us be clear about the source of benefits of the usury law. Total societal output is the same, so there is no gain to total consumption. The market equilibrium has the usual Pareto property of a market—there is no other allocation that leaves someone better off and no one worse off. In contrast, at R_U, a poor individual would want to borrow more and pay more for it while a rich individual would want to lend more in return for a greater payment. But in participating in the market, the poor are subject to a pecuniary externality as they bid against each other. Behind the veil of ignorance, individuals would want to eliminate this externality—improving their lot when they turn out to be poor in exchange for a somewhat worse out-come when they are rich.

The Effect of Initial Inequality   How would inequality affect whether a society adopts a usury law behind the veil? Glaeser and Scheink-man find that a usury law is more likely and the rate of interest R_U lower when:

1. Income is distributed unequally. So one consequence of more in-equality would be stricter usury laws. This would be consistent with the passage of usury laws in the nineteenth-century United States, when income appears to have been less equally distrib-uted than it was in the mid-twentieth century.

2. Income is volatile. Volatility in the Glaeser-Scheinkman model is captured by how much the share of the pie going to the poor changes from one period to the next. So we are talking mainly about the volatility of income going to various subgroups of the

population. If there is no volatility, there is no incentive for the poor to pay interest to smooth their consumption. Note that if the poor are more subject to bouts of unemployment, their income may be more volatile than that of the rich. This is captured by the following interpretation of the model. The first period represents a time of downturn in the economy, so the poor have low income. In the second period, the economy recovers. The pie expands, but the poor have relatively larger gains than the rich.

3. Growth rates are low. If growth rates are high enough, the rich will have no incentive to lend to smooth consumption, even if their period 2 share falls. If the rich do not want to lend in the first place, a usury law has no bite.

4. The supply of loans is inelastic. When the supply is inelastic, the benefits of cheaper rates are not offset by a reduced supply of credit.

5. Loans are for consumption. If the rich have investment opportunities, they will be less willing to lend to the poor to finance consumption.

A usury law is essentially a form of price regulation. With price regulation, supply does not equal demand. So the aggregate supply must be rationed among consumers. Lenders and borrowers will look for a variety of means to evade the regulation including commissions and other charges. George Holmes (1892) provides a large list of evasive strategies.

In the United States, usury laws are largely a matter of state law. As long as credit markets were local, these laws could be somewhat effective.[9] The development of a national credit market, particularly with regard to credit cards, has essentially resulted in a race to the bottom in which out-of-state lenders represent the uncontrolled sector. From the perspective of the Glaeser-Scheinkman model there is a case for a national usury law as a form of social insurance.

The Effect of an Optimal Usury Law on Inequality   Let us compare inequality with R_M, R_U and $R = 0$. First period consumption inequality is actually decreasing in the interest rate since the poor borrow more as the interest rate increases for $R < R_M$. The reverse is true for second period consumption inequality, which increases in the interest rate. With respect to overall utility, inequality is worst when credit markets collapse and $R = 0$. The overall utility of both poor and rich is least at $R = 0$. For any interest rate for which loans take place, the transaction must be beneficial to both parties. The poor have higher utility at R_U than R_M, and vice-versa for the rich. So R_U has less inequality than the market rate. Note, however, that R_U is not the interest rate that would minimize inequality in a regulated credit market. An even lower rate would make the poor better off at the expense of the rich. But such a rate is not chosen behind the veil. Citizens take into account that they may be rich as well as poor. There are two policy lessons from this analysis:

1. When redistribution is not direct but indirect via credit markets, some ex post inequality may be a desirable social policy. The comment holds even when, as in the Glaeser-Scheinkman model, we do not need to consider disincentive effects from labor supply or capital flight but do need to consider the voluntary participation of the rich in the credit market. Behind the veil, ex ante, the society should accept some inequality ex post.

2. Obtaining a reduction in inequality in the short run is not always a compelling argument for a policy. Although the unregulated market has relatively low first period consumption inequality, this short-term reduction in inequality is not worth the increase that occurs in the second period. In other words, government policy may seek to protect the poor from borrowing too much. Paradoxically, at least in a Glaeser-Scheinkman framework, the way to do this is to see that the poor are charged low interest rates.

INTERIM POLITICAL INTERVENTION   If usury laws are decided not behind the veil but after types know whether they are rich or poor, interest rates will depend on the relative political power of the rich and poor.

• Poor are decisive. One might think that Populism would destroy credit markets. This would happen only if the poor were irrational. Utility maximization by the poor leads to an interest rate at which credit markets still operate. The poor are better off borrowing. Rational poor simply act as monopsonists.

- Rich are decisive. Similarly, rational rich would not just go above the behind the veil rate to an unregulated market. They will vote to have governmental authority enforce a lenders' cartel in the form of higher than market rates.

The Glaeser-Scheinkman model is very easy to think about in terms of majority voting. There are only two types of agents, rich and poor. The rich have one most preferred interest rate, the poor another. I should point out that interim politics would become more complex in populations made heterogeneous by a continuum of types of either utility functions or endowments.

EMPIRICAL EFFECTS OF USURY LAWS   Glaeser and Scheinkman present only anecdotal and very exploratory empirical work in support of their model. John Caskey (1997) adds an interesting twist in his empirical examination of usury laws in the American states as they affect pawnshops, a source of consumption loans to the poor. Pawnshop outlets are largely one-person operations that need a minimum profit level in order to be viable. Usury laws reduce the profit per loan, which must be made up in greater loan volume. This results in a lower geographic density of pawnshops. The winners here are urban borrowers, who pay lower interest rates and do not have to travel much farther to find a lender. The losers are rural borrowers. Thus, usury laws on pawnshops redistribute among the poor. Caskey also notes that the rich elite once recognized the social benefits of low interest pawnshops and financed non-profit pawn organizations. The only one to remain in existence in the United States is the Provident Loan Society in New York City. The non-profits charge lower interest rates than profits but give a lower loan amount for a given collateral and may restrict the type of collateral accepted.[10]

Bankruptcy Policy as Usury Law

The regulation of payments to creditors in a bankruptcy reorganization can also be seen as a problem of regulating an interest rate. I use the work of Ayotte (2002) to illustrate this point.

A MONOPOLY LENDER AND A HIGH ABILITY BORROWER   Ayotte (2002) first considers a situation where a monopoly lender confronts an entrepreneur (or many identical ones) of known ability level. In period 0, the lender makes investment funds I_1 available to the entrepreneur. The probability the project succeeds in period 1 and returns R_1 is increasing in costly effort expended by the entrepreneur. If the project succeeds, the contract is over and payoffs are made. If the project fails, the lender will, because the entrepreneur is of sufficiently high ability, want to invest an additional amount I_2. Again the return R_2 depends on effort. If the project succeeds, payoffs are made. If the project fails, there is no return. The "game" ends.

The monopoly lender is profit-maximizing and chooses repayments F_1, F_2 to maximize profits, taking into account the entrepreneur's incentives to expend effort. As in any monopoly problem, prices are too high to maximize social surplus. The first-best would be for a government to both order the lender to make the necessary investment transfers to the borrower and to mandate higher effort levels by the entrepreneur. If, as is my stance throughout, the government is limited to regulating voluntary loan contracts, it can still improve social surplus. Ayotte considers solely the regulation of F_2, the loan contract of a "reorganized" failure at the end of period 1. He shows that the government should choose a lower repayment than the monopoly repayment. The direct benefit is that more effort is expended in period 2, resulting in a greater chance of garnering R_2. This benefit is offset by the entrepreneur's expending less effort in period 1, given that the government regulation gives a higher continuation payoff than monopoly. This lesser effort is in fact what underpins the standard argument in favor of tough bankruptcy policies. But in contrast to the standard argument, the soft policy does not drive up interest rates. On the contrary, the monopolist lowers F_1 in order to induce the entrepreneur to expend more effort in period 1. Regulating the monopolist does, as is standard, increase social surplus.

HETEROGENEOUS BORROWERS WITH REGULATED INTEREST RATE AND WORKOUTS   Ayotte shows his results are quite robust to having a heterogeneous population of entrepreneurs, as long as their abilities are known in advance. There will be a minimum ability level needed to receive a loan. For projects that fail at period 1, there will be a cutpoint.

Below the cutpoint, entrepreneurs (or at least their firms) will be liquidated; above it, they will secure additional financing. If the government sets a regulated F_2 following the filing of bankruptcy, it would appear that this would lead to more liquidation, thereby enlarging the poor. But this problem can be solved by allowing for voluntary workouts where a firm, knowing it otherwise faces liquidation, will agree to pay a higher rate than the regulated rate. If workouts are costless, there again is a gain to social surplus. In particular, there is a gain for relatively high ability firms that would have to pay a higher rate in period 2 without government regulation. With regulation, these entrepreneurs produce more period 2 effort and reap higher expected returns than in the unregulated market.[11]

Regulation with Workouts: Benefits Accrue Only to the More Able   One might think of Ayotte's entrepreneur as a small startup business. Only a slice of the entrepreneurs benefit from a fresh start policy. Government regulation of F_2 combined with costless workouts gives no benefit to the least able entrepreneurs. Moreover, regulation benefits only some of those receiving loans. After period 1, "luck" creates successful and failed projects. The "lucky" are the big winners among borrowers and naturally do not benefit from a fresh start given to the failures. Among the "unlucky," less able types either continue to be liquidated or agree to a workout where they pay an unregulated interest rate. So these less able types do not benefit. The only beneficiaries are the relatively high ability types who secure additional financing for period 2 at the regulated rate. Moreover, there is, in the absence of transfers, no salvation for the doubly unlucky, those with failed projects after period 2.

Ayotte's model begs the question of regulating F_1 as well as F_2. In terms of social surplus, it would clearly pay to attack monopoly power at every point, albeit paying attention to the participation constraint of the lender. The case for such a double-barreled usury law, however, becomes weaker as lenders become more competitive. Interestingly, however, the case for a "usury" law limited to F_2 does not depend on the government being able to fine tune its policy. It turns out that any F_2 less than the market rate is better than the market rate. The basic reason for this interesting result is that workouts increase as F_2 is reduced. For any F_2 below what the monopolist would charge, there is no loss with respect to entrepreneurs that are liquidated or undergo workouts while a gain persists for those that are refinanced at the regulated rate.

Majority Voting and Regulation   Finally, it is interesting to ask—although the issue is not explored by Ayotte—how the political process would operate at an interim stage after types are known. The lender is worse off as the government imposed rate gets lower. Borrowers are better off as the rate gets lowered until it gets so low that the threat of liquidation forces them into a workout, a situation that returns them to the high private market rate. Thus, the preferences of the borrowers are single-peaked, with the most preferred F_2 being the lowest rate that leads to a fresh start in bankruptcy rather than a workout. If the lenders do not vote, the median ability type will decide the policy under standard majority rule assumptions. This policy, Ayotte's results show, will be better than the private market but it may be far from the behind the veil policy that would maximize social surplus.

Collateral Wealth and Enforcement of Debt Collection

Jappelli, Pagano, and Bianco (2002) model the process of legal enforcement. Their model differs from that of Ayotte in two important ways. First, it is one-shot. It concerns only debt collection and not refinancing. Second, loans can be collateralized. A common thread, however, is the analysis of government policy in the case of failure. Jappelli and his coauthors interpret leniency to borrowers as weak enforcement. Another way to view the model, however, is to assume that the "rule of law" prevails but, re household exemptions in American bankruptcy law, the state constrains the extent of recovery.

Here's the setup. Entrepreneurs, to simplify just a wee bit, can undertake a project that returns an amount $1 + \pi$ with probability p. They need to borrow 1 unit to finance the project. Lenders require a return of at least $1 + \bar{r}$ to break even. Entrepreneurs are heterogeneous in the amount of collateral c_i that each entrepreneur has to back up the loan in case the project fails. The regulatory environment is captured by two parameters, ϕ_P and ϕ_c. These parameters need not be interpreted in terms of deadweight costs of enforcement. Rather they specify how the debtor's assets are shared with the creditor in case the debtor fails to repay the loan. If a loan is defaulted, the lenders can grab $\phi_c c_i$ of the collateral. In the case of a successful project, they can also recover $\phi_P(1 + \pi)$.[12] The loan repayment amount $1 + r_i$ is endogenous. The repayment amount is the most lenders can recover in the case of default. The authors consider two scenarios, one with competitive lenders and one with monopoly lenders.

COMPETITIVE LENDERS   With fully competitive lenders, there should not be political conflict. Lenders earn zero profits for any values of the parameters, so they are indifferent about enforcement. Similarly, conditional on receiving a loan, borrowers are indifferent about the values of both ϕ_P and ϕ_c. Competition among lenders gives these borrowers the entire expected surplus from their project. Moreover, as either parameter is increased toward the maximum value of 1, fewer entrepreneurs are credit rationed and unable to secure financing. There is thus no political economy problem here. A status quo policy of $\phi_P = \phi_c = 1$, strict enforcement, will be weakly preferred to any other policy, both behind the veil and after the endowments, c_i are known.

(The result of support for strict enforcement arises because the borrowers are risk neutral. Except for borrowers with very high levels of collateral, the interest rate r_i is decreasing in ϕ_c. Risk averse borrowers will prefer a lower ϕ_c, retaining more when they fail, in return for making a higher payment when their project succeeds. In contrast, for constant ϕ_P, credit rationed entrepreneurs would like to see ϕ_c raised enough to permit their becoming borrowers.)

BORROWER PREFERENCES UNDER MONOPOLY LENDING   Political problems arise when there is not perfect competition. Monopoly banks will now like better enforcement. Better enforcement allows the bank to extract a higher surplus by raising interest rates. Moreover, fewer borrowers will be credit rationed, so a larger number of profitable loans will be issued.

Preferences and the Social Choice Problem   The preferences of borrowers under monopoly are more complicated than under competition. Assume a bank makes a loan as long as its profits are weakly positive. Jappelli, Pagano, and Bianco (2002) show that the bank's zero profit combinations of ϕ_P and ϕ_c for an entrepreneur of type c_i satisfy the linear locus:

$$c_i = \frac{1 + \bar{r}}{\phi_c} - \frac{p\phi_p(1 + \pi)}{\phi_c}$$

Entrepreneur type c_i's most preferred policies are any points on this locus. The bank breaks even and the borrower keeps the entire surplus. The entrepreneur likes points on a locus for $c > c_i$ less because she will be credit rationed. Points on a locus $c < c_i$ are also less preferred because the bank uses the better enforcement to extract some of the entrepreneur's surplus. The most preferred loci are monotonic in c_i. Without getting further into the social choice problem generated by the individual preferences, it is clear that complete enforcement will no longer be an equilibrium, either behind the veil or at the interim stage. From the viewpoint of equality of ex post returns, however, it is clear that the less well endowed and the monopolist benefit from strict enforcement to the detriment of those with more collateral. Thus, when there is monopoly (or oligopoly) banking there will be political conflict among debtors over enforcement policies. In the context of the Jappelli, Pagano, and Bianco model, the Robin Hoods are not the poor but the rich. There would be a political coalition between the rentier class and the poor. The poor—again within the specific context of this model—are best off with a strong degree of enforcement. This result echoes the Ayotte (2002) paper—leniency most benefits those borrowers who have the highest endowments, either in ability or in collateral.

Limiting Collateral In the monopoly model, borrowers who get loans under a policy ϕ_p, ϕ_c would seek to hide the value of some of their collateral. Alternatively, they could push for legislation to limit the collateral that could be attacked by the lender. Such a law would reduce the profitability of the monopolist and increase returns to some borrowers without hurting the least well endowed. This might correspond to making ϕ_c a decreasing function of c_i, perhaps effectively the case if the better endowed receive more effective legal representation.

In their article, Jappelli, Pagano, and Bianco (2002) had the objective of deriving theoretical predictions about how variation in enforcement would affect the performance of credit markets. I have tried to take a small step beyond their model to show how the choice of policies could enter into a political process, one that can have substantial impact on the equality of outcomes for participants in the market.

Corrupt Enforcement, Liquidation Value, and Social Costs

Biais and Récassens (2002) present a different model of enforcement that also leads to the rich favoring leniency. The poor favor leniency as well, while the middle class may favor "tough" enforcement. Their model differs from that of Jappelli, Pagano, and Bianco (2002) in several respects. Entrepreneurs need I units of capital to finance a project. But they only need to borrow $I - A_i$ where A_i is the endowment of type $i \in \{p,m,r\}$ for poor, middle, and rich. The entrepreneurs can exert either high or low effort. The project either succeeds and returns an amount R or fails and returns 0. The probability of success depends on effort. In the case of success, loans are always repaid and the entrepreneur is continued, receiving a continuation rent E. In the case of failure, if the entrepreneur is continued, the lender receives 0 and the entrepreneur again gets E. If the entrepreneur is liquidated, the lender receives L and the entrepreneur receives 0. The capital market is competitive.

The first best is for all types to be funded, for all types to exert high effort, and for all entrepreneurs to be continued, even after failure. Liquidation is inefficient since $E > L$ is assumed. To get the first best, suppliers of capital have to take an equity participation in the firm. To both satisfy the participation constraint of the capitalists and the incentive compatibility constraint of the entrepreneurs, the entrepreneur must need to borrow only a relatively small amount of capital. In fact, the authors assume that only A_r is sufficiently large for these constraints to be satisfied. So only the rich get equity financing.

The other type of contract is a second best debt contract. The lender gets a high payment in the case of success and L in the case of failure. Again incentive compatibility and participation constraints must be satisfied. No deal is workable for the poor, who are credit rationed. The middle class gets debt contracts. If there is perfect enforcement of the contracts, we have a "tough" law.

A "soft" law allows entrepreneurs to be continued in the case of failure. Two forces drive to continuation. One is that a failure is seen as imposing exogenous social costs, which are unknown when the contract is signed. Law mandates continuing when the costs pass a threshold value. The other force is corrupt judges. They will, for a bribe paid by the entrepreneur, continue the firm even when the social costs are below the threshold. The probability of the judge not being corruptible is fixed. The chance that a failed entrepreneur will continue, robbing the lender of L, obviously leads to more credit rationing.

OPTIMAL BEHIND THE VEIL POLICIES   There are two cases to consider in discussing optimal policies in the Biais and Récassens model:

1. Middle class is relatively rich and receives financing under both "tough" and "soft" laws. In this case, a "soft" law is preferred, because E > L and the social costs of liquidation are avoided.

2. Middle class is relatively poor and receives financing only under "tough" law. In this case, a "soft" law is preferred only if social costs are sufficiently high. That is, it is better not to have these entrepreneurs financed at all if the cost of bad apples is too high. Of course, this result would change if it were thought that social costs also resulted when entrepreneurs were credit rationed.

It is direct to see how inequality is affected by the choice between "soft" and "tough." Inequality between the poor and middle classes is always reduced by a "soft" law in the first case whenever the continuation rent E is less than the social cost born by the poor in the case of liquidation; in the second case, "soft" law also reduces inequality because the middle lose financing. Analysis of inequality between middle and rich is similar.

POLITICS   The poor and the rich will always favor a "soft" law because their own financing is unaffected by the law while they share in the social costs of liquidation. The middle class will prefer a "soft" law if they are relatively rich, unless bribes become too expensive. In contrast, a relatively poor middle class prefers a "tough" law. It is easy to see that, depending on who has political power, the political decision, made once endowments are known, can readily differ from the optimal policy.

An interesting extension to the model occurs when entrepreneurs can hire labor. The important distinction here arises with a relatively poor middle class. If there is a "soft" law such that they are credit rationed, the middle class is thrown onto the labor market. If there is a "tough" law, only the poor become laborers and their wages are bid up. Thus, bankruptcy law creates a pecuniary externality for the poor, as in Bolton and Rosenthal (2002). The effect of a "soft" law is to depress wages, making the rich even more favorable to a "soft" law and making the poor less favorable—the poor must now trade off social costs and wages. Thus, as in Ayotte (2002) and in Jappelli, Pagano, and Bianco (2002), "softness" exerts its greatest charm on the most highly endowed.

Credit Markets with Incomplete Information

Dewatripont and Maskin (1995) and Bolton and Rosenthal (2002) represent two situations where politics will respond to information flows as well as to inequality in endowments and market power. In both models, borrowers vary in productive capacity. In Dewatripont and Maskin, the setup is one of asymmetric information at the time of the loan. The borrower knows his or her ability but the lender is ignorant. This leads to a problem of adverse selection. Aggregate output will be greater if the bad types do not get loans. The credit market may undergo endogenous organization that screens out the bad. Political intervention could take the form of preventing this organization to achieve redistributive goals. This intervention need only be an ex ante policy. Because the borrower type becomes known to the lender after the loan is made, a complete contract can be written. Government intervention would affect financing decisions but not repayments. In contrast, in the Bolton and Rosenthal model, neither borrowers nor lenders know productive abilities when loans are contracted and an individual borrower's type cannot be verified after production takes place. In this case, intervention takes the form of a political process that allows penalties for default to be contingent on the average level of productivity, that is the overall state of the economy. Loan contracts are unaffected, but all borrowers are allowed to default in bad times. The political process partially completes the contracts by conditioning them on the macroeconomy.

Asymmetric Information and the Structure of the Credit Market

In the Dewatripont and Maskin (1995) model, there are two types of potential entrepreneurs, whom I will term good and bad. Entrepreneurs borrow one unit in an initial period 0. The good complete their projects at the end of period 1 and produce a return $R_g >$ 1 after extracting a rent $E_g \geq 0$. Clearly a good project is socially beneficial and should be financed. The bad require an additional unit of financing in period 1 and complete their project only at the end of period 2. The bad take a loan only if they know it will be refinanced since, to simplify slightly, they enjoy rents that satisfy $E_b > 0 > E_t$, where E_b is the rent from a completed project and E_t the rent from a project that is terminated after period 1. Since the net return from a bad project is less than the two units of investment required, the social value of financing the bad is dubious.

THE BASICS OF THE MODEL   The bad can get financed, however, because of adverse selection. Dewatripont and Maskin (1995) first show this by looking at a simple situation in which there is a single lender, with two units of capital, and a single borrower. The lender does not know the borrower's type when writing the loan contract but does know the type at the end of period 1. He can, therefore, write a complete contract. The lender has all bargaining power and walks away with the total return from the project (net of rents). Moreover, the lender can engage in costly monitoring in period 2 that increases the chances of getting a relatively high return from the bad project. Because the first unit of capital is sunk in period 0 and because the lender is unable to credibly commit not to refinance at period 1, the lender refinances since the expected return, net of monitoring costs, exceeds one. Knowing they will be refinanced, the bad entrepreneurs take loans. This structure was chosen to mimic the "soft budget constraint" problem in socialist economies.

Loans to the bad can be avoided with an alternative, "decentralized" market structure. Here the borrower faces two lenders, each with one unit of capital. A lead lender makes a loan in period 1. Again this lender can monitor in period 2. Because the lender must share the return from a completed bad project with the second lender, the "decentralized" lender will monitor less than the "centralized" lender. For some technologies, the first lender will not monitor enough for the second lender to expect to break even on the loan. So the second lender will not lend. In turn, if the bad type entrepreneur gets a negative rent E_t from a project that is not refinanced, the poor type will not borrow. The decentralized structure can thus screen out bad projects.

THE MODEL IN A LARGE ECONOMY WITH EXCESS CAPITAL   Dewatripont and Maskin (1995) proceed to extend the simple model to one where there are many entrepreneurs and an even larger number of potential lenders so capital is in excess supply. Consequently, lenders earn zero profits. The organization of the credit market is endogenous. Lenders can either operate in a decentralized fashion, each lending at most one unit of capital, or combine into banks with two units. (There is no incentive to form larger banks.) The two-unit banks have the option of sinking all their capital immediately in two projects or of investing in just one project in period 0 and possibly refinancing the project in period 1. When productivity and monitoring technology lead to relatively low returns from bad projects, the (essentially unique) equilibrium has decentralized creditors offering contracts that are accepted only by good types. In contrast, when conditions for bad projects are more favorable, only big banks offer contracts and all projects get financed.

The interesting political economy questions posed by the model arise in the former case, where only good projects get financed. First, it is not always efficient to finance only good projects since the lenders do not consider the rent E_b enjoyed by bad types whose projects are financed until completion. Second, even when project returns and entrepreneurial rents together do not justify an investment of two units of capital, not financing bad projects is the worst outcome for bad entrepreneurs. (I focus on inequality between entrepreneurs and ignore the fact that excess supply of capital leads to no net income for lenders.) In the absence of ex post transfers, there can be a case for financing bad projects.

GOVERNMENT REGULATION OF THE MARKET   How might government intervention proceed in the Dewatripont-Maskin economy? Assume that the total expected return from financing all projects, net of monitoring costs, at least equaled the capital costs. Then legislation could mandate that loans be made only by big banks restricted to lending only one unit in period 0 (a capital requirement). Competition among the big banks would then result in contracts that would lead to all projects being financed. Clearly, intervention would be expected if a political decision is made after borrowers know their types and if the bad are politically pivotal. If entrepreneurs are risk averse, to hark back to Glaeser and Scheinkman (1998), intervention might also be adopted behind the veil as long as the implicit cross-subsidy of good to bad is not too great. In contrast, if good types are pivotal, they will impose a small bank structure even when the market would endogenously organize as large banks.

In summary, I have indicated how regulatory issues, ones with implications for inequality, arise in the relatively simple economy studied by Dewatripont and Maskin (1995). Here the questions pertained to the organization of creditors. But a very similar approach might well be applied to the extensive literature on the organization of credit markets for the poor that has developed largely in the context of developing nations (Besley 1995). For example, one policy decision might concern whether entrepreneurs are forced to borrow in cooperatives with joint liability. Questions of interim intervention will then arise for debtor as well as creditor organization.

Incomplete Contracts and Debt Moratoria

In contrast to the Dewatripont and Maskin (1995) model, Bolton and I (2002) have focused on an environment where returns are not observable. Incomplete contracts must be written. The poor are "farmers" who start with only their labor endowments and are unable to produce unless they can borrow capital from the rich. Farmers are further differentiated in terms of productive capacity. There are good, average, and bad types in order of decreasing ability. The model also features incomplete information with regard both to the productive capacity of individual agents and to the state of the macroeconomy. Loan terms and repayment cannot be made dependent on the productivity types or the state of the economy. A single commodity, thought of as wheat, is used for both investment and consumption. To produce wheat for consumption, invested wheat must be matched with labor. A farmer with sufficient capital may choose to hire labor in a labor market. There is no money in the model. All the initial stock of wheat is in the hands of the rich, who might be thought of as rentiers rather than bankers.[13]

The model takes place in three periods. Loans contracted in period 0 are repaid or defaulted in the period 1. At this time additional investment can take place from retained earnings. Labor markets are potentially open in both period 1 and period 2. Production takes place in periods 1 and 2. After period 1 production occurs, individual agents learn their productivity types and the state of the economy. All production is consumed at the end of the period 2. Thus there is no room for consumption smoothing. For both production periods, the economy is either in a High (H) state or Low (L) state for both production periods.

In the interesting equilibrium to the model, the rich lend to the poor in period 0. No labor is hired at that time. Good types are always able to repay their loans in period 1. Average types can repay only in the high state, and bad types can never repay. In the absence of a mechanism for political intervention, defaulting farmers keep their period 1 output but are "kicked off the farm" for period 2.

Political intervention takes the form of a referendum on a moratorium on the debt repayment. When a moratorium is voted, no one repays. Good types face a trade-off between getting cheap labor when there is no moratorium and getting out of their debts when there is one. They favor a moratorium only in the low state, when investment opportunities are weak. In contrast, the bad and average types are either unable to repay or have no demand for labor when they can repay, so they always favor a moratorium.

After a moratorium is voted in state L, the bad types are indifferent between keeping their farms or working for a wage equal to the value of the farm's output. In contrast, in the absence of a moratorium, the bad can only earn wheat as laborers. Because their labor is in excess supply, their wage is bid down to zero. A moratorium thus creates a pecuniary externality in the labor market to the benefit of bad types. The average types benefit from a moratorium in the low state by being able to add capital to their farms.

In state H, if there is not a majority for a moratorium, bad types are defaulted, average types repay but have no surplus for additional investment, and good types expand their farms, both by adding capital and by hiring labor.

When the good farmers are politically pivotal, a debt moratorium occurs only in state L. Then, no one repays. Nonetheless, if the low state is not too likely, credit markets do not collapse, and the outcome leads to higher expected aggregate output than were moratoria constitutionally proscribed.

A contingent moratorium equilibrium is worse for the rich than no intervention. As to the borrowers, the moratorium equilibrium is always better for all of them, when it exists, than the no intervention equilibrium that would hold were moratoria constitutionally proscribed. But if the bad or average poor are politically pivotal, the contingent moratorium equilibrium collapses. When the rich anticipate that a moratorium will be voted in both states, credit markets collapse and there is no lending. This is the worst case scenario for the poor. Thus, for some economies, the poor are better off when they are allowed to intervene and for others they are worse off.

The lesson here is that political equality in the form of majority rule and one-person one-vote may not always be desirable. Contingent moratoria dominate credit markets with no moratoria which in turn are better than the collapse of credit markets. But to have moratoria only in the low state, one group in the society, the good poor, must be politically pivotal. In essence, the good poor must be a dictator. If majority rule happens to make them dictator, so much the better. Otherwise, we will get more inequality. If the average and bad poor are pivotal, credit markets collapse and there will be no lending. If the rentiers are pivotal, there is never a moratorium and the bad and average poor are "kicked off the farm" in the low state. Admittedly this finding arises in a model that is specialized in its technology, its contracting structure, and its political institutions. Nonetheless, there is a general lesson that more political equality does not always mean more economic equality.

Types of Inequality   We now explore how changes in initial inequality affect the viability of political intervention.

Three types of inequality appear in the model:

1. Inequality in initial endowments. There are two types of agents. The poor agents have 0 endowment. The rich rentiers have endowment $\bar{W}$. There are N rich agents and M − N poor agents. Thus, the fraction that are rich is N/M. Obviously, for fixed N/M society

becomes more equal but poorer as $\bar{W}$ is decreased. The society becomes more equal as N/M is increased.

2. Inequality in abilities. The bad, the average, and the good differ in productivity. Obviously, the society becomes less equal if the expected productivity of the good is increased while the productivity of the other two types is held constant. Similarly, the society becomes more equal if the productivity of the bad type is increased. The effect on inequality of raising the productivity of the average types is ambiguous and depends on the productivity of the other two types and the population proportions of the types.

3. Inequality in outcomes. This is captured by the distribution of final consumption in the model. This distribution is determined by initial inequality, by uncertainty concerning the state of the macroeconomy, by technology, and by political institutions. The interaction of the economic model and politics is complex. It is quite possible that higher initial inequality in productive capacities will lead to lower inequality in consumption because higher initial inequality may prevent expropriative politics that causes the collapse of credit markets. In other words, there must be enough productive poor types with a "stake in the system" to prevent the unproductive types from causing a collapse of the economy.

ANALYSIS OF EQUILIBRIUM WITH A DEBT MORATORIUM In equilibrium, rentiers lend all their endowments to the poor in return for a repayment per unit lent equal to the productivity of average types in state H. In state H, a moratorium is rejected. In state L, a moratorium is voted and all types do not repay. This equilibrium holds for a range of values of the probability of state H, the productivity parameters, parameters that give the population distribution of good, average, and bad types, $\bar{W}$, N/M, and a technological parameter, $\bar{k}$, which describes maximum firm size.

This equilibrium exists only for certain combinations of parameters. Here is the intuition. For the rich to be willing to lend when moratoria are anticipated, the good state of the economy must be sufficiently likely. Interestingly, for some parameter values, however, the equilibrium can be sustained even when the low state is more likely than the high state. For the interest rate to be pegged to the productivity of average types, these types must be relatively productive in the high state, and the good types must not be too numerous. Bad poor types must be sufficiently numerous to provide an ample supply of labor. The high productivity of good types in state H affords this type with ample liquidity for investment; for investment opportunities to exist $\bar{k}$ must be relatively large. Note, finally, that it would be easier to sustain the equilibrium if a supramajority vote were required to enact a moratorium.

How Inequality Affects Equilibrium   How is the equilibrium influenced by the parameters that effect initial inequality?

- If we make the endowment of the rich, $\bar{W}$, too small we cannot sustain the equilibrium because the good types among the poor will vote for a moratorium even in state H. The reason is that their initial borrowings become so small that they have limited earnings to spend on additional capital and labor. Knowing that the good poor will vote for a moratorium causes the credit market to collapse. Nothing is lent. Thus the poor benefit if the rich are very rich to start with.

- Similarly, if the poor become too numerous (N/M small), the equilibrium collapses because the average and bad poor, who always vote for a moratorium, are the majority. In this sense a large number of unproductive poor undermines a democratic society because their incentive to cancel debts ex post prevents investment ex ante. Such societies can only get investment if they limit democracy and commit to ruling out moratoria in their constitutions. Such ideas seemed to pervade the drafting of the U.S. Constitution (McCoy 1989).

- There must be sufficient inequality in productivity for the good poor to have insufficient investment opportunities in state H. On the other hand, the good types must not to be too productive in state L or they will always oppose a moratorium. The state H productivity of average types must be sufficient to make loans profitable. The population proportions of the average types must also be large enough to make loans profitable. The bad poor also have to be relatively numerous in order to furnish a pool of cheap labor. Most interestingly, the bad poor cannot have productivity that is too low in state H. In this case, the good poor will always support a moratorium, since cheap labor will be available even with a moratorium. The equilibrium fails to hold; credit markets collapse.

Summary of Equilibrium Analysis   Sustaining an equilibrium in which credit markets are open but in which debt relief is provided in unusual circumstances appears to require both some moderate degree of inequality within the poor and substantial capital for the rich to lend.

INEQUALITY IN FINAL CONSUMPTION   Credit markets Pareto dominate the absence of a credit market. The society without a credit market is poor and unequal. Opening up a credit market allows, for typical parameter values, enormous increases in average consumption, even when moratoria are proscribed. But the credit market creates a winner-take-all society in which the good farmers become very wealthy. Moratoria, from the perspective of average consumption do not seem to make a great deal of difference. Compared to no moratorium, average consumption increases only slightly. Moratoria, however, sharply improve the lot of the least well off members of the society; bad farmers see their expected consumption increase substantially. (Since their initial consumption is low, this substantial increase contributes little to the overall average.) The big gain to the bad poor comes in state L. The bad (and average) farmers greatly benefit from a low state moratorium since they remain on their farm and do not become penniless laborers.

Summary of Inequality Analysis   In our illustrative economy, credit transfers achieve a first best in terms of initial investment. The rentiers lend all their wealth to the poor. This wealth is invested fully, hence optimally, given the information available in period 0. In terms of aggregate production, however, we are not at a first best in period 2. The first best would involve reinvesting wheat available at period 1 on good farms until the good farms reach their capacity constraint $\bar{k}$. To obtain the participation of the lenders, however, some wheat needs to be repaid rather than reinvested. Moreover, average and bad farmers retain output, which should be reinvested on good farms. Nonetheless, credit markets greatly benefit the society in that they provide an incentive for rentiers to transfer capital to producers. In our illustrative example, the first order benefit from government is clearly that of "rule of law," where debts are repaid in the absence of a moratorium. By eliminating repayment in the low state, moratoria have a second order effect and move the economy closer to the first best.

The resulting distribution of consumption, however, is highly unequal because of the winner-take-all technology. From a policy perspective however, it is worth emphasizing that this inequality is much to the advantage of the poor as a class. In absolute terms, no poor individual is left behind.

True, in our example, creditors suffer from a moratorium. Interestingly, this need not always be the case. Bolton and Rosenthal (2002) cover the scenario where creditors would actually prefer to have a contingent contract, where the repayment was set to the productivity of average types in state H but was reduced to the lower productivity of average types in state L. Because the state cannot be verified, they cannot obtain such a contract privately. If a moratorium, rather than completely eliminating repayment, could just reduce the repayment, the resulting political intervention could be Pareto optimal.

Credit in an Industrial Economy

The work of Perotti and von Thadden (2002) represents a very stylized investigation of the role of debt versus equity in a capitalist economy. An extension of the model investigates the use of taxation to reduce the ex post consumption inequality that arises, for example, in the Glaeser and Scheinkman (1998) and Bolton and Rosenthal (2002) models. Perotti and von Thadden tweak the model technically such that preferences are single-peaked and a median voter-dictator makes all political decisions. I will, as a short-hand, refer to this politically decisive agent as "government." The government regulates debt contracts by making the following policy choices:

1. Control of firms is given either to equity holders or lenders. If lenders are chosen, the lenders are prevented from diversifying their risk.

2. The loan exposure of the firm, L.

3. The maximum rent, H, available to stakeholders and employees in firms.

4. Whether incomes will be taxed.

After the initial political decision, firms choose between a "safe" and a "risky" investment strategy. (All firms make the same choice.) Each agent's final return is then the rent from the firm where the agent is employed plus a portfolio return from the aggregate economy. When taxation is introduced, individual returns are subjected to redistribution.

Each agent in the economy is associated with a firm and with an exogenous share α_i of the net returns to all firms in the economy. That is, every individual has a fully diversified equity portfolio but some individuals have greater exogenous wealth than others. The government then becomes the agent with median α. The return of each firm is a random variable $R \geq 0$. The distribution from which this return is drawn depends on whether the firm's investment strategy is "safe" or "risky." Individuals are risk-averse. The initial decisions of the government determine the investment choices of firms and the ultimate payoffs to agents. The economy faced by the government is as follows:

1. A parameter H bounds the firm-specific returns of individuals, h_i. These are given by:

$$h_i = H \text{ if } R_i \geq H$$
$$= R_i \text{ if } R_i < H$$

2. The firm's debt obligation L determines the return to lenders. Lenders seek to maximize their return. Since they have lower priority than stakeholders, the return is given by:

$$L \text{ if } L + H \leq R_i$$
$$R_i - H \text{ if } H \leq R_i < L + H$$
$$0 \text{ if } R_i < H$$

3. "Equity" controllers seek to maximize the firm's total return net of stakeholder rents and debt repayments.

4. An "equity" controller will always choose the risky investment

strategy that is high return, high variance. A "debt" controller may, because debt returns are upwardly limited, choose a "safe" investment strategy.

5. The government, in an extension, is free to tax firm returns and then give each individual a common lump sum payment. Tax collection involves deadweight loss. If tax-collection is not too inefficient, a government that would have chosen control by lenders in the absence of taxation will switch to control by equity followed by redistribution.

Note that the total return to any agent consists of a risky return h_i and a risk-free return which is aggregate per-capita net returns to firms, weighted by α_i.

The model has several nice insights, all of which arise with or without ex post redistribution:

- If lenders are to be induced to take the safe strategy, debt must be limited. Beyond a critical value of L, lenders will shift to a risky investment strategy.

- Say political power is held by an individual with very low α_i perhaps because the median voter has few equity holdings. It might be thought that such an individual would always opt for debt control of firms in order to avoid a risky investment strategy by the firm. But for the lender to take the "safe" strategy, H must not be too large. Thus, the median agent faces a potential trade off between a high H with a risky return and a lower but safer rent.

- As long as the politically decisive agent has at least an equal share of equity, $(\alpha_i \geq 1)$ rents within firms are eliminated ($H = 0$) and the society pursues a high return strategy. This implies that stakeholder rents arise only as a consequence of wealth inequality combined with political power being held by a relatively poor individual. These rents increase as the politically decisive agent has a lower share of equity returns but decrease as this individual becomes more risk averse. Very risk averse individuals would want to get a bigger crumb from the aggregate economy rather than bet on the success of their firm.

- If the "risky" strategy is very attractive (that is, very high expected return with only a small increase in risk) compared to the "safe" strategy, the society will unanimously prefer equity control. If the "risky" strategy is substantially less attractive, there will be a cutpoint in α such that types below the cutpoint impose lender dominance in firms. However, there is an intermediate situation where there are two cutpoints such that lender dominance is chosen only if the politically decisive individual is between the two cutpoints. When the pivotal voter has a very small share of the aggregate output, she prefers to bet the ranch on a large h_i.

- In a nutshell, the model calls attention to an interaction between inequality and "technology," embedded in the distributions of investment returns. As political power shifts to the "equity poor," it may not always be the case that they prefer the safety of "debt" finance. For some distributions, lenders are empowered only when the pivotal agent is moderately poor.

- Ex post consumption inequality without taxation reflects two effects. First, there is the effect of the initial inequality in wealth, which is reflected in the overall portfolio return. Second, there is the effect from the dispersion of rents induced by the random return of firms. For a given investment strategy, inequality in this component increases with H. While increasing stakeholder rents decreases the dispersion of consumption that arises from initial wealth, since the average net earnings of firms decrease in H, the rents introduce another source of inequality. The net effect on inequality of the model depends in complex ways on the "safe" and "risky" distribution of returns to the firms and the distribution of initial wealth. Say, for example, political control was given to the poorest individual, one with an α_i near or at 0 but who was not too risk averse. This individual could choose equity dominance combined with a high H that left little net earnings to firms. The resulting distributions of consumptions could be extremely unequal. An inequality based on an exogenous distribution of wealth would simply be replaced with an inequality based on random returns to firms. Thus it may be inappropriate to conclude that an observed ex post distribution of inequality is not in the interest of the poor.

- Perotti and von Thadden (2002) cite data from Luigi Guiso, Michael Haliassos and Tullio Jappelli (2001) to observe that the proportion of share-holding households in the United States, the archtypical equity finance country, is sharply higher than in Germany, the archtypical bank dominance country. Shareholders in Germany are not more than 30 percent of the population in any quartile of the income distribution. In contrast, shareholding in the United States is at 38 percent in the second quartile and reaches 87 percent in the top quartile. The sharp break in the United States comes between the second quartile and the first where only 4 percent hold shares, actually slightly less than the 7 percent for the same quartile in Germany. Thus, it is possible that the political process in the United States is biased to equity governance where firms pursue high growth but risky strategies whereas Germany plays it safe. The thick equity markets of the United States, partly fueled by pension funds, may contribute to a lessening of those policies, such as regulated markets, that protect stakeholder rents and insulate individuals from the effects of market competition.[14]

The Perotti–von Thadden model is very stylized, perhaps more believable for European societies where stakeholder rights are established in a centralized fashion than for the United States. It also would appear to need some fleshing out in terms of how debt and equity are actually supplied to firms. It nonetheless points to interesting linkages between individual wealth inequality and the structure of industrial finance and corporate governance. In particular, if those who hold little wealth are politically powerful they may prefer to incur a loss in aggregate output by imposing governance by individuals who have nondiversifiable risk with upwardly bounded returns from debt contracts.

Final Thoughts

The examples I have considered contain some lessons for the future modeling of the political economy of credit markets. There is certainly an air of "anything goes":

1. Policy is likely to be very sensitive to the degree of monopoly power or, alternatively, supply elasticity of credit.

2. Policy is dependent upon technology, represented by capacities in basic productivity, effort, and monitoring.

3. Policy responds to the flow of information.

4. Policy responds to the allocation of political power. While the basic economic point of some of the models can be made by ignoring some forms of heterogeneity among agents, such heterogeneity is likely to be critical to a political process.

5. When redistribution is not possible or limited, successful credit markets can be accompanied by increased inequality. Forces that drive toward increased inequality are the participation constraint of lenders and the differential returns of borrowers. These returns will depend on inequality in initial endowments and on sheer luck. Credit markets probably have more potential to reduce poverty—all boats rise—than to reduce inequality.

While it is instructive, from a viewpoint of thinking normatively about policy and inequality, to consider "behind the veil" politics, the actual process is always going to be influenced by self-interested interim preferences. In such cases, "democracy," most typically thought of as majority rule, can have ambiguous consequences for inequality. Moreover, the political alliances will not always be rich vs. poor. In both the Ayotte model and the Jappelli, Pagano, and Bianco model, the beneficiaries of lenient policies are only the high end debtors.[15]

As to how work might proceed in the future, it obviously would be nice to put together some of the models in more general settings. One could, say, think of considering monitoring and leniency together. Perhaps an even more productive channel would be to look at regulation and redistribution in a common framework. As either regulation or redistribution increases the distortion of market outcomes, the distortions are likely to generate increasing costs in efficiency. This is most evident of any policy that would violate the participation constraint of lenders. These increasing costs suggest that an ounce of redistribution and an ounce of regulation are probably preferable to two ounces of either one alone.

Notes

1. Education illustrates the range of options. Education can be thought of as an investment in human capital. Equality in human capital can

contribute to reducing other forms of inequality. Direct redistribution, where the state uses tax revenues to finance free education is one option. Another is one where the government makes loans to students or their parents to finance education. Finally, parents or students can borrow in private markets. Although this chapter treats only the purely private possibility, many of the issues raised with respect to loan repayment in private markets would also carry over to the repayment of government loans.

2. In particular, in Kiminori Matsuyama's (2000) model, the wealth of a society evolves only through the use of credit to fund investment. In the model, it is quite possible for a society to evolve into a polarized wealth distribution, where there are only two wealth levels, one rich and the other poor.

3. This is not to say that parties may often do better by agreeing to procedures, such as binding arbitration, that are outside of government courts. What matters is that final, physical enforcement remains in an ultimate public authority with a high degree of legitimacy.

4. But see Tullio Jappelli and Marco Pagano (2001) for discussion of cross-national variation in regulatory processes with respect to the flow of information.

5. The models we look at are finite period models. Thus, it is straightforward to characterize initial inequality and both interim and final inequality in terms of utility or consumption. The treatment of infinite horizon models is more complicated since each period then involves both ex-ante and ex-post considerations

6. The technical work can be briefly summarized:
   a. The rich pick L to maximize their two-period utility taking R as given (supply condition).
   b. The poor do the same (demand condition).
   c. That is, plugging into the two utility functions and differentiating gives two first order conditions that must be satisfied simultaneously.
   d. Solving the two equations gives the market-clearing values R_M and L_M.

7. Similarly, I am going to ignore other types of private transactions. For example, an insurance market might operate behind the veil in a fashion that would give all citizens equal consumption. See Townsend (1994) for a discussion of consumption smoothing mechanisms that might operate in addition to credit markets.

8. Adding a small enforcement cost would not change the substantive import of the model.

9. See Holmes (1892) on the myriad ways in which deals were structured to avoid the usury limit.

10. The Provident Loan Society's website indicates that it accepts only diamond and gold jewelry as collateral. If so, large segments of the poor cannot approach its windows.

11. A subtler version of the model treats the case where workouts are pro-hibitively expensive but where lenders can sell defaulting firms on an open market to uninformed investors. Because all defaults up for sale are pooled, the lender is able to obtain more than the liquidation value for marginal firms. The lender is thus willing to finance more firms than in the workout case. Moreover, higher social surplus, with no decrease in the fraction of firms receiving startup funds, can be achieved by having debtors, rather than creditors, in possession dur-ing bankruptcy. This result, however, depends heavily on the infor-mational asymmetry affecting potential purchases.

12. In equilibrium, there is no strategic default. Debtors who successfully complete their projects always repay.

13. In a somewhat more complicated version of the model, the rich can also be farmers.

14. On this point, see Raghuram Rajan and Luigi Zingales (2003).

15. Similarly, Bolton and I have shown (Bolton and Rosenthal 2001) that bailouts can engender a coalition between the least productive debtors and creditors.

References

Aghion, Philippe, and Patrick Bolton. 1997. "A Theory of Trickle-Down Growth and Development." *Review of Economic Studies* 64(2): 151–72

Alston, Lee J. 1983. "Farm Foreclosures in the United States During the In-terwar Period." *Journal of Economic History* 43(4): 885–903.

——. 1984. "Farm Foreclosure Moratorium Legislation: A Lesson from the Past." *American Economic Review* 74(3): 445–57.

Ayotte, Kenneth J. 2002. "Bankruptcy and Entrepreneurship: The Value of a Fresh Start." Paper presented at the conference "Understanding Fi-nancial Architecture: Financial Structure and Bankruptcy." Oxford, U.K. (September 13–14).

Balleisen, Edward J. 1996. "Vulture Capitalism in Antebellum America: The 1841 Federal Bankruptcy Act and the Exploitation of Financial Dis-tress." *Business History Review* 70(4): 473–516.

Benabou, Roland. 1996. "Inequality and Growth." In *NBER Macroeconomics Annual*, edited by Ben S. Bernanke and Julio J. Rotemberg. Cambridge, Mass.: MIT Press.

Besley, Timothy. 1995. "Nonmarket Institutions for Credit and Risk Shar-ing in Low-Income Countries." *Journal of Economic Perspectives* 9(3): 115–27.

Biais, Bruno, and Gilles Récassens. 2002. "Corrupt Judges, Upwardly Mo-bile Entrepreneurs, and the Political Economy of Bankruptcy Laws." Working paper. Toulouse, France: University of Toulouse.

Bolton, Patrick, and Howard Rosenthal. 2001. "The Political Economy of Debt Moratoria, Bailouts, and Bankruptcy." In *Defusing Default: Incen-*

tives and Institutions, edited by Marco Pagano. Washington, D.C.: Inter-American Development Bank.

———. 2002. "Political Intervention in Debt Contracts." *Journal of Political Economy* 110(5): 1103–34.

Caskey, John P. 1997. *Fringe Banking: Check-Cashing Outlets, Pawnshops, and the Poor.* New York: Russell Sage Foundation.

Dewatripont, Mathias, and Eric Maskin. 1995. "Credit and Efficiency in Centralized and Decentralized Economies." *The Review of Economic Studies* 62(4): 541–55.

Diamond, Douglas W. 1984. "Financial Intermediation and Delegated Monitoring." The Review of Economic Studies 51(3): 393–414.

Glaeser, Edward C., and Jose Scheinkman. 1998. "Neither a Borrower Nor a Lender Be: An Economic Analysis of Interest Restrictions and Usury Laws." *Journal of Law and Economics* 41(1): 1–36.

Guiso, Luigi, Michael Haliassos, and Tullio Jappelli, eds. 2001. *Household Portfolios.* Cambridge, Mass.: MIT Press.

Holmes, George K. 1892. "Usury in Law, in Practice and in Psychology." *Political Science Quarterly* 7(3): 431–67.

Jappelli, Tullio, and Marco Pagano. 2001. "Information Sharing in Credit Bureaus: Theory and Evidence." In *Defusing Default: Incentives and Institutions,* edited by Marco Pagano. Washington, D.C.: Inter-American Development Bank.

Jappelli, Tullio, Marco Pagano, and Madga Bianco. 2002. "Courts and Banks: Effects of Judicial Enforcement on Credit Markets." Working paper 58. Salerno, Italy: CSEF, Dipartimento di Scienze Economiche e Statistiche Università di Salerno. Available at: www.dise.unisa.it/WP/wp58.pdf (accessed January 31, 2005).

Kroszner, Randall S. 2003. "Is It Better to Forgive than to Receive? An Empirical Analysis of the Impact of Debt Repudiation." Unpublished manuscript. Chicago: University of Chicago.

Kroszner, Randall S., and Philip E. Strahan. 1999. "What Drives Deregulation? Economics and Politics of the Relaxation of Branch Banking Restrictions." *Quarterly Journal of Economics.* 114(4): 1437–67.

Mann, Bruce H. 2002. *Republic of Debtors: Bankruptcy in the Age of American Independence.* Cambridge, Mass.: Harvard University Press.

Matsuyama, Kiminori. 2000. "Endogenous Inequality." *Review of Economic Studies* 67(4): 743–59.

McCoy, Drew. 1989. *The Last of the Fathers: James Madison and the Republican Legacy.* New York: Cambridge University Press.

Nunez, Stephen, and Howard Rosenthal. 2004. "Bankruptcy 'Reform' in Congress: Creditors, Committees, Ideology, and Floor Voting in the Legislative Process." *Journal of Law, Economics and Organization* 20(2): 527–57.

Pagano, Marco, ed. 2001. *Defusing Default: Incentives and Institutions.* Washington, D.C.: Inter-American Development Bank.

Pagano, Marco, and Paolo Volpin. 2001. "The Political Economy of Finance." *Oxford Review of Economic Policy* 17(4): 502–19.

Perotti, Enrico C., and Ernst-Ludwig von Thadden. 2002. "The Political Economy of Bank- and Market Dominance." Unpublished manuscript. Lausanne, Switzerland: University of Lausanne.

Persson, Torsten, and Guido Tabellini. 2000. *Political Economics: Explaining Economic Policy,* Cambridge, Mass.: MIT Press.

Pinheiro, Armando Castelar, and Celia Cabral. 2001. "Credit Markets in Brazil: The Role of Judicial Enforcement and Other Institutions." In *Defusing Default: Incentives and Institutions,* edited by Marco Pagano. Washington, D.C.: Inter-American Development Bank.

Posner, Eric A., Richard Hynes, and Alup Malani. 2001. "The Political Economy of Property Exemption Laws." Unpublished paper. Chicago: University of Chicago Law School.

Rajan, Raghuram, and Luigi Zingales. 2003. "The Great Reversals: The Politics of Financial Development in the 20th Century." *Journal of Financial Economics* 69: 5–50.

Rothbard, Murray N. 1962. *The Panic of 1819: Reactions and Policies.* New York: Columbia University Press.

Rucker, Randal R., and Lee J. Alston. 1987. "Farm Failures and Government Intervention: A Case Study of the 1930s." *American Economic Review* 77(4): 724–30.

Straub, Stephane, and Horatio Sosa. 2001. "Ensuring Willingness to Repay in Paraguay." In *Defusing Default: Incentives and Institutions,* edited by Marco Pagano. Washington, D.C.: Inter-American Development Bank.

Townsend, Robert M. 1979. "Optimal Contracts and Competitive Markets with Costly State Verification." *Journal of Economic Theory* 21(1): 1–29.

———. 1994. "Risk and Insurance in Village India." *Econometrica* 62(3): 539–591.

Warren, Charles. 1935. *Bankruptcy in United States History.* Cambridge, Mass.: Harvard University Press.

INDEX

Boldface numbers refer to figures and tables.